"*Outsmart Crime!* presents excellent tips for preventing the types of crimes that most Americans fear. Shadel and Ward put their considerable crime expertise to good use by presenting a vulnerability continuum, drawing upon interviews with convicted felons, and focusing on citizen empowerment strategies. Time spent reading this text will be time well spent."

—B. M. (Mac) Gray II, Executive Deputy Director,
the National Crime Prevention Council

* * * * * * * *

"*Outsmart Crime!* by Doug Shadel and Al Ward is a must for those interested in empowering themselves and their communities rather than living in fear. Shadel and Ward model values of community building by writing a book on crime designed to educate and empower rather than promoting sales through sensationalism and fear. Through this very readable book we are shown how to start to break the cycle of learned helplessness and to begin to use our two greatest weapons against becoming victims of crime—ourselves and each other."

—Jane Middelton-Moz, best-selling author of
***Will to Survive: Affirming the Positive Power of the Human Spirit* and**
Shame and Guilt: Masters of Disguise

* * * * * * * *

"We're all concerned about crime and avoiding becoming statistics. *Outsmart Crime!* offers commonsense approaches to crime prevention, incorporating the points of view of convicted auto thieves, burglars, wife batterers, and gang members. It is clear that average citizens can take steps to make their lives safer."

—Betsy Cantrell, Crime Prevention Director,
the National Sheriffs' Association

* * * * * * * *

"Citizens who act on the practical crime prevention recommendations presented by Shadel and Ward will substantially reduce their chances of becoming crime victims. This book encourages citizens to be confidant and assertive. Using the techniques outlined by the authors, citizens can help lower their fear of crime and increase criminal's fear of citizen action."

—Dr. Wilbur Rykert, Director,
National Crime Prevention Institute

OUTSMART CRIME

200 Creative Strategies for Baffling the Criminal Mind

by Doug Shadel and Al Ward

Newcastle Publishing
North Hollywood, California

Cover and interior design © 1995 Michele Lanci-Altomare

ISBN: 0-87877-198-0
A Newcastle Book
First printing 1995
10 9 8 7 6 5 4 3 2 1
Printed in the United States of America.

*This book is dedicated to all of you
who are working to ensure that the homes,
neighborhoods, and communities of America remain
safe for every citizen and for the generations that follow.*

TABLE OF CONTENTS

FOREWORD

BY KEN EIKENBERRY,
Former Attorney General of Washington

There is a mood in the country these days that should disturb us all. Part of it is an anger at the perception, probably justified, that government is not serving our best interests but rather is manipulated by special interest lobbyists and career politicians whose main concern is not their country but themselves. Even stranger is the sense that our justice system metes out compassion for criminals and does not care about victims.

Still these impressions pale in comparison to America's fascination with crime and the growing perception that our country is becoming a mosaic of lawless streets and criminal ruffians who care little about the public good.

At the heart of the problem is the word "perception." Each night on the evening news, our living rooms are filled with images of teenage violence, drugs, and gangs. Some studies estimate that there has been as much as a 300 percent increase in the number of stories of violence reported on television news in the past four years while actual violent crime rates have remained the same.

Very little is ever mentioned about the variety of positive things going on in the world: responsible parents watching carefully over their children; good Samaritans volunteering at their local church or senior center; a big brother or sister mentoring a troubled youth who otherwise would be without a positive role model. These things happen every day in America without fanfare or material reward . . . or television coverage.

The great paradox of our time is that while we are angry about the level of violence in society, we are nevertheless fascinated by it and feel compelled to watch it. Stories about murder and gang warfare are dramatic, and we are strangely drawn to the macabre and to the unusual. The effect of this focus on the negative generally and crime in particular is to foster a kind of bunkering down mentality among citizens and especially older folks. Many people are literally afraid to leave their homes for fear of being caught in the cross-fire of rival gang warfare.

Outsmart Crime! provides a comprehensive look at crime from the law enforcement practitioner's standpoint and for the first time gives us cold, hard facts about the so-called "crime epidemic." The authors point out that overall rates of crime have actually gone down over the past twenty years, even though it is true that certain categories such as youth violence have gone up. They also make it clear that while the overall rates of crime have gone down and the chances of any one person becoming a victim are relatively low, it is still essential to take some precautions to ensure that you avoid victimization.

My experience with crime and crime victims was somewhat different than what Doug Shadel describes in the introduction of this book. He suggests that he was sympathetic to the plight of criminals, especially those who had difficult childhoods, but that changed when he himself became a crime victim. When one is personally touched by crime, whether oneself or through a loved one, it no longer seems as important *why* the perpetrator did what he did. The only thing that matters is that he gets his just due.

My family has been personally touched by crime several times over the years and as Attorney General of Washington, I worked hard to establish specific constitutional rights for crime victims. The determination to make this happen also came from my work as a deputy prosecuting attorney in an urban county and having firsthand experience in how criminals can make a farce out of our system of rights and duties.

But the ultimate revenge on the criminal element is prevention. It is important for all of us to read the material in this book in order to understand how to thwart the criminal mind. Between the clearly presented crime data, the interviews with convicted criminals describing how they selected their victims, and the empowerment strategies which provide tips for avoiding crime, *Outsmart Crime!* will provide you with the tools you need to all but eliminate crime from your life and ensure that your community is a safe place to work and live and raise a family.

ACKNOWLEDGMENTS

I would like to thank the following individuals who have been instrumental in this project's completion: Al Ward, who spent hundreds of hours teaching me the fundamentals of crime prevention long before we ever decided to write this book; Bill Stiles, for his support of this project and for clearing the way for me to go inside the New York State prison system; Judy Armstrong, for her help in securing prisoner interviews in Washington State; Gina Misiroglu and Michele Lanci-Altomare, for their tremendous talent and commitment to this project; the Bureau of Justice Statistics staff, especially Ronet Bachman and Marilyn Marbrook; the inmates who agreed to share their stories in the name of crime prevention; and Al Saunders, for taking the risk of publishing my books in order to promote social justice.

I would also like to acknowledge my son Nicholas, who has been a consistent source of joy and learning for me and who reminds me to "lighten up" every so often; Bill Shadel, for his long-standing advice and counsel; and the rest of my relations—Julie Shadel, Dave Shadel, Cindy Shadel, Tuyet Shadel, Gerry Shadel, Donna Trombly, Hans Halt, Peter Halt, Hiedi Halt, Dorothy Trombly, and Donna Stiles—who together have combined to make my life a most interesting and joyful journey.

—DOUG SHADEL

I would like to thank and recognize some individuals who have had a part in this endeavor. Doug Shadel has given me a unique perspective regarding life, profession, and people that has kept me going through ups and downs of this endeavor and for several years before.

To Ed, my son, who has become an adult, thank you for sharing your adult wisdom with me. To Jane, my sister, teacher, and friend, thank you for your continued support and advice. To Mike, my partner, my confidant, and best buddy, thanks for always being there to bounce new ideas off of.

For my friends and mentors in the crime prevention field, especially Joe Anderson, Margaret Boeth, Timothy Crowe, Jerry Germeau, Heather Hall, Joe

Harpold, Bill Hartung, Betsy Lindsay, John Marx, Joe Mele, George Sunderland, and Daryl Pearson, I thank you for sharing your knowledge and your friendship. Unfortunately it would take too many pages to acknowledge all the people who have led me to this particular moment in time but you are all included in the millions of crime prevention practitioners who have said this all before. I salute your efforts, your dedication, your sacrifices—an effort of selfless love for all humankind that is difficult if not impossible to understand.

—AL WARD

INTRODUCTION

ON BEING A CRIME VICTIM

As this book was being completed in the fall of 1994, Al Ward, my co-author, and I were having lengthy discussions about the direction of the manuscript. The majority of the material we had put together was fine: interviews with convicted burglars, car thieves, and robbers, and the two hundred plus empowerment strategies were all useful to the reader as a way of understanding the criminal mind and taking concrete measures to avoid victimization. Further, we agreed that the empowerment quizzes would reinforce the prevention messages we were trying to convey.

The one area with which we struggled was the statistics. We both felt that the media had overblown the so-called "crime problem" and that in many ways we as a society were scaring ourselves to death. Fear of crime, we believed, was becoming more of a problem than crime itself. The solution to this perception problem was to cite statistics from the Bureau of Justice Statistics (BJS) which disclosed the "rates" of crime victimization each year. This would tell a person what his or her chances were of becoming a crime victim. We believed that once a person knew for example that his or her chance of having his car stolen *was* two out of one hundred (that's how many people had their car stolen in 1992 according to the BJS), then they wouldn't be afraid.

The difficulty was that many of the people who read early drafts of the manuscript said that we were sending a mixed message. They said if you tell people their chances of being victimized are only two out of one hundred, then they will stop reading and will never bother to adopt any of the empowerment strategies listed later on in the book.

Others had told us candidly that we were shooting ourselves in the foot by disclosing the true rates of crime. They said crime was an incredibly hot issue and we could probably make a fortune by just fanning the flame of fear with things like the crime clock (every seventeen seconds someone is murdered in America). They cited America's fascination with crime as evidenced by the publicity surrounding the O. J. Simpson trial as a further reason not to douse the flames of fear with a cold bucket of reality.

I personally agonized over this point for months. Should we jump on the bandwagon and ride the popular tide by scaring people into buying our book? Should we put a big "crime clock" on the cover and tell people that in the time it takes to read chapter one, fourteen people in the U.S. will have been murdered? I even began to rationalize that at least if people were really scared, they would be more inclined to incorporate the empowerment strategies we had outlined into their lives.

After months of reflection on this point, it came to a head the weekend before the final manuscript was due on the publisher's desk. On a Sunday in October, I had a long discussion with Al on this topic and we decided to include the total number of crimes committed in each category (in addition to the rates) in order to underscore the fact that there are indeed a huge number of crimes committed in this country each year even though the chances of any one person being victimized are low.

I remember tossing and turning in bed that night, wondering if we were making the right decision. At about 4:00 A.M. I decided I couldn't sleep and should go for a run. Running is always a form of catharsis for me and something I do to focus and reflect on a subject. So at four o'clock on a Monday morning, I put on my jogging clothes, grabbed the Sony Walkman which always accompanies me and headed out the door. As I looked out onto the street, I noticed something was wrong. I said to myself, "Where is my minivan!?"

That's right, at the very moment I was struggling with the question of whether crime was a real problem or just something conjured up by the media, a group of gang members was stealing my van. I had left my car parked in front of my house on a somewhat busy street in West Seattle which is definitely an urban area and had been, as I would find out later, a hotspot for criminal activity during the past month.

Forget the fact that the car was locked and the keys were in my house behind a deadbolted door. Forget the fact that I had parked it there for four years without an incident. Forget the fact that my chances of having my car stolen were only two out of one hundred. Forget that I served for four years on the board of directors of the Washington State Crime Prevention Association, worked for the attorney general for fourteen years, and have now written two books about crime prevention.

At the moment that I went out jogging that morning and found my van gone, none of that mattered. The only thing that mattered was that someone had stolen my van. The thoughts that ran through my head were things like: "But all my stuff was in there," "My nine-year-old son's favorite football was in there," "A bunch of drug addict gang members are driving around in the same car I take the kids to soccer games in," and "If I ever catch the little jerks who did this. . . ."

All of a sudden, it occurred to me at that moment that I had never been a crime victim before. Here I was this supposed "crime expert" but that expertise had been limited to the relatively sheltered, antiseptic world of statistics, police conferences, and state prisons with remorseful criminals and dozens of corrections officers nearby. All of a sudden, I had become one of those two victims out of one hundred who had had his car stolen.

I did what one is supposed to do—called 911 to report a stolen car. The Seattle police responded quickly and within ten minutes of my calling there was a police officer at my door. The officer said there had been a flurry of car prowls and thefts in the area and "the gangs love minivans because they can all ride around together in them." He filled out the report and gave me a file number to use in contacting my insurance company. I was then faced with the immediate question of how to get to work. I hitched a ride with a co-worker who lives close by and started the process of renting a car and wondering where my car was and, more importantly, what condition it would be in when I found it.

I found my minivan the next day when I was driving home from a meeting. The thieves had parked it about two blocks from my house on the street. When I saw the vehicle, I slammed on the breaks of my rental car and backed up to inspect it. There was very little damage done to the vehicle. The passenger side lock had been picked with a screwdriver and the ignition had been pulled (see chapter 3, Outsmarting Auto Theft, for more information on car theft). It was full of empty purses, bank receipts, identification cards, foreign currency, telephone numbers on small slips of paper, and it quickly became apparent that this group of gang members had spent the evening using my van to rip off other cars in the neighborhood.

I speculated that when they were done, probably at dawn, they simply parked the car close to where they had stolen it and took off. In some ways, it is the perfect crime because they steal a car in the middle of the night while the owner is sleeping, and drive it around breaking into other cars before the owner can call it in as stolen.

I called the Seattle police to tell them I had found the car and they sent a police officer out to check it out. The officer looked through the empty purses and the collection of identification and foreign currency that had been spewn throughout the van and said, "I take it you didn't leave it this way?" He took one of the IDs out of the van to return to the owner and then he said to me, "Well, you're lucky you got your van back without too much damage." I said, "Aren't you going to take the rest of this evidence or dust for fingerprints or investigate or something? I mean, isn't this grand theft auto?" He said there wasn't much he could do to find the people and, besides, he said this happens every single day and they rarely catch the person. He told me I should just feel fortunate to have the car back.

I was incredulous at the lack of interest by the police. I nevertheless secured the van and the next morning had a tow truck tow it to the repair shop. The gang members had not stolen anything of value in the vehicle. All of my cassette tapes were still in there, a box of my first book, *Schemes & Scams*, was ripped open but no copies were stolen (I guess gang members aren't big readers). The only thing they did take were some law enforcement pins which I had placed on the visor over the driver seat.

The total bill for damage was under $400 and my insurance company paid most of it, but despite the minimal financial loss, this event changed me. I have fundamentally changed my view of crime and of criminals. I had been a person full of compassion for the criminals I interviewed in prison. At the time I had been reading Alice Miller's *For Your Own Good* which chronicled the violent childhood of Adolf Hitler and reviewed two hundred years of German child-rearing manuals which imposed cruel standards on children as a means of breaking their spirit. I had learned that most of those who became criminals were merely projecting anger and hostility onto the world that was the result of a cruel upbringing.

I began to conclude that criminals are not born, they are grown by society and therefore we should have compassion for them. And while I still believe that criminals are grown, not born, it has become significantly more difficult for me to be compassionate.

The experience of becoming a crime victim is such a violation of one's emotional and physical existence that it creates a lasting anger that makes you want to just lock all thieves up forever. I found myself saying "I don't really care what made these kids this way, they messed with my stuff and I want them to pay, damn it!"

The week after it happened, I wrote a letter to each one of my neighbors describing what had happened and soliciting interest for starting a block watch in the neighborhood. The response I received from this letter was simply amazing. People came out of the woodwork to say they had had bikes stolen, homes burglarized, ornaments ripped off of their back porch, gang members following them in their cars.

I had not met many of my neighbors during the four years I had lived in this neighborhood and I certainly had never heard of any crimes being committed until I told others of my experience. This seemed to open the floodgates of interest. It was not that our neighborhood was crime-free. To the contrary, numerous crimes had been committed, but everyone was keeping the information to themselves. It wasn't until a major felony—auto theft—occurred that everyone woke up to the fact that we were in the middle of a crime spree.

Since this event, I have organized a block watch on our street, complete with maps that list everyone by name, address, and telephone number. We are going to be installing big medal block watch signs at either end of the street and, in effect, we are taking back our street from gang members who have been silently ripping off almost everyone who lives there for the past year.

Al and I decided to open the book with the story of my victimization for three reasons. First, it is important that as you read the statistics about "rates of victimization" contained throughout the material, you recognize that low rates do not make you immune to crime. The mistake I made with my car was that I knew the chances were roughly two out of one hundred that my car would be stolen, so I didn't take the simple precaution of parking it in the safety of my backyard.

If I had taken this precaution, I am certain the gang members would have chosen someone else's minivan. My backyard is off of a dead-end alley and there are numerous infrared motion detector lights which would turn on if anyone were to snoop around there at night. The reason I didn't take this precaution was because I was willing to risk the odds and I was always in a hurry and it took a couple of minutes longer to park there.

The second point is that prior to the theft, my neighbors and I were a model of poor communication, so much so that none of us realized we were all being victimized by crime. Each one of us thought it wouldn't do any good to report a stolen bike or a stolen basketball and it certainly wasn't worth bothering the neighbors. The only reason I decided to bother my neighbors was because the gang members stole my $18,000 car! That is a pretty big item to lose.

Once we began to organize and communicate with each other, the crime went away. Our block became more trouble than it was worth for the bad guys and so they began to go elsewhere. Don't make the same mistake my neighbors and I made. Don't wait until a big crime has been committed to meet your neighbors and take precautions to avoid crime. The strategies listed throughout this book will help you know what to do, but don't wait to become a victim to employ them.

A third and final point to this story is that the police cannot protect you from crime. As the officer said as he was explaining why he wasn't going to even attempt to investigate the theft, the police rarely catch the culprits and there are so many car thefts going on, they can't even begin to keep up with it.

This should underscore the central message of this book: crime prevention is up to you and your neighbors. The police do the best they can with limited budgets and limited man (and woman) power. But ultimately, safety, law and order, and peace is up to you. This book is about providing you with the tools you need to establish and preserve law and order in your community.

THE TRUTH ABOUT CRIME

1

M y t h :

> *There is an epidemic crime wave crashing*
> *over the land in the 1990s which threatens*
> *the very fabric of our society.*

REALITY:

WHILE ANY AMOUNT CRIME IS A PROBLEM,
OVERALL CRIME VICTIMIZATION RATES HAVE
ACTUALLY GONE *DOWN* IN THE PAST TEN YEARS.

THE ISSUE OF CRIME HAS BEEN ON THE MINDS OF AMERICANS every year since the founding of this country 218 years ago. While the threat of becoming a crime victim has worried people for decades, that concern has peaked in the 1990s as the media and its constituents (viewers and listeners) have become enthralled by violence on the news and in programming. Some studies estimate that between 1992 and 1993, the number of stories about crime and violence reported on the major networks doubled.

A central theme of this book is that it is not crime victimization that has dramatically increased but America's fascination with it. This chapter explores the statistical truth about crime victimization in an attempt to quell the hysteria and fear which this fascination is creating within some segments of society, especially older adults. By knowing your real chances of becoming a crime victim, you will be free to live your life without constantly looking over your shoulder.

WHAT ARE YOUR CHANCES OF BECOMING A CRIME VICTIM?

There is much debate in the media these days about just how bad the crime problem has gotten. Organizations like the Federal Bureau of Investigation (FBI) and the Bureau of Justice Statistics (BJS) will say that crime in general is going down, but youth violence is going up. By watching the nightly newscasts however, one could easily conclude that crime has not only gone up but is in fact the only activity happening in any given community.

While it is impossible to predict with certainty whether you or anyone else in particular will become a victim of crime, it is possible to look at victimization rates based on specific characteristics and get a clearer picture of the crime milieu.

There are many factors that help determine one's vulnerability, but we are going to focus on four factors—age, sex, race, and location. The Bureau of Justice Statistics each year publishes what is known as the *Sourcebook of Criminal Justice Statistics*—it is a big book full of statistics which are the result of a survey they make of approximately 100,000 randomly selected people twice per year. The survey asks people about their experiences and attitudes toward crime during the preceding six months whether or not they have been victims themselves.

Throughout *Outsmart Crime!*, we quote from the *Sourcebook* and another BJS publication, *Criminal Victimization in the U.S.* This book is also updated twice yearly, although we have used the 1992 edition for our charts. You can write to the Bureau of Justice Statistics to obtain a copy, but beware that the *Sourcebook* is bulky and can get confusing given the fact that it consists of almost eight hundred pages of statistics. The statistics in this book describe the number of victims per one hundred people in any particular age group.

The chart below lists the ten highest rates of victimization and the ten lowest.

TEN MOST COMMON VICTIMS OF VIOLENCE—1992

Category	% Victimized	% Not Victimized
1. Black Males (16-19)	15.8%	84.2%
2. Black Males (20-24)	13.1%	86.9%
3. Black Females (16-19)	9.3%	90.7%
4. Black Females (12-15)	9.3%	90.7%
5. White Males (12-15)	9.1%	90.9%
6. White Males (16-19)	8.9%	91.1%
7. White Males (20-24)	8.4%	91.6%
8. Black Females (20-24)	7.8%	92.2%
9. Black Males (12-15)	7.4%	92.6%
10. White Females (12-15)	5.8%	94.2%

TEN LEAST COMMON VICTIMS OF VIOLENCE—1992

Category	% Victimized	% Not Victimized
1. White Females (65+)	.27%	99.73%
2. White Males (65+)	.64%	99.32%
3. White Females (50-64)	.76%	99.24%
4. Black Females (65+)	.96%	99.04%
5. White Males (50-65)	1.14%	98.86%
6. Black Females (50-65)	1.21%	98.79%
7. Black Males (65+)	1.24%	98.86%
8. Black Females (35-49)	1.29%	98.71%
9. White Females (35-49)	2.0%	98.0%
10. White Males (35-49)	2.2%	97.8%

Source: *Criminal Victimization in the U.S.*, the Bureau of Justice Statistics, 1992, Table 11, page 29.

We have included the percentage of people victimized and not victimized as a reminder that the majority of citizens are not victimized in any category and vulnerability to crime is very much a relative issue.

For anyone who has been a victim of a violent crime like rape or murder, these statistics are of little comfort. In fact, the whole goal of this book is to provide you with strategies to eliminate crime from your life. But we provide both the positive and negative data to you as a reminder that, notwithstanding the media and the public's fascination with violence and crime, it's still a relatively safe world out there. If one were to put these on a continuum, it might look something like the following:

THE VULNERABILITY CONTINUUM — AGE AND RACE AS RISK FACTORS

Violent Crime Victim Rates—1992

.27% --------→	1.24% ----------→	7.8% -----------→	5.8% ---→
White Females (65+)	Black Males (65+)	Black Females (20-24)	Black Males (16-19)

Source: 1992 *Sourcebook of Criminal Justice Statistics*, published by the Bureau of Justice Statistics, Table 11, page 20.

These statistics will become important as we begin to explore the concept of the "path of least resistance," the idea that criminals will look for opportunities where there are weaknesses or little resistance. Many of those who are victimized could have avoided it by following a few simple precautions. Clearly, the age category which is most at risk in terms of violence is the twelve- to twenty-five-year-olds, both white and Black. The least victimized age group is the fifty-plus crowd. Whatever your category, it is important to know your odds of victimization in order to outsmart crime.

Another statistic to look at is the crime rate for each type of crime. These are 1992 figures for various crimes:

VARIOUS CRIMES

Crime	No. of Victims	% Victimized	% Not Victimized
Burglary	4,757,420	4.89%	95.11%
Auto Theft	1,958,780	2.01%	97.9%
Robbery	1,225,510	.59%	99.41%
Assault	5,254,690	2.55%	97.45%
Rape	140,930	.07%	99.93%
All Violent Crimes	6,621,140	3.21%	96.79%

Source: *Criminal Victimization in the U.S.,* Table 1, page 16.

The interesting fact about this data is its comparison to another survey question the BJS asked citizens: Do you feel any sense of danger from gun violence where you live and work? In 1992, 50 percent of those in urban areas said yes, 33 percent of those in suburban areas said yes, and 29 percent of those in rural areas said yes. Yet the overall victimization rates for violent crime was only 3.21 percent in 1992. We belief this wide discrepancy between actual victimization rates and citizens' perception and fear of crime are having a crippling effect on how people live their lives.

To conceptualize where you fall on the vulnerability continuum, you must think about whether you are Black or white, young or old, and whether you live in a city or a rural area.

THE VULNERABILITY CONTINUUM—LOCATION AND SEX AS RISK FACTORS

Violent Crime Victim Rates—1992

1.87% --------------- ➤ 3.22% ----------------- ➤ 7.64% -------- ➤

Rural White Female   Suburban White Male   Urban Black Male

Source: *Criminal Victimization in the U.S.,* Table 18, page 38.

In addition to these national statistics which point out differences in crime rates based on population density, within cities there are areas which the police refer to as "hotspots." A hotspot is an area where there are greater than average rates of crime. The 1992 Seattle police report on residential burglary shows a breakdown by precinct of crime rates for various types of crimes (see Figure 1). The heavily shaded areas are hotspots. Most police departments in the United States, whether they are in urban or suburban or rural areas, will be able to provide you with such information in order to assess the risks associated with moving to a particular neighborhood. This is an example of what you can expect the hotspots chart to look like for your area.

Each area is numbered, so you can find out exactly how many crimes occurred in that area in that year. This is an excellent resource to check *before* moving into a particular neighborhood. It is also helpful when comparing one neighborhood to another.

The reason for citing these statistics is to provide you with trends of victimization so you can make rational choices about how to protect yourself based on the real threats that exist. Often the fear of crime which is generated by news media and other glamorizations of crime and violence is often as debilitating as actual victimization.

As you read through chapters on the various types of crime, it is important to remember that where you fall on the vulnerability continuum is generally based upon where you live, your age, your sex, and your race. If, for example, you are a white male over the age of sixty-five living in a rural area, your chances of being victimized by any crime are incredibly small. This is not to say you should consequently take no precautions against crime, but the information should help reduce your fear.

If, on the other hand, you are a Black male between the ages of twelve and sixteen and living in an urban area, you are the most vulnerable segment of the population living in the highest crime area and must take maximum precautions.

FIGURE 1: SEATTLE HOTSPOTS — Residential Burglary

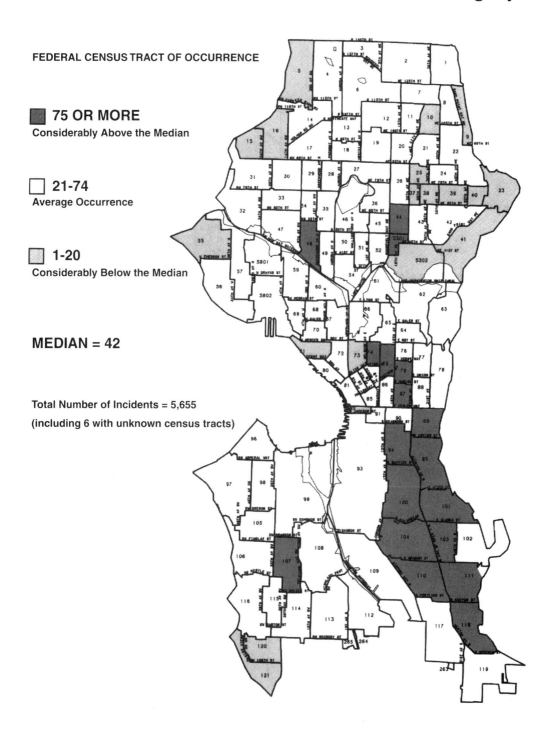

FEDERAL CENSUS TRACT OF OCCURRENCE

75 OR MORE
Considerably Above the Median

21-74
Average Occurrence

1-20
Considerably Below the Median

MEDIAN = 42

Total Number of Incidents = 5,655
(including 6 with unknown census tracts)

Finally, the chart below lists how crime rates compare with the rates of other life events. We include this here to give you some perspective of what it means when we say two out every one hundred people are victims of a particular crime.

HOW CRIME RATES COMPARE WITH THE RATES OF OTHER LIFE EVENTS

Events	Rate per 100 per year
Accidental injury, all circumstances	22.0%
Accidental injury at home	6.6%
Personal theft	6.1%
Accidental injury at work	4.7%
Violent victimization	3.1%
Assault	2.5%
Injury in motor vehicle accident	2.2%
Death (all causes)	1.1%
Victimization with injury	1.1%
Serious assault	0.8%
Robbery	0.6%
Heart disease death	0.5%
Cancer death	0.3%
Rape (women only)	0.1%
Accidental death, all circumstances	0.04%
Pneumonia/influenza death	0.04%
Motor vehicle accident death	0.02%
Suicide	0.02%
HIV infection death	0.01%
Homicide/legal intervention	0.01%

Source: Multiple, including highlights from *20 Years of Surveying Crime Victims*, the Bureau of Justice Statistics, 1993, page 5.

Chapter 1

COMMON QUESTIONS ABOUT CRIME

During the past decade, we have given hundreds of speeches to community groups about crime and how to prevent it. From local church groups, Kiwanians, Rotaries, Chambers of Commerce, and American Association of Retired Persons (AARP) chapters to retired teacher units, you name the organization, we have spoken to them.

At the end of each presentation, there is always a question and answer period during which the audience has the opportunity to ask follow-up questions on a variety of topics. What follows are the most common questions we encounter during these sessions. Rest assured that the questions are very similar from group to group and geographic region to geographic region.

So, to abate your fears and provide further clarification on crime issues, we thought we would try to answer the common questions on the minds of citizens before offering specific empowerment strategies to eliminate crime from your life. One goal we have in doing this is to address some of the myths about crime and how to prevent it. The questions are listed in no particular order.

QUESTION 1:

Is crime on the rise, staying the same, or going down? It seems like it must be going up because it's in the news so much.

The quickest way to see whether or not crime is on the rise is to look at the three charts in Figure 2. Chart one shows total number of victimizations from 1973 to 1992. You can see that of the four generic types of crime listed, the overall rate is down (-6 percent), household crimes are down (-3 percent), personal theft is down (-18 percent), and only violent crimes are up (+24 percent).

Chart two shows crime trends for the specific crimes of personal larceny, total violent crime, assault, robbery, and rape. Chart three shows twenty-year trends for household larceny, burglary, and motor vehicle theft. Motor vehicle theft is the only property crime which has shown an uptrend during the past twenty years.

FIGURE 2: WHAT ARE THE TRENDS IN CRIME?

The number of victimizations rose from 1973 until the early 1980s and has since declined

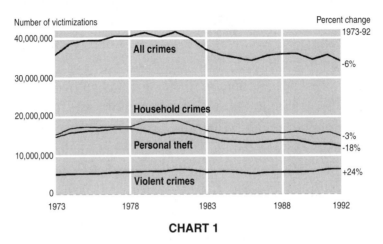

CHART 1

Note: Household crimes include burglary, larceny, and motor vehicle theft.
Violent crimes include rape, robbery, and assault.

Victimization rates for most property crimes have also declined

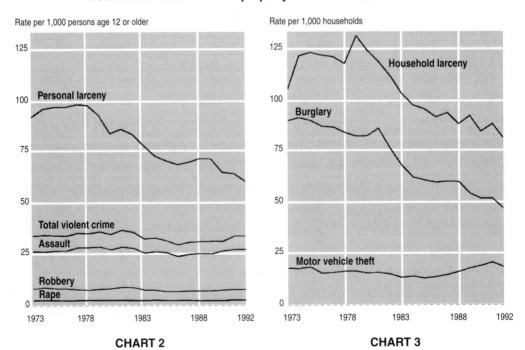

CHART 2   CHART 3

So if the crime trend is generally down, why is it all we hear about on the news and in the halls of Congress these days? The reason is that violent crimes, which indeed are on the rise, are the most spectacular and the media tends to focus on them because the American public is fascinated with violence. It is exhilarating, and while many blame the media for creating panic and the perception that crime is everywhere, they wouldn't put it on television if the public didn't watch it. In many ways, we are creating our own hysteria by continuing to watch violent drama series, news magazines, and newscasts which focus on gruesome crime.

QUESTION 2:

I see so much violence on television every night, it worries me. Is it a good idea to buy a gun to protect myself and my family?

There are many people who have grown up with hunting weapons and have been carefully trained in firearm safety by their fathers or others. For these folks, gun ownership is not a problem. But you will be hard pressed to find a police officer or law enforcement official of any kind who thinks that weapons are a good deterrent to crime.

In fact, even convicted burglars say it is not a factor in how they chose their victims because when they look for a house to burglarize, they have no idea which homes have guns and which do not.

Increasingly in the United States there is a perception that with so many handguns on the streets (200 million at last count) if you are the only one without a gun, you must by definition be at risk.

A fundamental question one needs to ask about gun ownership is this: When was the last time you found yourself in a situation where you thought to yourself, "If only I had a gun in this situation, I'd be better off?" Discounting times when fear of crime made you think it would make you safer, the question is, Has there ever been a real-life situation where you felt you needed a gun? If the answer is no, that should tell you whether to buy one or not. Very few people even know someone who has had to use a gun or who has been in a situation when a gun helped save his or her life.

Even police officers don't use guns very much. In the Bellevue (Washington) Police Department, there has only been one police officer who has ever shot anyone in the past twenty-five years. This is obviously not true in other cities like New York and Los Angeles, but it is a rare event even in large cities. A study called Citizens Killed by Big City Police conducted by researchers L. W. Sherman and E. G. Cohn of the Crime Control Institute in Washington, D.C., looked at police shootings from 1970 to 1984 in the fifty largest cities in the U.S. There were a total of 353 people killed by police officers during that time. That is less than one death every two years per city on average.

The vast majority of police officers will tell you to use your head instead of a gun for protection. If you are buying a gun to prevent a street rape or a burglary or some other kind of property crime, it is a foolish thing to do. The chances are greater that the gun will be used *against you* by the mugger or bad guy since he has more experience typically with fighting and with weapons than you do.

As you will see in interviews with Drew, the convicted burglar, and Joseph, the convicted robber, both say that the victim having a gun would in no way deter them and in fact may endanger the victim if he or she does not know how to use it. Joseph says he took guns away from victims and used it against them (see the section in chapter 4, Inside the Mind of a Robber).

QUESTION 3:
Would chemical sprays like mace help protect me from muggers?

Personal safety products are everywhere in the marketplace now and they are selling like hotcakes. Just like those who sell guns say it is a panacea and will eliminate crime from your life, many of those companies who sell personal security products also say their product is all you need to remain safe. It isn't that simple.

Chemical sprays, noise makers, or other kinds of self-defense weapons can be used as tools in an overall strategy, but in and of themselves they are not going to eliminate crime from your life.

Mace is tear gas and has been corrupted over the years in terms of how it should be used. It doesn't work the same way on all kinds of people—some people get irate when it is used and can become more dangerous after it is used than they were before. The latest kind of chemical spray is cayenne pepper spray which seems to work more consistently than mace.

Recognizing that, in a struggle, it could be used against the victim, if it makes you more confident by having it in your purse or in a coat pocket, then it is worth buying. This is because the biggest deterrent to being attacked is to look like you are *not* a victim—by walking tall, looking around, walking with a definite purpose. If knowing you have mace or spray in your pocket or purse increases your ability to look confident and in fact *be* confident, then it is worth carrying.

The fact to remember about a noise maker or a chemical spray is that it does no good lying at the bottom of a purse. If you are going to buy something like that, get it on the end of a key chain so that when you go out to your car, you will have it in your hand. Also, these sprays have safeties on them, so you need to take the safety off when you think you might need it. Another drawback is that the spray can accidentally discharge and hit a child in the face or stain your clothing.

Noise makers can be effective because if used properly when you are in danger, the noise attracts the attention of anyone around which will cause a robber to flee. Some people are so terrified when they are confronted with a bad guy that they literally can't scream, so noise makers can essentially scream for them.

The biggest problem with chemical sprays and noise makers is that people don't use them or they don't learn how to use them and so they don't work properly. If you buy one of these noise makers or chemical sprays, make sure you know how they work and that you do indeed use them.

QUESTION 4:

Are alarm systems a good deterrent to being burglarized?

Alarm systems certainly act as a deterrent to the burglar. Most burglars we have interviewed say they would never hit a house that had an alarm system. However, buying an alarm system isn't the first thing a person should do. The first thing to do is to examine the need for that type of security. If you live in a safe neighborhood that hasn't been burglarized for twenty years, you may not need an alarm system. If none of your neighbors have alarm systems, if you have deadbolt locks, if you use your locks, or have locking devices on your windows, you may not need an alarm system either.

The first step is to see if you can break into your own house. If there are gaps, fix them. If you still feel the need for an alarm, then get one. People get into trouble with alarms when the alarm is not handy for them. They will cut corners by installing only one touch pad to activate and deactivate the alarm system when they should have had at least two. If there is more than one entry/exit point frequently used and you have only one touch pad, you are going to run the risk of setting off the alarm by not deactivating it in time.

The second problem with alarms is their activation with your children. Kids are a lot harder to teach about an alarm system than adults. So often the adults will leave the alarm system off at night so they don't have to worry about the kids coming home late and activating the alarm system.

The main concern we have about installing alarms is that once installed, the homeowner does nothing else to avoid problems. Just like the chemical sprays and noise makers, an alarm is a tool which should be only one part of a security system. That system includes block watch, operation identification, appropriate locks, and many other things we discuss in chapter 2, Outsmarting Burglary. It is a mistake to assume that an alarm alone will be all you need to protect your home.

Another point to remember about alarms is that according to the National Burglar and Fire Alarm Association, there is a monthly monitoring fee involved and

98 percent of all alarms that go off are false. This has led many local city governments to have false alarm ordinances that call for a fee to be imposed after a certain number of false alarms. If you have children who are constantly tripping the alarm, this could become costly and this cost, along with the cost of installing the system and the monthly monitoring fee, should be weighed against its deterrent value.

Alarms should be the frosting on your security system cake, not the entire cake.

QUESTION 5:

Isn't it true that the biggest threat to my safety is a stranger attacking me?

Well over half of all crimes of violence are committed by someone the victim knows, not strangers. For example, according to the BJS, 71 percent of the rapes that occurred in 1991 were committed by either a family member or someone well known to the victim. Similarly, 68 percent of the assaults committed in 1991 were committed by family or people well known to the victim.

Women in particular are fearful of street assaults from strangers, but they are more likely to be victimized by a boyfriend. Remember to establish clear boundaries with your boyfriend and to act if the person goes past those boundaries. Women are often caught off guard by acquaintance types of crime.

Also, acquaintance rape is not reported nearly as often as stranger rape because the person is embarrassed about it. From the standpoint of personal crimes, the biggest threat is not from a stranger, but from someone you know.

QUESTION 6:

If I move out of the city to a rural area, will I be safe from crime?

While it is true that the crime rate is less in rural areas than it is in suburban areas and less in suburban areas than in urban areas, crime nevertheless still exists in rural areas.

One explanation for the lower crime rate in rural settings is that there are more sophisticated communication networks within the community. In the city, block watches are formed typically after someone has been burglarized and usually the victim of that burglary calls and sets up an appointment to have a police officer come out and meet with the neighbors.

In rural areas, often the neighbors already know each other and the police and so it is very hard for a stranger or a burglar to come and go without being discovered.

But to think that living in the country in and of itself is going to eliminate crime from your life is a fallacy. Many gangs from the big city are shopping around for smaller communities to move into because the competition for the drug trade in the city is so fierce and deadly.

Also, as drug lords and gang leaders begin to accumulate wealth, they are actually moving into the suburbs. Sanyika Shakur, a sixteen-year veteran of the L.A. gangs who was nicknamed "Monster" from his brutal treatment of rival gang members, explained why gangs are moving into previously unexplored areas in his autobiography *Monster*:

> *It was an escape to a peaceful enclave for a couple of hours. The places she took me, bangers (gangs) didn't frequent. This was before the influx of narcotics, primarily crack. We were all of the same economic status—broke. Now, with so many "ghetto rich" homeboys from every set, no place is beyond the grasp of bangers.*

One of the reasons the L.A. gangs began to move out to other areas is because gangs are primarily economic enterprises, with the product being drugs. And there was so much competition in urban areas that the price of drugs was down. There were discounters and the equivalent of K-Mart blue light specials and the profits were being eliminated.

Given this economic environment, why not go to a town of 65,000 instead of a city the size of Los Angeles and have a complete monopoly on the drug trade and charge whatever prices you want to? Given the natural community communication networks in such a town, a newly arrived gang operation needs to operate at particularly low visibility until they get established, but to the gangs the added precautions they need to take are generally worth it.

QUESTION 7:

As an adult over the age of sixty, I feel particularly vulnerable to crime because I am not as strong as I once was. Do criminals target older adults?

Older adults comprise the lowest category of victims of all crimes. There are a number of explanations for this. They tend to not be in areas that are hotspots like downtown where younger people would be going to work, and they tend to shop in the middle of the day when a minimum of threats might present themselves.

They are also the lowest victimized category when it comes to property crimes. The best neighborhood to live in is one that is filled with active older adults because they are home all day.

Older adults are victimized by the fear of crime. Older adults (and the rest of the U.S. for that matter) watch the news every night and it is filled with stories about violence and mayhem. It is important to realize that much of the violence we see on television is happening among rival gangs and, while gangs are moving out from what used to be the center of a core ghetto area, they are still by and large focusing their violence in those core areas. The chances of an older adult getting in the middle of one of those incidents is extremely low (see the section in chapter 7, Inside the Mind of a Gang Member, and the section in chapter 8, The Truth About Crime and Older Adults).

QUESTION 8:

Am I more at risk of becoming a crime victim at night than during the day?

People can be at risk anywhere, anytime, especially if they look like victims. Chapter 4 addresses how to avoid looking like a victim. If you are slouched over and walking as though you don't know where you are going and would not resist if a bad guy confronted you, you are at risk whether it is day or night.

It is also important to understand that where you are is as important as whether it's day or night. If you are walking down a back alley in a ghetto area in broad daylight, you may be at more risk than if you were walking down a suburban sidewalk at 3:00 A.M.

The most important step you can take to be uniformly more safe is to always pretend you are in a dangerous area like New York City. Anyone who goes to New York City or who lives there realizes that it can be a very dangerous place at any time of the day. Therefore, New Yorkers are alert, aware of their surroundings and the people around them, and walk with a purpose and with confidence.

For those people who are from New York, they don't act a certain way because they are constantly thinking, "Oh my gosh, if I don't act confident and walk with a purpose, I'll be mugged." In fact, it becomes so second nature to them that they just normally look and act empowered and consequently will not likely be victims of crime.

QUESTION 9:
Do most criminals look the same or are they all different?

Over the years, there have been a lot of gangster movies that have stereotyped criminals in such a way that the American public thinks criminals, thieves, and hoodlums are supposed to look a certain way. Ted Bundy was a great example of someone who looked like the all-American boy, the kind of guy every mother would love her daughter to go out with. The only problem was that he was a serial murderer. We also have a false stereotype that many African Americans or bedraggled-looking people are dangerous.

However, it is more important to look at behavior of individuals than the way they look physically. If you see someone in your neighborhood whom you do not recognize, irrespective of how he or she looks, its a good idea to become territorial and, in a nice way, go up to the person and say hello and try to engage him or her in some conversation.

This sends a message to the person that you know who he is and if anything happens, you are going to recognize him. Some burglars will drive into an upscale neighborhood in a Mercedes just to avoid detection. If the burglar drove into that same upscale neighborhood in a run-down car, he would immediately attract attention from those in the community.

We discuss the "chameleon effect" later in this chapter. This refers to the practice some burglars and others have of matching their clothes to the neighborhood they are victimizing. It is important not to look at the person as much as at the behavior. If there is an attractive-looking male in a jogging suit in your neighborhood, you might normally think nothing of it. But what if you noticed he wasn't jogging? And not only that, what if you noticed he was writing down notes on a small notepad? This is an example of an unsuspicious-looking man engaging in suspicious kinds of behavior.

You can't tell a book by its cover. Criminal con artists almost always seek to first convince their victims they are legitimate before stealing their money. They might sound nice and friendly and they might give you names like Visa and Dun & Bradstreet as business partners so you'll believe them, but then they tell you you've won a car. Legitimate in appearance, illegitimate in behavior.

QUESTION 10:
Is it dangerous to leave my child unattended even if there are other adults around?

There is a perception among parents that as long as their child is around a lot of other people, he or she is safe. For example, if the child is on a playground with one hundred other kids and a supervisor, one would think he or she will be safe. There was an interesting project done by a local television station which sent an undercover producer onto a playground with a picture of what was supposedly his lost dog. The producer went up to kids and asked them to go with him into the bushes to help find his lost dog. He showed them a picture of the dog and, because he looked legitimate, *70 percent* of the kids he approached went with him.

Part of this gets back to the concept of what is a stranger. Here you have children with lots of people around and it is possible to be abducted. Another situation which can be serious is when a mom lets her child go into a restroom unattended, reasoning that there are a lot of people around. This is not a good idea because although lots of people are around, they are virtually all strangers.

Another example is when a mall has a big toy or some other kind of play equipment for kids to play on and their parents drop them off there and go shop. There are lots of people around, but it is not a safe place at all because the child is surrounded by strangers whom he or she does not know. You should never, ever, leave your child unattended. If you cannot personally watch your child, leave him or her with a trusted friend, baby-sitter, or neighbor.

QUESTION 11:

I am a single woman and have been thinking about taking a self-defense course in order to protect myself from attackers. Is this a good thing to do?

There is no doubt that people who are strong and in shape or who have learned karate or other self-defense type of strategies are typically less likely to be victimized by street crime. But not for the reason one might think. The main reason these folks are less victimized is because of the increased self-confidence that comes with conditioning and refinement of physical movements.

This self-confidence is a deterrent to the criminal who wants to find the most vulnerable victim, not the one who will put up the greatest struggle. This will become clear when you read the interview with Joseph, a notorious New York City street robber who clearly indicates he always looked for the easiest victims.

The danger in thinking that all one has to do is bulk up or learn karate is the same as thinking that all one has to do is buy a gun or install an alarm.

There is no substitute for using your brain to outsmart crime instead of overpowering it. Not everyone is capable of bulking up or learning karate, but that doesn't mean he or she must become a crime victim.

To the burglar who is cruising through neighborhoods looking for the best house to burglarize, if all you have done is bulk up, and failed to trim your hedges, mow your lawn, or install deadbolts or start a block watch, the fact that you are in great shape is of little deterrent value to that burglar. The 120-pound weakling may have gone to great lengths on the other hand to present the impression an empowered person lives in his house, which means the burglar will avoid it like the plague.

QUESTION 12:
Crime is the police's problem. Why should I have to worry about it?

Many people feel that as long as their taxes are paying for police officers to patrol neighborhoods, they shouldn't have to do anything themselves. As we said in the introduction to this book, to the extent that law and order exists in a given community, it is because the citizenry choose to live that way, not because the police have caused it to be that way.

There are never going to be enough police to forcibly keep the peace in any given community without the active participation and support of the members of that community. Local law enforcement departments are increasingly moving to community policing concepts which is really nothing more than a return to the cop walking the beat and getting to know the citizens in advance of having to investigate crimes.

The idea is to link up law enforcement more closely with those who would operate as the eyes and ears of law enforcement: the public. Without your help, the police cannot do their job and the best way to help is to adopt the empowerment strategies in this book and become actively involved in your community.

Just as individual criminals look for the weakness and vulnerability in their prospective victim, so do gangs and other organized criminal operations look for weakness and vulnerability in communities. The movement of gangs from large urban areas to smaller communities is disturbing, but your community can avoid it by demonstrating empowerment, a lack of tolerance for disorder, and a close connection with the police.

RECURRING THEMES IN CRIME PREVENTION

There are some common themes in this book that will run through all of the empowerment tips and descriptions of how to avoid crime. It is important to cover these common themes and to repeat them over and over because it is difficult to predict every kind of encounter one might have with crime and develop prevention strategies for each one.

Therefore, if you remember some basic themes about how criminals think and how they operate, you can adapt your behavior to specific situations whether or not specific empowerment strategies have been provided.

The Path of Least Resistance

Criminals don't want to get caught and the best way to avoid getting caught is to find the easiest possible target. So if you are talking about street crime, the robber or assailant is going to look for a victim who is looking vulnerable, with shoulders hunched over, not looking around at his or her environment and not walking with a purpose. They are looking for someone who they think they can steal from with a minimum amount of struggle and a minimum amount of noise. They are the easiest to overpower, the easiest to sneak up on, and the easiest to get away with.

In the context of the burglar, the home that looks like it is the easiest to victimize would be the burglar's primary target: unkept, no real visible signs of any security going on, no one home, lights on during the day on the front porch, garage open, no cars around, papers and mail stacked up. This kind of a home might as well have a neon sign that says Welcome Burglars! There is an alarm company that actually has a television advertisement with a neon sign that says Rob Me, because these disheveled characteristics are there. This book covers numerous empowerment strategies one can employ to avoid being the path of least resistance.

The concept here is important to remember because convicted burglars in interviews have said that they always looked for the most vulnerable homes to steal from. They would avoid neighborhoods that had block watch signs, homes with alarms, homes with deadbolt locks, and areas with dogs because there were so many homes that didn't have *any* security that it was pointless to take the additional risk of hitting a house that showed any security at all.

The implications for preventing crime are obvious here. If you do anything at all to show that you want to avoid crime, you are significantly less likely to be victimized, whether in your home, on the street, or at work. Theoretically, as long as you are not the path of least resistance, the typical criminal is going to avoid you. We are suggesting that you take considerably more steps than just avoiding this minimum level of action, but something is better than nothing.

The Chameleon Effect

Whereas the path of least resistance addresses what the criminal is looking for in a "desirable" victim, the "chameleon effect" addresses steps the criminal takes to avoid being detected and ultimately caught. If the criminal stands out to the point that everyone notices him, he is not going to be successful. Some criminals are that way. These are the people who are addicted to drugs, look bedraggled in appearance—they are always being contacted by the police because they obviously look dangerous or don't fit in anywhere except in a dark back alley.

The successful criminal is the one who will disguise him- or herself in order to blend into the environment—the burglar who rents a Mercedes in order to drive into an upper-class neighborhood; the burglar who puts on a jogging suit before going into a middle-class neighborhood; the burglar who drives up to a neighborhood in a maintenance type of vehicle; or the office thief who puts on a maintenance uniform before entering an office to steal purses from people's desks.

Con artists who use the telephone to swindle people will do everything they can to convince the victim that he or she is legitimate before asking for a cashier's check to enter a contest.

The best tip to remember to overcome the chameleon effect is to focus on what people do, not what they look like. Behavior is a much more important clue in detecting crimes than appearance. We respond to people based upon our own stereotypes. So if a person of a race that is different from the predominant race in your neighborhood comes down the street, you are going to notice that person. In so doing, you are going to miss the person of like race who is dressed up as a city water department meter reader who is really casing the neighborhood for a later burglary. So we have to get rid of our stereotypes and focus on what kind of behavior a person is engaged in that makes you uneasy.

The Importance of Empowerment

The empowered person is confident and not fearful. One of the chief sources of confidence is knowledge, and hopefully the information and insights provided by this book will provide people with enough information to be able to avoid fear and consequently avoid victimization. It is a great irony that the person who most fears crime and communicates that fear to the criminals is in fact the most likely to be victimized. It becomes almost a self-fulfilling prophecy.

By contrast, the powerful person who walks with a purpose and who has taken specific and significant steps to avoid appearing to be the path of least resistance, whether at home or on the streets, is the least likely to be victimized because the person appears strong.

This is why we call all of the crime prevention tips in this book empowerment strategies. If you adopt any of these strategies, you will not only feel more powerful but, importantly, you will appear more powerful to would-be attackers and other criminals. And because there are so many people who do not take the initiative for whatever reason to become empowered, there will always be easy targets for criminals to victimize. The main message you want to convey is "Not me, not here, not now." You can do this by becoming an empowered citizen.

The Role of the Police

There are two primary roles for the police: investigating crime reports and preventing crime. Unfortunately, up to 90 percent of what a police officer does is reacting to crime rather than preventing it. This is an important point to recognize especially for those who have held on to the myth that crime prevention is exclusively a police matter. For if 90 percent of the resources of the police department are spent on reaction to crimes that have been committed and answering citizen calls, and only 10 percent at most is spent on prevention, that means that you and your neighbors are primarily responsible for preventing crime.

Notwithstanding the fact that police patrols can be a deterrent to some degree, ultimately there will never be enough patrol cars in any given jurisdiction to prevent criminals from plying their trade.

While some more progressive police departments are beginning to create substations in neighborhoods and are launching creative community policing programs, the simple fact is that the police department in your community will never spend anywhere near a majority of its time preventing you from becoming a crime victim. It is up to you, in essence, to "take your neighborhood back from crime." Fortunately, we walk with you through every step of this process.

Understanding the Mind of the Criminal

Another theme that runs through this book is the importance of understanding how the criminal mind works so that you can outsmart it. It is for this reason that every chapter of this book includes a section called Inside the Mind of. . . . This section contains a statement from a convicted criminal about how he or she went about committing crimes and what steps you can take to avoid being a victim of this crime.

Why is it important to know what a criminal thinks? Take the burglar as an example. Once you know that burglary is a "sneak" crime and that the primary objective of a burglar is to look for and steal from only those houses that have no one in them, you have an important piece of information in structuring your strategies for avoiding burglary.

The behavior that you engage in to protect your "kingdom" is going to be dramatically altered by your knowledge of what a criminal is thinking. Of equal importance in understanding the criminal mind is the extent to which it allays what for many is unjustified fear that results from television coverage of violence. If you know how gang violence operates and understand that the vast majority of violence caused by gangs is between one gang and another, and you know that only those who accidentally get caught in the cross-fire between rival gangs are the ones who get victimized, your fear would be mitigated by the knowledge that you can avoid certain dangerous areas.

As we have already pointed out, being victimized by fear can often be as debilitating as actual victimization, so the more you know, the lower your fear. The lower your fear, the less victimized all of us will be by crime and the more empowered and confident we become. And, of course, empowerment is in itself a deterrent.

The material relating to the mind of the criminal is based on a series of interviews Doug Shadel conducted at Clinton Correctional Facility in Dannemora, New York, in May 1994 and from other interviews conducted with inmates at the Clallum Bay Correctional Facility, a maximum security prison near Forks, Washington. Nine interviews were conducted. In each instance, the inmate's real name has been concealed and an assumed name has been used. Below is a brief introduction to each inmate:

1] DREW ➤ Thirty-three years old, serving seven to fifteen years for burglary at Clinton Correctional Facility. Has committed over 350 burglaries and has been in and out of prison for the past fifteen years. At the time of his most recent arrest, Drew was addicted to alcohol and was a cocaine addict.

2] ED ➤ Twenty-eight years old, serving three to six years for burglary at Clinton Correctional Facility. Claims to have committed approximately 250 burglaries.

3] JOSEPH ➤ Thirty-three years old, serving ten years for armed robbery at Clinton Correctional Facility. Has been in prison for twenty of his thirty-three years—a career criminal who has robbed over two hundred people at gunpoint on the streets of New York City and elsewhere. Joseph has also committed rape, burglary, and a variety of other offenses during his "career."

4] NOVA ➤ Thirty-one years old, serving fifteen years to life for first degree rape at Clinton Correctional Facility. Has been in and out of prison for most of his life. Claims to have raped over two hundred women, abused his wife, and been a crack addict and an alcoholic.

5] SAD CAT ➤ Twenty-five years old, serving fifteen years to life for attempted murder at Clallum Bay Correctional Facility. A Samoan gang member from Long Beach, California, who was transplanted to Seattle, he has been involved as a gang banger since the age of eight.

6] CHRISTOPHER ➤ Twenty-four years old, serving fifteen years to life for attempted murder at Clallum Bay Correctional Facility. A professional auto thief who has stolen over two thousand cars since the age of fourteen, Christopher has been incarcerated off and on for the past ten years.

7] JEFF ➤ Thirty-two years old, arrested in 1984 for spousal abuse, released on his own recognizance. Was a habitual batterer and alcoholic for about ten years before his arrest and subsequent rehabilitation.

8] ROGER ➤ Twenty-eight years old, serving fifteen years to life for second degree murder at Clinton County Correctional Facility. A career drug dealer whose father was part of the Metayeen Drug Cartel in Miami, Roger ran drugs from the East to West Coast. Prior to his arrest, he specialized in robbing drug dealers of their cash and stash.

9] LINDA ➤ Twenty-five years old, arrested for twenty-eight counts of passing bad checks. She is on probation after serving time in the county jail.

From their insights into prevention strategies to how to keep your kids from turning out like they did, the individuals in this book bear their souls. What will you learn? Probably more about the inside scoop on crime than you would have ever imagined.

When It Comes to Reporting Crime, "If It Bleeds, It Leads."

The phrase "If it bleeds, it leads" is a great way to sum up the misimpression the media is giving Americans in the 1990s. We interviewed a former assignment editor for a local Seattle television station, Denny Fleenor, who explained why television has so many crime stories on the nightly news:

> *Television is a visual medium and there is no better picture than a fire blazing or a crime scene with the yellow tape around an area and a bloodied body. When I was at the assignment desk, I would spend eight hours a day listening to a bank of police radios blaring crime calls the police were headed toward. We needed to know exactly where the crimes were so we could send a film crew out to report on it. There was tremendous pressure to air stories that had drama and would hold the viewer's interest. Our research showed us that people love to watch stories about crime and violence and so we were just giving them what they wanted—lots of blood and guts. I had probably a hundred different stories I could have aired on any given day, but the crime stories got the best ratings and that is what it was all about. Unfortunately, we ended up providing a very distorted view of the world.*

The pressure to focus on crime stories has created an environment in which people are afraid to move about freely in their neighborhood or in their city. While the chances of being victimized are low, the rates of fear which the Bureau of Justice Statistics records are getting higher every year. There is a danger of encountering a sort of "bunkering down" mentality in neighborhoods where people are afraid to talk to anyone and they feel imprisoned in their own homes.

If this book does nothing else, we hope you walk away less fearful than you were before. We think once you understand what your real (not perceived) risks are of becoming a victim, once you understand how criminals think, and once you have learned some powerful prevention techniques to avoid crime, you will be empowered to walk anywhere in your community without the fear of victimization.

The Vulnerability Continuum

One of the themes we keep coming back to over and over again is the idea of the vulnerability continuum. Each chapter in this book opens with the Bureau of Justice Statistics which provide a statistical picture of your chances of becoming a victim of a particular crime.

Wherever possible, we provide statistical breakdowns of your chances of victimization based primarily on location and other important variables. Wherever this is not available, we suggest that you conceptualize your risk based upon the Vulnerability Continuum charts provided in this chapter.

These charts provide you with a general picture of who is being victimized the most based on the factors of age, sex, and race. Overlay on top of that whether you live in an urban, suburban, or rural area in order to further assess your vulnerability and therefore the extent to which you should employ some or all of the empowerment strategies listed in this book. The only way to determine the level of prevention and protection you need is to determine where you fall on the vulnerability continuum.

Three Principles of Safety

Although we describe literally hundreds of empowerment strategies in this book, there are three general principles which run through all of the empowerment strategies. They are:

Be aware of what's going on around you: This simply means whether you are in your car, walking down the street, or in your home, be aware of your external environment. This is not to say that every moment of the day you must worry about crime. Rather, it just means get into the habit of being observant.

You might want to practice this by spending ten minutes each day concentrating on everything around you. If you are at home, become aware of the neighborhood and what is going on in it; notice the temperature inside your house and then go outside and notice the outside temperature. Check the area in the immediate vicinity of your house. Check out the neighbor's yard and the general atmosphere of the street you live on.

By training yourself to be alert in the normal course of your day, you will become safer on a daily basis. This is because when a suspicious situation presents itself you will be more likely to notice it and avoid it.

Trust your instincts: Once you have become a trained observer, it is important to trust your instincts when a questionable situation arises. Too often, people ignore their instincts and walk into situations which in retrospect they knew to be dangerous. When you are walking down the street and the knot forming in your stomach tells you someone is following you, listen to it and take action. Later on in this book we talk about actions you should take given certain situations.

Have a plan: The empowerment strategies in this book are designed to help you avoid becoming a victim. It is important that you read through them and think about how you would employ them in the event you were confronted by crime. Having a plan is very much a theme that runs through all of the material in this book. In some ways, this book is nothing but one big plan for eliminating crime. Use it.

PRINCIPLES TO LIVE BY

As you read the chapters and decide for yourself what aspects of your lifestyle you are willing to change to become more empowered, here are the principles we suggest informed crime fighters live by:

1] THE MAJORITY OF CITIZENS ARE NEVER VICTIMIZED ➤
The world is still an orderly place, notwithstanding the media's preoccupation with violent crime. The overall crime rate in 1992 was actually lower than it was in 1973 and over 90 percent of American citizens were not victimized in 1992. While any

amount of crime is unacceptable, it is important to put what you see on the news in perspective and recognize that the sky is not, in fact, falling.

And with more and more people, especially older adults, locking themselves in their homes afraid to go out at night, it is increasingly important that one understands the true statistical chances of becoming a crime victim.

2] UNDERSTANDING HOW CRIMINALS THINK IS KEY TO AVOIDING CRIME ➤ The statements from prisoners are designed to give you a true understanding of how criminals think and specifically how they choose their targets. Once you become armed with this knowledge, it is important to incorporate it into your daily life. For example, when you go to the lake to go swimming, it is important to remember that Christopher, the car thief, lists it as one of his favorite locations to break into cars because people typically leave their wallets and checkbooks behind when they go swimming.

Likewise, when it comes to walking down the street on your way to work, it is important to walk with your head up, looking around confidently like you know exactly where you are going. Why? Because Joseph, the convicted armed robber, says that he would only rob the person who looks the weakest, one who is not aware of his or her surroundings and therefore looks vulnerable to a surprise attack.

3] IT IS UP TO YOU (NOT THE POLICE) TO ENSURE THAT YOU ARE NOT A VICTIM ➤ While your chances are relatively low of becoming a crime victim, it is ultimately up to you to ensure that you avoid crime. There are concrete strategies you can employ to avoid crime, irrespective of where you live, your age, or your gender. It is a cop out (so to speak) to rely exclusively on the police for protection. The only way to lower the crime rate is to take charge of your life and employ the empowerment strategies listed herein.

4] MAKE YOUR COMMUNITY A CRIME-FREE ZONE ➤ This book provides numerous strategies to help you avoid crime individually but we have also attempted to stress the value of communities working together to ensure that law and order predominate. Whether it is starting a block watch on your street, volunteering to help clean up vacant lots which otherwise might attract crime, or just agreeing to watch your neighbor's house when he's on vacation, it is clear that communities have got to work together in order to reduce crime.

The best way to start building a community that is crime free is to meet with the neighbors on your block to discuss their experiences with crime. You can certainly invite a crime prevention officer from your local police department to such a meeting who can give you crime statistics for your community. He or she can also usually provide your block with block watch signs, stickers to go on the windows of each house, and even engravers that enable residents to engrave their valuables.

Remember, however, that the real deterrent to crime is not the police who might periodically patrol the area or visit a block watch meeting. The real deterrent is you and your neighbors, who decide that you will not tolerate any crime on your street or in your lives. Once that happens, you are on your way to ensuring a safe environment for yourself, your belongings, and your family.

5] WE MUST ATTACK THE ROOT CAUSES OF CRIME ➤ It is pretty clear to us that the root cause of much criminal behavior starts with the family. The single most important element you can provide as a parent is to listen to your kids, and nurture and love them. The interviews we conducted of prisoners brings this point out clearly. We asked each one of them what they would tell parents to do that their parents didn't do. To a man, each one said "listen."

This may sound like an oversimplification but in our research, it is painfully obvious where the root causes of criminal behavior lie: in parenting. We believe that bad kids are not born, they are grown. And if you want to attack the root causes of crime, providing a positive mentor relationship with children is the single most effective way to do it. It is perfectly fine to mount campaigns to keep kids off drugs and alcohol and to educate them about AIDS and the problems associated with teen pregnancy and all of the other social ills besetting our young people. But we believe that most of these problems are symptoms, not root causes.

The root cause of crime is the failure to provide kids with a steady diet of principles adhered to by a lawful, orderly society. Increasingly, the difficulty is that in order to provide these principles, one must first possess them. And as more and more kids are giving birth to kids and our prison population soars, there are fewer and fewer people available to mentor solid lawful principles.

We believe one solution to this is volunteerism. Organizations like Big Brothers and Big Sisters hold the key to turning the tide on youth violence and gangs. If we as a society can begin to encourage more lawful citizens of all ages to volunteer to mentor just one kid during their lifetime, we may begin to attack this problem.

The growing population of retirees may very well be the best source of such volunteerism. Organizations like AARP are literally teeming with volunteers who have led successful lives and could provide positive directions for otherwise directionless kids.

We know from study after study that kids who have made it out of the inner city against seemingly overwhelming odds all had one thing in common: they had at least one person who was in their corner, someone they could talk to and who provided them with unconditional love. This is precisely what all the prisoners we spoke to said was lacking in their lives.

The great poet Henry David Thoreau once said:

There are a thousand hacking at the branches
of evil to one who is striking at the root.

If we are going to significantly reduce crime in America, more of us must attack its root causes. And that means taking care of kids whether they are ours or someone else's, hour by hour, day by day, month by month. Big government programs may or may not work, but what does work is one human being taking the time to guide a young person toward a positive future. Individual, personal, direct service. You don't owe it to your country to help in this way, you owe it to yourself. Every young person we turn away from crime and toward hard work, community, and responsibility brings us one step closer to a time when empty jails can be turned into community centers; when hospital emergency rooms stop treating shooting victims and are preoccupied with the delivery of healthy babies; when juvenile detention centers house study groups for gifted Asian, Black, and Samoan youths who previously would have been in trouble for gang banging.

Beyond taking steps to outsmart crime for yourself and the sake of your family, take the next step. Find a young person who is at risk of losing his or her way and intervene. Spend time with the youth, get him or her involved in sports or other positive, interesting activities. Teach him or her the benefits of deferred gratification and hard work.

The most selfish thing you can do is to give your time to someone who needs it: you will be rewarded beyond your wildest imagination.

OUTSMARTING 2
BURGLARY

Myth:

> As long as I have a deadbolt lock on my door
> and keep a light on when I'm gone, I will not
> be burglarized.

REALITY:

> **BURGLARS USUALLY BREAK IN THROUGH
> WINDOWS AND ARE ALMOST NEVER FOOLED BY
> HAVING A SINGLE LIGHT ON WHEN YOU'RE AWAY.**

ONE OF THE MOST DISTURBING ADS ON TELEVISION THESE DAYS shows a burglar breaking into a house while the owners are gone, ransacking it with little or no regard for the damage being done and then smirking as he sneaks off with all of the valuables in the house. The ad ends with a statement like, "Don't let a creep like this in your house."

In this chapter, we dispel some of the myths about burglary, provide an overview of your chances of being burglarized, share some very revealing interviews with convicted burglars, and provide an extensive series of empowerment strategies which enable the reader to take action to avoid becoming a victim.

THE TRUTH ABOUT BURGLARY

Burglary is defined as: unlawful or forcible entry or attempted entry into a residence.

What are your chances of being burglarized? It depends on where you are on the vulnerability continuum. While age, sex, and race play a role, perhaps the most important factor is location. In 1992, the BJS estimated that overall burglary rates for city, suburban, and rural dwellers were as follows:

BURGLARY BY LOCATION—1992		
Location	% Victimized	% Not Victimized
City	6.01%	93.99%
Suburban	4.46%	95.54%
Rural	4.17%	95.83%
All Areas	4.89%	95.11%

Source: *Criminal Victimization in the U.S.*, Table 34, page 50.

While burglary rates have been going down over time, largely due to the increased number of burglar alarms installed in homes and increases in auto theft as the property crime of choice, it is still important to understand how the burglar thinks and therefore how to outsmart him or her. Remember that in 1992 there were 4.7 million burglaries committed in the United States and it is important to take measures to ensure that you are not included among those who are victimized each year.

And while the overall burglary rate of 6.01 percent of households means 93.99 percent of households are *not* burglarized, the burglar is looking for that 6 percent of the population who may not have taken any precautions to prevent the crime.

If you live in a so-called hotspot as described in chapter 1, where there is a concentration of criminal activity for one reason or another, your chances of being victimized increase dramatically. Therefore, as we mention in the opening chapter, the extent to which you need to be concerned about outsmarting crime is directly dependent on your location on the vulnerability continuum.

The following is an interview between the two of us during which Doug asks Al to profile the typical burglar and what kinds of houses he is after. Al's responses are based on dozens of interviews he has had with convicted burglars during his twenty-five-year-long law enforcement career. Al provides an excellent profile of just who these people are in order to know how to stop them.

DOUG: Give me a profile of the typical burglar in terms of age, gender, and socioeconomic status.

AL: The typical burglar is between the ages of twelve and twenty-six, usually male, and often has a substance abuse problem. Burglars are often scared out of their gourd when they enter a house and consequently they never spend more than three to five minutes in the house.

DOUG: What kind of a house are they looking for?

AL: One that is vacant. Burglary is a "sneak" crime, meaning the burglar wants to find a home where he can enter, take your stuff, and leave without ever being noticed by anyone, including neighbors. So when he is driving through a neighborhood, he will look for obvious signs that a house is unoccupied like papers stacked up on the porch, mail piled up in the mailbox, that kind of thing.

DOUG: What other signs would he look for that make a house an attractive target?

AL: Burglars look for signs that the homeowner is sloppy and therefore might have left a window or door unlocked. If the lawn has not been mowed or the hedges haven't been trimmed, these are signals to the burglar that the homeowner doesn't have his or her act together.

Another thing they look for is the absence of people around in the neighborhood. If the house they are looking for is on a block where everyone goes to work during the day, that makes it attractive.

DOUG: Do burglars spend a lot of time casing a neighborhood to find the best house to break into?

AL: Some burglars are very premeditated. A couple of years ago, we had a case where a couple of burglars stole a reverse directory from the library and actually charted out neighborhoods and called them at different times to find out who was home. They spent the better part of a week charting out neighborhoods to get a feel for when the best time was to be there.

Then they had CB radios and the person who was going to be on foot would put on a jogging outfit and would jog through the neighborhood and knock on the door of the house of his choice based upon signals he got about the way it looked from the exterior. Then if no one was there, he would break in, steal valuables, and call his accomplice on the CB to tell him where to pick him up.

The jogging suit allowed him to blend in. A lot of burglars don't blend in and that is why a person who is out doing yard work, out for a walk, or riding a bicycle can easily notice suspicious activity or people who don't belong.

In other cases, the burglars might live in the neighborhood, so they just wait and observe their own neighbors to determine when the best time to hit would be. Others are just passing through and make some quick assessments about which house to hit. The house they are looking for is the path of least resistance.

DOUG: What do you mean by the path of least resistance?

AL: The path of least resistance is simply the house where the chances of getting caught are the smallest. So an attractive house would be one in a community where the neighbors all work, the lawn and yard are not kept up, papers and mail are overflowing.

But there are other things they look for. Every burglar I have ever interviewed has told me there are some specific things that scare him away. Any indication that a house has an alarm system is a big deterrent. The burglar will say to himself, "Why should I risk having a loud siren go off and the police called through a monitoring station when there are so many houses without alarms?"

Second, if the burglar sees signs that there are dogs on the premises that would make a lot of noise, that becomes a deterrent. Third, they look for signs that indicate whether the neighborhood is well organized and whether neighbors are watching out for each other. Whether that means they have posted block watch signs or are generally attentive to the activities going on in the neighborhood, it tells the burglar he will likely be seen if he tries to burglarize someone.

All of these deterrents relate to noise and the risk of being caught as opposed to the difficulty of getting in. So it is important to keep up physical security by locking doors and windows and having deadbolts, but it is also important to evaluate your whole environment.

DOUG: Are most burglars looking to break into nice houses in wealthy neighborhoods or will they try any neighborhood?

AL: The typical burglar can find what he wants in any house, so he is not looking just for a nice house. Almost everyone has stereos, TVs and VCRs, and some kind of jewelry, which are the top items burglars are after.

Some burglars think that if they get into too high class of a neighborhood that the homes will have sophisticated alarms, a safe in the house, watch dogs, and the like and that puts them at greater risk.

DOUG: What percentage of burglaries occur during the day versus at night?

AL: Fifty percent of all burglaries are done at night, 50 percent during the day. Daytime is attractive simply because so many people are at work, and there are fewer people home. However, night time can be advantageous because often the signals are clearer at night about whether someone is home. If it's 7:00 P.M. in the winter and there are no lights on, the chances are there is no one home. Also, at night, the darkness provides good cover.

DOUG: What percentage of burglaries occur with no forced entry, meaning a door or window was left open?

AL: Forty percent of all burglaries are the result of a window or door being unopened or a key being found: no forced entry. This is perhaps the most frustrating statistic of all and most revealing in terms of the path of least resistance. In fully 40 percent of the burglaries that occur, the homeowner left a door open or a window open.

The majority of burglars I have interviewed say they look exclusively for homes with open windows or doors and if they have to use forced entry, they go on to the next house.

DOUG: Once a burglar has decided which house to hit, how does he do it?

AL: The typical way a burglar goes about it is he drives into a neighborhood, parks his car, looks for the house he is going to hit, then goes up to the house and knocks on the door. If nobody answers, that means there is nobody home. The next step is to try the door. If the door doesn't open, he'll see if the window is locked. This technique is mostly done during the daytime when most neighbors are at work.

DOUG: Are most burglars armed or not armed?

AL: It depends on where you are. Usually the burglar is hoping to get in and get out without anyone being the wiser, so while some may be armed just because it is a nasty part of town, it is not because he is hoping to be able to blow away the victim. People get in their way and they seek to avoid any confrontation with people. Therefore, I'd say most burglars are not armed.

INSIDE THE MIND OF THE BURGLAR

No matter how many statistics or brochures with tips on burglary prevention one reads, there is no substitute for hearing from burglars themselves. The following is a statement made by a convicted burglar named Drew who has committed over three hundred burglaries. We asked him to give us his perspective on three basic areas relating to burglary:

1] Choosing targets

2] Breaking into houses

3] Choosing a neighborhood

The statements that follow are adapted from a thirty-page transcript of a tape recorded interview conducted inside Clinton Correctional Facility in May 1994.

"My name is Drew. I have been a criminal on and off since I was about thirteen. I am thirty-four years old now and I am serving seven to fifteen years for burglary. By the time I leave the New York prison system, I will have spent fifteen of my thirty-four years in prison. I have committed over three hundred burglaries in my life and have been caught only twice. Most of the time, I was stealing money in order to support my drug habit. In the early 1980s, I was addicted to cocaine, snorting an ounce per week (at that time it cost about

$2,500 per ounce). I hope that the following information will help people avoid those who are out there right now taking the risk."

On Choosing Targets

"The main thing for doing burglaries is to find a house that is empty. I became very skilled at knowing whether someone was home or not. A lot of times, people think that if they just put a light on in the front window when they are not home that will convince the burglar. Let me tell you something, if I am cruising through a neighborhood and I see a house that is completely dark except for a front light on in the window, that tells me the house is empty. If the people were really home, they would be watching television or something and there would be a dim kind of light projecting out of the window from the back of the house.

"The other thing I look for is oil stains in the driveway. If I'm driving by or walking through a neighborhood and I see a house that has no car parked in the driveway, but there are oil stains in the driveway, that tells me that no one is home.

"I used to go out right before it got dark, like at dusk—that was the best time to look for a house because people were still at work and you could see if windows were open. I wanted to hit a house before the people came home but while it was still light enough to see what I was doing. You might think that nighttime would be better to do a burglary because of the cover of darkness, which is true, but it also means there is more of a chance for someone to be home. In today's age of two-income families, I realized that most people work during the day.

"Anyway, I would look for a house where there were no cars in the driveway and no one inside. I liked to hit houses that didn't have a garage because a lot of times the garage had a car inside. If the house looked empty and there was a garage, I would go look inside the garage to see if a car was in it.

"I had a rating system of one through ten, with ten being the riskiest house and one being the least risky. Any house that was over a three, I would avoid. The reason is we were always looking for the easiest house on the block to hit.

So if I went up to a house and saw a big Beware of Dog sign on the door or an alarm sticker, I still might hit the house, but those types of things would definitely increase the risk factor. I'll talk more about alarms in a minute.

"If someone had a sign on the door that said This House Protected by Smith and Wesson, it wouldn't affect me at all. Some people think that if they buy a gun, it will stop them from being burglarized. What they don't realize is that a gun is only good if you are home to use it. I was always looking for empty houses. That's 'cause burglary is a 'sneak' crime. We want to get in and get out without anyone seeing us—I mean anyone. I don't want the neighbors to see me, the mailman, the milkman—anyone! So let me give you a piece of advice, if you're thinking of buying a gun to protect you from burglary, don't do it. Chances are I'll just break into your home when you're not there and steal everything, including the gun.

"Another thing I would look for in a good house to hit was one that had a lot of trees on the sides of the house or in front to block the view from the neighbors or from the street. This was pretty common and so there was lots of houses to choose from. Also, some people had fenced off their house for privacy and it made it real easy to get in and take stuff without being seen. If I saw a house that had a lot of trees around it and a solid wood fence completely surrounding it, I owned that house—that's the first one I would hit.

"I really liked to hit houses that were on a street corner. This is because there was only one neighbor to watch out for and you could see cars coming from four different directions. That's not to say I wouldn't hit houses in the middle of a block, but, given the choice, I'd probably go for the corner house.

"So the perfect house to hit would be one with a solid fence around it, no garage, oil stain in the driveway, no alarm, on a street corner, no dogs, and a back alley where I could pull up my van to load the stuff. It was pretty rare to find all of these things in a target, but most of the time, my houses had two or three of these characteristics."

On Breaking into the House

"I would almost always take someone with me to keep watch while I was inside getting the stuff. The typical thing we would do is I would go up to the house and knock on the door while my friend watched for neighbors. Now remember that we had already scoped it out and saw something that made us pretty sure there was no one home: oil stains in the driveway, no lights on or if there were lights on, it was a light near the front window. I'd knock on the door just to double check. If someone came to the door, I'd ask for a girl like Jane or Sandy or something. They would say I had the wrong house and I would get the hell out of there.

"More commonly there would be no answer, so I'd go around to the side of the house and check to see if any windows were open. I would also look for alarm stickers and the control box or tape around windows to prove they really had an alarm. Just putting up the stickers wasn't good enough—most burglars are hip to that trick. The thing that always amazed me is that at least 40 percent of the houses I broke into had a window or door open somewhere. This made it pretty easy to get in.

"If there were no open windows and I wasn't sure about the alarm situation, I would go to the side of the house and take a small rock and throw it through the side window. Then I would wait for fifteen minutes to see if a silent alarm had been tripped. If no police came during that fifteen minutes, then I would just break the window and climb in.

"A lot of times, people think that they are fully protected if they install an alarm. And it is true that I would rather hit a house that didn't have an alarm than one that did. But if you are going to spend the money to get an alarm, make sure you get it for all levels of your house. A lot of times, I would see that a house had an alarm on the first floor, but there was an open window and/or no alarm on the second floor. If that was the case, I would just climb up onto the second story and break in that way.

"So the main thing I would avoid was houses with full on alarm systems on all floors. A house has six sides, not four. Lots of times, I climbed in through a skylight or through a daylight basement.

"I also didn't like houses that had dogs like rottweilers or Dobermans. It was a combination of the noise they make when they bark and the fact that they would probably bite my head off. Besides, there were so many houses that didn't have dogs, it was stupid to risk it.

"Another thing I didn't like was houses that had infrared lighting—you know those kind of lights that come on at night when somebody walks through the beam—man those were a bummer 'cause when I was taking the risk and doing the burglaries at night, I'd scope out a house that I thought was empty and go up to it and then this light would all of a sudden flash onto me and it made me jump about ten feet in the air. Even after I realized what it was and that there was still probably no one home, I was so nervous that I split. I didn't know if the neighbors had seen me or what.

"Lighting is the big thing. I think it is important to have timers on your lights so they come on and go off at certain times. It's also important to put timers on more than one light and also to hook the timer up to a radio or a television or something that makes it sound like someone's home. The thing that I look for is the way the television looks from the outside of a house through the window. I know exactly how it looks cause I have peered into so many houses from the outside and if I see that the television is on, I'm gone. Watching television is the one thing everyone does when they come home."

On Choosing a Neighborhood

"The one thing I never did was burglarize an apartment. That was just too scary—too many people around. I almost always would hit individual homes in neighborhoods. The best neighborhoods are middle- to upper-middle-class neighborhoods with large-sized lots. The more trees and space around a house, the easier it is to get in and get out without being seen. Unfortunately, I did most of my burglaries in New York City and the houses are pretty close together, so I had to be careful. I didn't hit expensive neighborhoods too much because they all had expensive alarms and security systems.

"The kind of neighborhood I was looking for was one where no one was home. So I would look for the kind of yuppy neighborhood that had kid's toys in the backyard which meant the family which had a couple of kids but both parents worked and were never home during the day. The worst neighborhood to hit was one that was full of older adults. Not only are they home all day, but a lot of them got nothing better to do but to stare out the window and look for unusual-looking people walking around.

"That's another thing, for awhile I did burglaries with this girl—she was a great cover because when you go into a neighborhood, you want to look like you fit in. So if a couple of seventeen-year-old kids are walking down the sidewalk during the middle of the day, somebody might look at that as funny, you know? But if you're walking down the street with your girl, arm in arm, no one thinks twice about that.

"You know those little stickers people put on their houses that say Operation ID or something like that? Those didn't mean anything. In the first place, most people don't mark their stuff like you're supposed to, they just put up the sticker. In the second place, even if they did mark their stuff, I would just take the stuff to New York City. I could fence anything in New York City, marked or not. And I think that is true for any big city, not just New York.

"I must admit that I would not go into a neighborhood that had block watch signs at the beginning of the block. You know those ones that say, 'This neighborhood reports all strangers to the police' or something like that. It wasn't so much that I thought I couldn't go burglarize that block, cause I know I could have. It was more like 'Why risk it?' I mean, it usually means there is some little old lady or more than one who spends her whole day just looking for something to report. You put a little old lady on the block and it adds about two points to my risk factor system. Since I wouldn't hit any house that was over a three on my scale, it didn't take too many little old ladies on a block to put a house over the limit, you know what I mean?

"The neighbors played a very important role in which house I would hit. I was constantly watching out for neighbors to see if they were paying attention to what was going on in the neighborhood or whether they were just into their own business. One time I remember hitting a house that was vacant but the neighbors next door were home having a barbecue. But because of the way the house was situated with the backyard facing away from the house I was hitting, I was able to get in and out without anyone seeing me."

"The best neighborhoods were ones that were filled with yuppies—two income families or single people who spent a lot of time at work or traveling. I found myself continually going back to those types of neighborhoods and it was pretty easy to identify them. People who live in these types of neighborhoods should all have alarms—big time.

"Another thing I would do is if you are going to be gone for awhile, I'd have a neighbor park his car in your front yard—cover up the oil stain you know? Another thing is make sure you know the people you let into your house. For awhile, I was a plumber working for this guy and I went into and out of dozens of houses, looking at all the different stuff people had. Then once I quit and started doing burglaries, I knew exactly which houses had the best stuff, which had alarms and which didn't, you know—the whole thing. It was like taking candy from a baby."

On How to Prevent Burglary

"A lot of guys I know would dress up like a TV repair man or a plumber or a pizza delivery man—anybody who would have a reason to be hanging around your door. So if you see someone like that in your neighborhood and he is acting in a suspicious way like walking around to the back of your neighbor's house, call the police.

"Also, I would suggest hooking up a police scanner to the timers you have hooked up to your lights. The thing that would scare me off the quickest was the static noise that comes from a police scanner—that's the sound a police officer makes when he is sneaking up behind you to arrest you. So if I hear that anywhere near your house, I'm going to high-tail it out of there.

"When you put lights up in the outside, make sure they are facing the house, not facing out toward the street. If the lights are facing out toward the street, then it will provide cover for a burglar since no one can see what's going on near the house.

"On the issue of dogs, I think if you had a Beware of Dog sign up in your yard, I would probably skip your house. This alone wouldn't stop me necessarily, but there are enough houses without a dog that I'd look for before risking finding out if you really had a dog or not."

BURGLARY VICTIM SCENARIO

● ●

Bill's neighborhood was a picture of safety. As far as he knew, no one on his street had ever been burglarized in the twenty years he had lived there. One fine sunny day, he was just returning from a trip to the hardware store when he saw a man whom he didn't recognize in his backyard. He got out of his car and greeted the man. "Can I help you find something mister?"

"Oh yes," said the man not missing a beat. "I am terribly upset because Sparky, my six-month-old Dalmatian, got loose from his chain and ran away. I live about six blocks from here and I have been looking for hours. You haven't seen him have you?"

Bill immediately could sympathize with the man since his dog Chester had died last year after living his life as the family dog. "I haven't seen him, no," said Bill. "I'd be glad to help you look for him though." So the two of them headed off down the street and spent the next two hours looking for "Sparky."

When Bill returned after leaving his new friend up the street and being unsuccessful at finding the dog, he went into his home only to find that he had been burglarized. The stranger he had found in his yard was really one of two burglars who had been hitting his house when he came home at the wrong time and, unbeknownst to Bill, caught them in the act.

Instead of questioning the stranger more about what he was doing in his backyard, he succumbed to the burglar's creative "pitch" that he was merely looking for his dog. Meanwhile, his partner was waiting in the garage with all of the items they had hauled out of the house, so he could finish the job.

Moral: Some burglars are bold and quick on their feet. If you see someone in your neighborhood or especially in your yard whom you do not recognize, no matter how respectable he may look, confront him and ask him what his business is. Be sure to look him directly in the eyes when you do this. If he does not have a believable explanation, tell him to leave. If you suspect foul play, call the police immediately.

BURGLARY PREVENTION
EMPOWERMENT STRATEGIES

——————————————————————→

The statement you have just read from Drew, along with the Burglary Victim Scenario, should have revealed some obvious empowerment strategies for avoiding burglary. Below is a list of strategies which we believe will virtually eliminate your chances of becoming a victim. Some of them are taken from Drew's comments and reflections on his career as a criminal and other are taken from our experiences.

➡ *EMPOWERMENT STRATEGY #1: Be selective about where you live. Before buying a house, investigate the neighborhood you are thinking of moving into:*

❑ Talk to the neighbors about whether they have had problems with crime.

❑ Look for junk cars, vandalism, run down houses, unmowed lawns, proximity to middle schools and high schools.

❑ Call the police department and ask them about the neighborhood you're thinking of moving into. A lot of departments have crime analysis people who have crime data which pinpoints where crime is happening (see Figure 1: Seattle Hotspots, page 7).

❑ Ask the personnel at your local school what they think of the neighborhood. A wall will be created between the neighborhood and the school when crime problems exist. If the neighborhood is involved with the school, crime may not be a problem.

❑ Look for block watch signs, operation identification stickers on windows, good locks like deadbolts on doors: all of these are signs of a neighborhood that is organized.

❑ Look at the neighborhood at different times during the day: at night, look for who is out, how many lights are on, etc. Is there a place near the neighborhood where kids congregate at night? During the day, determine how many residents are at work and how many are older adults or homemakers who stay home.

- Try to identify if there are pieces of land in the area with an easement which might represent a heavily used path where kids might walk through: a path between two schools. Telltale signs of heavy traffic are places where there are a lot of cigarette butts or a lot of litter, or where there is vandalism on the fences or graffiti.

- Look for vacant houses, especially those that are boarded up or have five or six junk cars in front of them. Look for traffic patterns during the day. If there is a lot of traffic, often the homes will close their drapes to avoid noise and gain privacy and people tend to move to the back of their houses to live. This is a sign to a burglar that if he goes to rob a house no one will see him because the family is looking out the back, they have given up the front yard.

- Drive a two-mile radius around the neighbor and look for good and bad things as indicators. Good things would be a fire or police station; bad things would be bars, topless bars, convenience stores that attract a diverse and heavy flow of potentially questionable people. If they draw shady people, this could be a threat.

- Studies have indicated that if the burglar is under sixteen (and many are) and is on foot, he or she will likely burglarize a home that is within a mile of where he or she lives. If you are thinking about moving into an apartment, walk around the entire complex, talk to tenants who already live in the complex to find out if there have been any problems.

➥ EMPOWERMENT STRATEGY #2: *Rekey your house when you first move into it. Change all the locks.*

This is because if the house was a rental before or it was a house that had been owned by several others during recent years, you have no idea how many people have keys.

➡EMPOWERMENT STRATEGY #3: *Make sure that you have a solid core as opposed to a hollow-core door on all exterior doorways. It is possible to break through a hollow-core door with your fist.*

It is also important to install deadbolt locks on all exterior doorways. Make sure the deadbolts you use are heavy in weight and are made out of brass—they are probably strong.

➡EMPOWERMENT STRATEGY #4: *Use lighting when you are not home to give the appearance your house is not empty.*

To give the appearance of someone being home, buy a timer and hook it up to at least two lights in different parts of the house and to a radio that is set to an all-talk station so that it will sound like there are voices in the room. Turn it on at a volume level so that it can be heard, but so you can't really tell what it is. Don't turn on a television because it sometimes presents more of a fire hazard.

The number one thing all burglars say they are looking for is an empty house. They also all agree that when they see a lot of lights on in the house, they will likely not risk hitting it either because they think someone will see them or because they think no one is around to see them in the first place.

Remember that Drew says a single light on in the front window of the house was like a open invitation to go in. You must do more than turn on a single light in order to have it be a deterrent.

➡EMPOWERMENT STRATEGY #5: *Have your neighbor park his or her car in your driveway when you are gone for extended periods of time.*

Drew says that the first thing he looks for when he is assessing a house is oil stains in the driveway. If there are stains and he can see them, he reasons, then that is where the homeowner's car is normally parked and he is not home. By parking your neighbor's car there, the burglar will think someone is home.

➥ *EMPOWERMENT STRATEGY #6: Consider buying an alarm system, especially if you live in an area which has a relatively high crime rate.*

Alarms are not for everyone, but each of our professional burglars say he would not mess with a house that had an alarm system. They also all say that just buying an alarm sticker would not deter them because it is so easy to verify whether or not they truly do have a system.

➥ *EMPOWERMENT STRATEGY #7: In order to determine how easy it is to break into your house, try pretending you are a burglar.*

Lock your house, drive a block away, and park your car. Then look at your neighborhood as though you were looking for a house to break into. If you find an open window or an easy way to break in, then you know what you need to do to increase your security.

Drew says he had a point rating system from one to ten, with ten being the highest risk house to break into and one being the lowest. If a house was greater than three on his risk scale, he would skip it. When you are assessing your house, use the same point system.

Think about how likely it would be that someone could see you break into your house given the amount of lighting, the landscaping, etc. If you determine the risk to be less than five, then you should take steps to increase your security.

➥ *EMPOWERMENT STRATEGY #8: Remember that a house has six sides, not just four, and when you evaluate your security, determine how easy it would be for a burglar to climb in a skylight or a daylight basement.*

Drew and Ed both say they would frequently break into the second floor of a house because only the first floor was "alarmed over." So if you are installing an alarm system, you should evaluate all potential entry points.

A common point of entry for a burglar can be a crawl space under a house, a window in a daylight basement, or a skylight on the roof. Many burglars have gotten in by climbing through an outside-loading wood box, where people load their wood from the outside.

➡️EMPOWERMENT STRATEGY #9: Lock your windows and doors when you leave your house.

This seems obvious, but when everyone, including crime prevention experts and burglars, agrees that four out of the ten houses broken into are through unlocked doors or windows, the simplest way to avoid burglary is simply to lock up!

➡️EMPOWERMENT STRATEGY #10: If you are out in your neighborhood and you notice someone who doesn't belong or whom you have never seen before in your neighborhood, strike up a conversation with him or her.

This will give the person the signal that you will remember him. Burglars don't want to ever be seen by anyone, so if the person was going to burglarize the neighborhood, your talking to him will likely scare him away. He will go to the next neighborhood.

Ask him if you can help him find an address or mention what a nice day is. Make it a real positive contact so that it is not threatening to you at all.

➡️EMPOWERMENT STRATEGY #11: Give people the impression that you care about your house. Mow the lawn, keep the paint up, and do this even if you're out of town.

➡️EMPOWERMENT STRATEGY #12: Fences can be an effective deterrent if they enclose your property and create a psychological barrier, but don't create concealment for a burglar.

Recall that Drew says that he was looking for concealment more than anything else. Some people install privacy fences that block anyone's view from the street. If no one can see inside your yard, a burglar can get in and out without being seen. So some fencing is okay, but recognize there need to be openings.

➡️EMPOWERMENT STRATEGY #13: Install passive infrared lighting in the front and the back of your house.

This is a light that detects motion and will come on when you come home at night. The infrared lights in the back of the house are to deter prowlers who don't want to ever be seen. When they cross the infrared beam, a bright light shines on them and scares them away. Infrared lights cost between fifteen and twenty dollars each and are easy to install.

➡*EMPOWERMENT STRATEGY #14: Put valuables you rarely use in a safety deposit box at your bank.*

Other valuables should be spread around your home so that a burglar cannot swoop in and grab everything at once and be off. It is called risk management. There is a risk associated with using some things that are valuable. Another tenet of risk management is risk transfer, meaning by putting valuables you don't frequently use in a safety deposit box in the bank, you are transferring the risk to the bank.

➡*EMPOWERMENT STRATEGY #15—When you are on vacation, leave a key with a friend or trusted neighbor and have him or her take in your paper and mail.*

It is not a good idea to stop the delivery of your newspaper when you go on vacation because that communicates your absence to the paperboy and others he might interact with. Since most burglars are between thirteen and nineteen years old, this is not a good idea.

➡*EMPOWERMENT STRATEGY #16—Take your camcorder (or rent one) and go from room to room identifying all of your personal belongings. Photograph them and narratively describe when you bought each item, how much you paid, and the approximate value of each item.*

A camcorder is an excellent way to inventory your belongings and make a record of what they look like and what their estimated values are. Any antiques and old sterling patterns you have can't be marked, so you should videotape them. Also, as you get to smaller items, make sure there is a ruler in the picture so that you convey their size. This is especially important with rings, to indicate the size of any precious gems. A jeweler's appraisal is also important.

Is it important to videotape the serial number on the back of the VCR? It is if you don't inventory it. Insurance adjusters often say it is much easier to pay people what their merchandise is worth if they have an inventory and or picture of it.

➡ *EMPOWERMENT STRATEGY #17: Start a block watch in your neighborhood whether or not you have been the victim of a crime.*

Block watch is valuable because it gets neighbors to meet each other and gets them thinking about security. The first step is to get a police officer to come out and hold a meeting. The police officer will let your neighborhood know what has been going on in the area, and he or she will highlight your responsibilities in particular situations.

The police officer will hand out a map and have all in attendance fill in their names, addresses, and home and work phone numbers so that communication lines will be opened. In addition to meeting every neighbor present, each member in attendance is given a block watch map and told to put it by his or her phone. Then when a stranger is seen in the area, a phone tree can begin whereby on neighbor tells another who tells another.

➡ *EMPOWERMENT STRATEGY #18: Always be able to see who is at your door before opening it. If you don't know the person at your door, there is no reason to open the door.*

It is important to remember that if a stranger comes to your door and you do not feel comfortable with that person, there is no reason to answer the door no matter what the person says. If it is a police officer, you still need not answer the door until you get his or her name, department, and badge number and independently call the station and verify this information.

➡ *EMPOWERMENT STRATEGY #19: Never leave your garage door open when you leave the house.*

Often a burglar will find tools or ladders or other equipment he can use to break into your house. It also helps him determine whether you are home when the garage door is open and there is no car parked in it.

➡ *EMPOWERMENT STRATEGY #20: If you decide you need an alarm system, apply the rule of three: shop for a system at three different companies.*

It is important to arm yourself with information by reading consumer reports or brochures from independent alarm associations before buying.

Features to consider are the perimeter system, internal infrared traps, monitoring of any intrusion by an alarm monitoring company, and a siren or bell that goes off as soon as an intruder comes into the home. This warns the occupant and enables him to call 911, but, more importantly, the path of least resistance theory applies here. As soon as the burglar hears the siren, he is usually off and running.

Central station monitoring notifies the police that an intrusion has occurred and a police unit will respond. The siren or bell warns the occupant and scares the intruder. Both are important features.

➡ *EMPOWERMENT STRATEGY #21: If you are burglarized, look at your checks to see if any have been stolen.*

Oftentimes, a burglary will occur and you will report televisions and VCRs stolen, but not notice checks. Checks are among the most lucrative thing a modern day burglar can steal because there are so many ways to obtain phony identification and pass bad checks.

➡ *EMPOWERMENT STRATEGY #22: Use a locking mailbox or a post office box to avoid having mail stolen.*

More and more white collar crime is perpetrated by people who steal documents from your mailbox in order to get checking account numbers, social security numbers, dates of birth, and other vital information which can be used to swindle you. Never leave outgoing mail in your mailbox for the same reason.

Bank statements are a prime target for white collar crooks. If a crook has your bank statement and steals somebody else's checks, he can go to the bank, deposit the check into your account by filling in a blank deposit slip using your bank account number, and get cash back.

➡️*EMPOWERMENT STRATEGY #23: It is a good idea not to have your name on the mailbox or on the outside of your house.*

Having your name on the outside of your house gives a person a connection to the phone book. If someone had untoward intentions, he could see the name (especially if it is a single woman's name like Jane Smith) and look the name up in the phone book and start making obscene phone calls.

➡️*EMPOWERMENT STRATEGY #24: If someone calls you and wants to take a survey of you, generally it is not a good idea to participate.*

If you are interested, before you start answering questions, have the person send you some written information about his firm and the nature of the research he is doing. If he is unwilling to send you such information, don't do business with him.

Occasionally, burglars will pretend to take phone surveys so they can find out what kind of merchandise you have in your house and when you're home so they will know what to look for and when.

Several years ago, there was a situation where the Seattle Supersonics were making a run at the championship and a group of clever burglars called a family in Bellevue pretending to be a radio station. They said if you answer some dumb question correctly, you win tickets to that night's Sonics playoff game for your entire family.

They answered correctly and two hours later the burglars delivered five Sonics tickets to the family. The family then went to the game and returned four hours later to find virtually everything of value they owned stolen.

In that situation, the burglars figured out a way to guarantee they wouldn't be caught and that they could spend a lot of time in the house. The average burglar spends between three and a half and five minutes in a house. Here the burglars knew the entire family would be gone for at least three hours.

➡️*EMPOWERMENT STRATEGY #25: When you leave a message on voicemail or an answering machine say, "We can't come to the phone right now, but if you leave a message we'll get right back to you."*

It is important not to reveal whether you are home or not when you record a message on your machine. The single worst message you can put on your machine would be, "I'm not home right now and I don't plan to be until I return from vacation in three weeks." This tells anyone who calls that the house will be vacant and therefore safe to break into for a long time. Even saying "I'm not home" is not advisable because a burglar could be sitting outside of your home calling your number on a cellular phone to see if the coast is clear.

➥*EMPOWERMENT STRATEGY #26: Post emergency numbers for security, police, and fire assistance near every phone.*

➥*EMPOWERMENT STRATEGY #27: If you notice any suspicious persons or vehicles, call security or the police.*

➥*EMPOWERMENT STRATEGY #28: Be alert when you go home. It is the hardest time to be alert because you're tired. Try to see if people are around.*

➥*EMPOWERMENT STRATEGY #29: Keep doors and windows locked at all times. On a warm weather day, don't leave a side door open.*

➥*EMPOWERMENT STRATEGY #30: Have keys ready when approaching your home.*

➥*EMPOWERMENT STRATEGY #31: If you arrive home to find that windows or doors have been tampered with, don't go inside but, instead, call the police from a neighbor's house.*

➥*EMPOWERMENT STRATEGY #32: Don't give personal information to unknown callers. If you receive an obscene or crank call, hang up immediately, saying nothing.*

➥*EMPOWERMENT STRATEGY #33: If you use flood lights on the exterior of you house, make sure they face toward the house, not away from it: the latter can provide cover for a burglar.*

➡*EMPOWERMENT STRATEGY #34: Consider installing a Beware of Dog sign in your window.*

➡*EMPOWERMENT STRATEGY #35: Hook up a timer not only to lights but to a police scanner or television to better replicate being home.*

➡*EMPOWERMENT STRATEGY #36: Beware of people calling unsolicited saying you've won free dinners or show tickets: it might be a burglar seeking to get you out of your house.*

➡*EMPOWERMENT STRATEGY #37: Look out for repair men, pizza delivery men, plumbers, or yard workers who are really burglars. If they walk around to the side of a house, call the police.*

➡*EMPOWERMENT STRATEGY #38: Never confront a burglar—always call the police.*

➡*EMPOWERMENT STRATEGY #39: Lock your garage. Also, lock the door that goes from the garage to the house.*

➡*EMPOWERMENT STRATEGY #40: Don't keep valuables in your master bedroom: that is the first place the burglar looks.*

➡*EMPOWERMENT STRATEGY #41: Stay away from places where there aren't many people, like isolated parking lots.*

➡*EMPOWERMENT STRATEGY #42: If you see someone strange in the neighborhood asking questions about a neighbor, don't tell him anything, especially if the neighbor about whom he is inquiring is out of town.*

➡*EMPOWERMENT STRATEGY #43: If you see someone suspicious, make a phone call—make it obvious that you're calling.*

➡*EMPOWERMENT STRATEGY #44: Don't make it obvious that you are trying to look like you are not home.*

➡*EMPOWERMENT STRATEGY #45: Keep skylights closed and locked wherever possible. It is a common access point for burglars.*

➡*EMPOWERMENT STRATEGY #46: Plant prickly shrubbery around your house; burglars won't want to hide in them.*

➡*EMPOWERMENT STRATEGY #47: Lighting is especially important for people who live on a golf course or adjacent to a greenbelt since that is perfect access for a burglar to get into the backyard.*

➡*EMPOWERMENT STRATEGY #48: Close your blinds when you are at home. That way a peeping tom can't see you.*

➡*EMPOWERMENT STRATEGY #49: If you live in an apartment or condominium on the second or third floor, don't forget to lock sliding glass doors that lead to balconies. A burglar could access them with a ladder easily.*

➡*EMPOWERMENT STRATEGY #50: Don't leave ladders lying around your house. If you live in a condo or apartment, get the manager to secure ladders in a storage facility.*

➡*EMPOWERMENT STRATEGY #51: If you are away from home a lot and you have a big house, consider renting out the downstairs or another part of the house so that there will always be someone home when you are gone.*

➡*EMPOWERMENT STRATEGY #52: When you are going on a trip, consider calling the post office and getting them to hold your mail for you while you are gone. This is useful if you do not have a neighbor who can collect it for you.*

➡️*EMPOWERMENT STRATEGY #53: Be sure there are no large trees with branches overhanging your house that could be used by a burglar to climb onto the roof.*

➡️*EMPOWERMENT STRATEGY #54: If you decide to build a fence, be sure it is one you can see through. Solid wood fences provide unlimited cover for burglars once they are in your yard.*

➡️*EMPOWERMENT STRATEGY #55: Make sure gates to your yard are latched securely before leaving.*

➡️*EMPOWERMENT STRATEGY #56: Consider marking the valuables in your home with your driver's license or your social security number.*

BURGLARY PREVENTION QUIZ

Now that you have heard from the law enforcement experts and the professional burglars and reviewed the proposals for empowerment strategies, it is time to take the burglary prevention empowerment quiz. Answer yes or no to the following questions.

Outside Security

	YES	NO	
1.	____	____	Are your doors fitted with deadbolt locks?
2.	____	____	Are your doors of solid construction?
3.	____	____	Do your doors fit their frames snugly?
4.	____	____	Are strike plates properly secured?
5.	____	____	Do you have key locks on inside doors within arm's reach of windows?
6.	____	____	Are door hinges vulnerable?
7.	____	____	Do you lock your porch and garage?
8.	____	____	Do you lock your doors when away from home for short periods?
9.	____	____	Do you lock the doors out of your view when working in the yard?
10.	____	____	Do you avoid leaving keys hidden near access doors?
11.	____	____	Do you leave notes on the door to indicate your absence?
12.	____	____	Are your windows fitted with locks and do you lock them?
13.	____	____	Are sliding doors and windows secured with a track pin or Charlie Bar?
14.	____	____	Do you keep tools, ladders, etc. in places inaccessible to potential burglars?
15.	____	____	Do you store lawn mowers, snow blowers, gas barbecues, etc. out of sight when not in use?
16.	____	____	Do you light the outside of your home to discourage prowling or loitering?

	YES	NO	
17.	____	____	When you move to a new residence do you hire a reliable locksmith to rekey all locks?
18.	____	____	Do you change you locks immediately if your keys are lost or stolen?

Inside Security

YES **NO**

	YES	NO	
19.	____	____	Do you refuse to provide information regarding your property to telephone surveys?
20.	____	____	Do you avoid leaving valuables, coin collections, or large amounts of cash at home?
21.	____	____	Do you leave lights on and a radio playing when out for short periods of time?
22.	____	____	Have you marked your valuables or recorded serial numbers for identification?

Vacation Security

YES **NO**

	YES	NO	
23.	____	____	Do you notify a neighbor of your travel plans and give a key with a request for a periodic house check?
24.	____	____	Do you leave window shades in the normal positions?
25.	____	____	Do you cancel all deliveries?
26.	____	____	Do you make arrangements for your yard to be kept up and any mail and brochures to be picked up?
27.	____	____	If you own a second car, do you park it in the driveway?
28.	____	____	Do you use a light timer on interior and exterior lights?
29.	____	____	Do you doublecheck all doors and windows to be sure they are properly secured before leaving?

Apartment Security

YES **NO**

	YES	NO	
30.	____	____	Do you refer unknown persons seeking entrance to the manager?
31.	____	____	Do you report suspicious activity to the manager or police?

32. ____ ____ Do you advise the manager of any travel plans and request apartment checks and mail pick-up?

33. ____ ____ Do you store valuable property in your apartment locker?

• • • • • • • • • • • • •

Count the number of yes answers you gave to these questions. Any question to which you answered no you should take steps to change. Look at the scale below to assess your vulnerability to burglary.

26-33 YES ANSWERS—Very empowered citizen. Lowest level of vulnerability to burglary.

18-25 YES ANSWERS—Empowered but needs improvement. This total means you have taken more steps than average to burglar-proof yourself and your house, but you could do more.

10-17 YES ANSWERS—If you are in this category, it is important to take action and make some improvements on your security.

1-9 YES ANSWERS—This is the bottom level of empowerment. If you fall in this category, you are extremely vulnerable to being burglarized unless you live in a rural area with a very low crime rate.

The primary message of this chapter to remember to prevent burglary is to make your house harder to break into than other houses in your neighborhood. The burglar is very lazy and is looking for the easiest target. He will go to great lengths to find the easiest house to burglarize and therefore anything you do to make it harder for him will likely deter the average burglar. Remember this as you utilize your empowerment strategies to make your home and neighborhood a safer place.

CHAPTER 3
OUTSMARTING AUTO THEFT

Myth:

> *I don't need to worry about auto theft as long as I am insured and make sure I lock my car.*

REALITY:

> **MODERN AUTO THIEVES ARE OFTEN MORE INTERESTED IN STEALING VALUABLES LEFT IN THE CAR SUCH AS CREDIT CARDS AND CHECKS, WHICH MAY NOT BE COVERED BY INSURANCE.**

I N THE INTRODUCTION TO THIS BOOK, DOUG RECOUNTED HIS story of having his car stolen and how it fundamentally changed his view about the subject. Even though most people have insurance for their automobile, it is a major violation of one's privacy to have a car stolen.

In this chapter, we review the statistics in order to provide an objective assessment of your risk of becoming an auto theft victim. In addition, we provide a statement from a convicted auto thief who reveals some of the tricks of the trade such as where his favorite locations were to steal a car. The theme which prevails throughout the rest of the book once again surfaces here: anything you do to make stealing your car harder than stealing someone else's will greatly decrease your chances of becoming a crime victim.

THE TRUTH ABOUT AUTO THEFT

While burglary rates have historically been going down, auto theft rates have gone up precipitously over the past fifteen years. In 1976, the rate was 1.65 per one hundred people in the U.S. By 1992, the rate had climbed to 2.01 per one hundred population. It is also important to note that there are significant differences between auto theft rates in urban, suburban, and rural areas. Note these Bureau of Justice statistics for 1992.

AUTO THEFT RATES BY LOCATION—1992		
Location	**% Victimized**	**% Not Victimized**
Urban	3.53%	96.47%
Suburban	1.73%	98.27%
Rural	0.62%	99.38%
All Areas	2.01%	97.99%

Source: *Criminal Victimization in the U.S.*, Table 33, page 50.

These regional differences are important considerations when you read through the empowerment strategies in the next chapter. The concentration of auto theft in urban areas is consistent with the fact that gang activity and drug activity is also concentrated in urban areas. Remember again, that there were 1.9 million auto thefts in 1992 and the material in this chapter is designed to help you avoid becoming one of those who will be victimized each year.

Another interesting set of statistics which sheds light on auto theft is the location of the car when it was stolen. According to the BJS, the following data reflects where cars are most often stolen.

Parking lot or garage	35.5%
Near home	21.7%
On the street near home	20.6%
On street not near own, friend's home	10.4%
At, in, or near friend's, relative's, neighbor's house	3.2%
On street near friend's, relative's, neighbor's house	2.5%
On school property	2.1%
At home	.5%
Other	3.5%

Source: *1992 Sourcebook of Criminal Justice Statistics*, Table 3.10, page 252.

These percentages are consistent with what you will read is the most favorite places to steal cars in our interview of Joseph, the car thief in the next chapter. One final category that it is useful to look at when thinking about how to outsmart the car thief is the distribution of thefts during the day:

Nighttime (6:00 P.M. to midnight)	36.8%
Daytime (6:00 A.M. to 6:00 P.M.)	22.8%
Nighttime (midnight to 6:00 A.M.)	15.2%

Source: *1992 Sourcebook of Criminal Justice Statistics*, Table 3.10, page 252.

When it comes to studies on auto theft, there are many available. The trend in the 1990s is clearly for teenagers to steal cars and use them for joyriding and/or drug dealing. The increase in auto theft from 1986 to 1991 was 45.4 percent and this compares with a 13.7 percent decrease for burglary during the same period of time.

Another interesting study conducted in 1992 by the British Columbia Association of Chiefs of Police (BCACP) reveals a number of interesting trends on the issue of auto theft. The study was conducted jointly by

BCACP, the Insurance Corporation of British Columbia (ICBC) and Simon Frazier University. Police throughout the U.S. have confirmed many of the findings of this study to be precisely the trends they have anecdotally observed over time. Among the findings of this study which was released in October 1993:

❑ Most auto thieves are young persons interested in joy riding.

❑ The average joyride results in approximately $2,500 in damage to the vehicle stolen.

❑ Repeat offenders are responsible for a disproportionate amount of auto theft. Persons who have stolen one or two automobiles constitute about 35 percent of the offending population.

❑ A high percentage of auto thieves use drugs and alcohol regularly. Of the auto thieves interviewed, the average amount respondents said they spent on drugs and alcohol per month was $615. Many said they were motivated to steal cars when they were high on drugs and alcohol.

❑ Eighty percent of the auto thieves interviewed said they stole cars for fun, 50 percent said it was to steal things (parts/goods) for themselves, 73 percent said it was to steal things (parts and goods) to sell, 48 percent said it was to show off, 33 percent said it was to get a car for another type of crime.

❑ Auto thieves said mall parking lots and out of view residential areas were preferred locations for auto stealing. Fifty percent of this group said auto theft prevention devices like car alarms were useful deterrents for auto theft.

❑ Twenty percent of the cars stolen in the survey were stolen with the keys left in the ignition.

❑ The cars most commonly stolen were Datsuns, Nissan, Toyotas, Mazdas, Hondas, and Acuras.

❏ Seventy-five percent of the auto thieves said they avoided cars that had alarms in them.

❏ Sixty-one percent of auto thieves said they would avoid a car that had a locking steering wheel like The Club on it.

 INSIDE THE MIND OF AN AUTO THIEF

The following statement is by a notorious car thief named Christopher whom we interviewed in August 1994 while he was serving time at the Clallum Bay Correctional Facility in Washington State for attempted murder. As you read through this statement, think about how his comments might affect your behavior in the future; like where you park your car, how often you lock it, and what kinds of things you keep in it when you leave it.

On Which Cars Are Easiest to Steal

"My name is Christopher. I am twenty-three years old and I have been an auto thief since I was fourteen years old. I am currently serving a sentence of fifteen years to life for attempted murder. I have stolen over two thousand cars in my life and most of the money I got from this activity went to feed my heroin and cocaine addiction. I am writing this to help law abiding citizens avoid becoming the victims of crime.

"I started out stealing Ford cars when I was about fourteen. A friend of mine and I had gone to a junkyard and found some old Ford keys and one day my friend said, "Let's go beat a Ford" and so we just walked around until we found one and the old keys we had fit the ignition so we drove away. A lot of the older American cars are pretty easy to steal because you can unplug the ignitions and plug a new ignition in to them without tampering with the wiring or anything and because there wasn't any locked steering like before 1967.

"The easiest cars to steal are Japanese cars. The reason is because the sheet metal on the side of the car is so easy to bend—I just use a screwdriver to bend the metal and then I can maneuver the back of the lock inside the sheet metal until the lock pops open. It takes me about as long to open a car door using a screwdriver as it would take the owner to open with his key. So Mazdas, Toyotas, Hondas, and Nissans are the easiest to steal because they make them cheap. I would be able to open any Japanese car with a screwdriver.

"With American cars, it's a little different. They are made differently—they have a catch switch or an electric lock and you have to go in through the sheet metal on the door and bend a triangle into the sheet metal. It takes a little bit longer, but I've done it lots of times.

"Devices like 'The Club' are not insurmountable. I can get around The Club easily but I'm always looking for the easiest car to steal, so I would start by looking for one that is unlocked. You'd be amazed how many people leave their car door unlocked—even today. I bet four out of every ten cars I tried was unlocked. So you want to know one obvious way to avoid having your car stolen? Lock your damn door!

"Even though I could break into a car that was locked, if there were two cars sitting next to each other and one was locked and the other one wasn't, which car do you think I'm going to steal? It's the same with things like 'The Club' or cars that have alarms on them. I can get by just about any stock alarm—you know those cheap ones that come with some cars—but if I am looking in a parking lot and one car has an alarm (or The Club) and one doesn't, I'm going to take the car that doesn't.

"The only thing that would change this is if I was filling an order. Sometimes, people would pay me to steal a particular car that they wanted. If that was the case, I would steal the car no matter what it had on it—The Club, an alarm, whatever.

"The main reason why I stole cars in the early days was to have something to mess around in—you know we would steal a car and then go joy riding in it for a few hours, drinking, doing drugs, then we would dump it. As I got older, I became more competitive and it became a game as to who could steal the most cars and not only the most cars, but the best cars.

"I also learned as I got older that people left valuable things in their cars like checkbooks and credit cards that I could translate into cash immediately. So I started breaking into cars just to steal the stuff out of them."

On the Car Thief's Favorite Place to Steal

"I definitely had favorite places to look for cars to steal. Most of these places had to do with the chances of getting caught. Here are my top ten places."

1] WAREHOUSES ➢ The good thing about warehouses is the people who work there go in to work in the morning and they don't come out for eight or nine hours. Also, warehouse buildings don't have any windows and so no one can see out to the parking lot. This makes it perfect for the car thief who can go there in the morning and steal a car or break into a car and not be discovered until later in the afternoon.

2] BALL FIELDS ➢ How many times have you gone to a park to play softball or soccer or to watch your kid play and leave your checkbook or wallet in the car? The car door is locked and so you feel its safe, right? Wrong. I would go to a ball park and wait for everyone to arrive who is going to be playing in the softball game. Then it would take me about ten seconds to break into a car where I noticed a purse lying on the front seat. I would steal the credit cards and go have one of my girlfriends (prostitutes) run a $1,000 on the card before the game was even over. This meant it was impossible for the card owner to call in the stolen card until it was too late.

3] PARK AND RIDES ➢ Park and rides used to be my absolute favorite place to hit because a person would park his or her car there and go to work on a bus and no one would notice the car missing until the end of the day. It is still a good place for car thieves to hit but they are beefing up on security in a lot of them now so it's getting harder.

4] SKI RESORTS ➢ You get your ski equipment on and you head for the mountain, leaving a lot of other stuff like checkbooks and other clothes in your car. You're gone all day and so just like the warehouse parking lot, nothing gets reported until it's too late.

5] HEALTH CLUBS ➢ Health clubs are good because you've got usually a couple of hours before someone comes out. I got to be so bold at times that I would go into a health club with a pair of bolt cutters in my gym bag and when no one was looking, I would go clip the lock off of someone's locker and take the person's wallet and car keys. If it was one of them types where you had a control for your alarm on the keys, I would just walk around the parking lot playing with the controls until I found the car it opened.

6] PROFESSIONAL SPORTS EVENTS ➤ Any parking lot where you know the people are going to be away from their car for a specific length of time is good. So if you are walking around the Kingdome during a Seahawk game, you know that the cars parked in the area are owned by people at the game and you know how long the game lasts. The only thing is a lot of times the cops are out in force for those kind of events so you have to be careful.

7] PARKING GARAGES ➤ Parking garages are kind of fun. They are out of view from most people and especially if you hit them during the middle of the morning or afternoon when most of the car owners are hard at work, it's a piece of cake.

8] AT THE LAKE ➤ When people go swimming, they never take their wallets or other valuables with them—they leave them in their car. That is why I would go to the parking areas by lakes—to steal the stuff in their cars and run the cards before they knew they were stolen.

9] PARK AND FLY ➤ The parking lots around airports are good because people are gone on trips for days at a time. You have to usually get around the guard but there are ways to do that. Some people are so stupid that they leave their slip for claiming the car in the car itself. One time I snuck into a park and fly lot, climbed into a car that had the owner's claim check in it—drove to the gate and paid the parking fee and drove away.

10] NATIONAL PARKS ➤ When people drive up into the wilderness and park at a trail head or a big parking lot that is at the entrance to a hiking area, they tend to leave stuff in their cars and be gone for at least a couple of hours if not for days. This is a good place to steal cars or the stuff in cars because people don't notice it's gone until they come back.

On How to Avoid Auto Theft and Other Car-Related Crime

"I think people should remember how easy it is for a professional car thief like me to break into their car. The simple thing is don't leave anything in your car that you don't want stolen. I would steal jockey boxes (radios), checkbooks, credit cards, tapes, even alarms from cars.

"The easiest way to avoid auto theft is to get a good alarm system, not a stock alarm that comes with some cars 'cause those are easy to beat. I mean a good alarm. If you want to reduce the risk of your car being stolen at your home, park it in your garage at night. Also, it seems silly to have to say this, but lock your car doors whenever you leave it parked. I could break into any car no matter how locked it was, but if there were cars that were unlocked, they would be my first choice just because they were easier, you know?

"Also, avoid parking your car in the areas I described above and if you have to park in these areas, don't leave anything in your car. If you have a radio or tape deck, get the kind that you can pull out and take with you.

"I have another tip for you on that. If you have a pull out tape deck, don't just pull it and leave a hole there in your dash, because I could tell when someone did that and nine times out of ten they would just put the radio under the seat or something. If you are going to pull the radio, put some wires in the space where you pulled it from so it looks like someone already stole it.

"One more thing I would like to give as advice. If you are driving down the road and someone comes into your lane or pulls up along side of you and begins to mess with you, ignore them. When I was driving around stealing cars, I was all coked up and was—well—dangerous.

"One time a car pulled in front of me and cut me off and I got so mad that I pulled my .45 out from under the seat and started to drive after them. My intention was to get even with them by shooting them in the head. If it wasn't for the girl I was with talking me out of it, I would have probably done it and instead of serving fifteen to life, I would be serving life—period. You never know how messed up some of the people are out there on the road—take my advice and leave well enough alone."

AUTO THEFT SCENARIO

• •

Jim and Kathy had been training all year to run in the Portland marathon. Although they lived in the Seattle area, they had driven down the night before and stayed in a hotel near where the race was going to be held the next day. Because money was tight, their plan was to run in the race in the morning and then, as weary as they knew they would be, drive home to Seattle later that day.

When the big day came, they packed up their stuff in their car and parked the car on a back street near where the race was taking place. Because they were both running in the race, they left all of their valuables in the car securely locked and out of plain view—his wallet, their credit cards, her purse. They felt confidant that the car and their valuables were secure because the car was locked and was off of the main street where vagrants occasionally frequented.

They also felt secure because there was a large force of security and police officers out and about that day to do crowd control for the marathon race they were about to run in. Finally, their car, a 1986 Subaru, was not exactly a prize possession nor, did they feel, a particular target for car thieves. With these assurances in mind, they left the vehicle and spent the next three and a half hours running in the race and participating in after race activities.

When they came back to their car, they found that the car had been broken into and all of their valuables had been stolen. Interestingly enough, the car thieves did not take the car, nor did they break windows to get into it. Rather, there was simply a small scratch on the passenger side car door and everything of value missing.

The thieves had left Jim's wallet after removing everything from it except his YMCA card. Kathy's purse was completely gone along with everything in it. Since Jim had taken a single car key with him during the race, they were able to drive home after filing a police report and reporting their credit cards stolen. It certainly took the thrill away from the fact that Kathy had just finished her first marathon and Jim had run a personal record time.

Moral: Thieves are more interested in the valuables locked inside the car than the car itself. Also, car thieves look for cars parked near sports areas, park and rides, hiking trails or other places where they know the owners will be gone for a prolonged period of time. From this perspective, what better place to look for cars to break into than the area around the start of a marathon. Even if you are a world class marathon runner, it's still going to take you over two hours to finish the race!

Jim and Kathy should have parked their car in a lot that had an attendant and they should have probably left their stuff in a hotel room or with a friend who could have watched it. Also, parking on a side street that has little or no foot traffic really provides cover for a group of teenagers who are seeking to commit car prowls.

Finally, while Jim and Kathy assumed their car would be particularly safe because of the extra security on the street during the race, the truth is that such security spends most of its time ensuring that runners and automobiles do not collide rather than preventing auto theft or other kinds of crime. Remember, crime is preventable!

AUTO THEFT PREVENTION
EMPOWERMENT STRATEGIES

The number of car thefts and prowls is up significantly in recent years as the number of burglaries goes down. One possible explanation for this is that people have more and more expensive things in their cars these days like stereos with CD players, car phones, etc. Another reason is that, as Christopher has described, often the auto thief is after personal items in the car such as checks and credit cards.

A third possible explanation is that drug dealers don't want to risk having their own car seized in the event they get busted. Under statutes known as RICO (Racketeering and Influence Corrupt Organizations), law enforcement can seize the vehicle used during a drug bust and confiscate it on the spot. Consequently, many drug dealers are stealing cars to make their drug transactions, then dumping them.

➡ *EMPOWERMENT STRATEGY #57: Lock your car door.*

The number one thing to remember about car safety is when you park your car, lock the doors. This may seem obvious, but you would be amazed how many people are lulled into a false sense of security when they are at home and their car is parked in the front yard or in their garage.

It is important to lock your car even when it is in the garage and the garage door is closed. Some people have even been known to leave the keys in their car when they park it in the garage, feeling it is safe. What happens however when the keys are left in it and the house key is on the key chain? Remember, Christopher said four out of the ten cars he stole were unlocked.

It is amazing in this era of increased car thefts that you still see people leave their car running when they go into a 7-11 to pick something up. They figure it'll only take a second. But a second or two is all it takes for someone to jump into your car and steal it.

➡ *EMPOWERMENT STRATEGY #58: Always have at least a quarter tank of gas in your car to avoid running out in a dangerous place.*

➡*EMPOWERMENT STRATEGY #59: Lock your car doors while driving.*

➡*EMPOWERMENT STRATEGY #60: Keep your car well-maintained to avoid breakdowns.*

➡*EMPOWERMENT STRATEGY #61: Check the back seat before getting into your car.*

➡*EMPOWERMENT STRATEGY #62: Have keys ready when approaching your car.*

➡*EMPOWERMENT STRATEGY #63: Park your car in well-lighted areas.*

➡*EMPOWERMENT STRATEGY #64: Keep area maps in your glove compartment, and always get directions before driving to an unknown location.*

➡*EMPOWERMENT STRATEGY #65: NEVER pick up hitchhikers.*

➡*EMPOWERMENT STRATEGY #66: Never leave packages or valuables in plain sight. Lock them in the glove box or the trunk.*

➡*EMPOWERMENT STRATEGY #67: Never keep personal identification, credit cards, or checks in the car.*

➡*EMPOWERMENT STRATEGY #68: Avoid parking lots where a key is left with an attendant or with the vehicle.*

If you must park in a valet lot, leave only the ignition key with the attendant after you have safely stowed valuables in the trunk.

➡*EMPOWERMENT STRATEGY #69: At night, park your car in a garage if possible. If you must park in a driveway or a carport, leave an outdoor light on.*

➡️*EMPOWERMENT STRATEGY #70: Don't leave your car parked at unattended railroad or airport parking lots for long periods of time.*

➡️*EMPOWERMENT STRATEGY #71: Consider getting a car alarm if you live in a high crime or "hotspot" area.*

Most insurance companies offer a 5 to 15 percent discount on auto insurance if you have a car alarm.

➡️*EMPOWERMENT STRATEGY #72: Consider getting a steering wheel locking device like a heavy-gauge steel bar.*

➡️*EMPOWERMENT STRATEGY #73: Park your car with the wheels turned toward the curb, making it difficult for a thief to tow your car.*

➡️*EMPOWERMENT STRATEGY #74: Consider installing a "kill" switch in your car. This is a hidden switch that prevents the car from being started.*

The good thing about this is a thief might not be able to find it and therefore couldn't start your car. Also, it is cheaper to install than a car alarm. The down side is it doesn't stop a car thief from towing your car away. Also, many sophisticated car thieves will be able to find the switch.

➡️*EMPOWERMENT STRATEGY #75: Keep a tool kit in the car.*

➡️*EMPOWERMENT STRATEGY #76: Keep title and registration on you or in a locked compartment in the car.*

➡️*EMPOWERMENT STRATEGY #77: Keep change in the car for emergency calls.*

➡️*EMPOWERMENT STRATEGY #78: Never park near a place where someone could be hiding, like the bushes or a dumpster.*

➡️*EMPOWERMENT STRATEGY #79: Before getting into your car, be sure no one was following you in order to trap you in your car.*

➡*EMPOWERMENT STRATEGY #80: Vary your route to work.*

➡*EMPOWERMENT STRATEGY #81: Keep doors locked and windows rolled up when driving.*

➡*EMPOWERMENT STRATEGY #82: Do not engage in hand gestures or making faces of any kind with other drivers.*

➡*EMPOWERMENT STRATEGY #83: Maintain one and one-half to two car lengths between you and the next driver.*

➡*EMPOWERMENT STRATEGY #84: Consider getting a cellular phone to keep in your car in the event of emergencies. Take it with you when you park your car.*

➡*EMPOWERMENT STRATEGY #85: Keep pen and paper in the car in order to write down suspicious activity and report it to the police. If you are a hit-and-run victim, be sure to write down the license plate number of the vehicle that hit you.*

➡*EMPOWERMENT STRATEGY #86: If you break down or get a flat tire on a major road, wait for a law enforcement official. Never accept a ride from a stranger.*

➡*EMPOWERMENT STRATEGY #87: Maintaining your car is an important prevention step. If you break down on a dark street, you are in more danger obviously than if you make it home trouble-free each night.*

➡*EMPOWERMENT STRATEGY #88: Don't drive through hotspots or high crime areas when you commute to work.*

➡️*EMPOWERMENT STRATEGY #89: When taking public transportation, be sure to travel during times when there are a large number of other commuters doing likewise.*

➡️*EMPOWERMENT STRATEGY #90: When taking a cab, it is a good idea to travel in pairs, especially for women.*

➡️*EMPOWERMENT STRATEGY #91: When traveling on a subway, travel in pairs.*

➡️*EMPOWERMENT STRATEGY #92: When riding on public transportation, carry yourself confidently, looking around and making firm eye contact with others.*

➡️*EMPOWERMENT STRATEGY #93: As you approach your car, look for signs that someone has been in your car.*

AUTO THEFT PREVENTION QUIZ

Now that you have heard from the law enforcement experts and the professional car thieves and reviewed many empowerment strategies, it is time to take the auto theft prevention empowerment quiz. Answer yes or no to the following questions.

	YES	NO	
1.	____	____	I always lock my car whenever I park regardless of how long I am going to be away from it.
2.	____	____	When I park my car in my garage, I nevertheless lock the doors for added security.
3.	____	____	I never leave valuables in my car when I park it even though it is locked.
4.	____	____	I always lock my car doors while driving.
5.	____	____	If another car drives into my lane cutting me off, I remain calm, not engaging in hand gestures at the offending party.
6.	____	____	I always look for a well-lit area to park in.
7.	____	____	Whenever possible, I avoid parking in valet lots. When I must park in valet lots, I put all valuables in the locked trunk.
8.	____	____	I always avoid driving through high crime areas, day or night.
9.	____	____	I have a rule to fill up my tank with gas before it gets below the three-quarter empty level.
10.	____	____	I always walk past my car and look around it before getting in.

• • • • • • • • • • • • •

Count the number of yes answers you gave to these questions. Assess your auto theft knowledge by referring to the scale on the next page.

8-10 YES ANSWERS—You have an excellent knowledge of auto theft and how to prevent it.

5-7 YES ANSWERS—You have a good knowledge of the basics, but could use a refresher course. You may want to go over the empowerment strategies again.

3-4 YES ANSWERS—Your car might be at risk of being stolen, especially if you live in a hotspot area.

0-2 YES ANSWERS—Don't tell Christopher or any other car thief where you live. Better reread this chapter and focus on the empowerment strategies section.

If someone like Christopher wants to steal your car, he probably would be able to. The trick is to get him to "want" someone else's car more than he wants yours. Whether you install devices like The Club or an alarm system or whether you simply ensure that you always lock your car and park it in well-lit areas, you can rest assured that anything you do will significantly reduce your chances of coming out to your driveway and experiencing that empty feeling described at the beginning of this book: "Where is my minivan?"

CHAPTER 4

OUTSMARTING ROBBERY

M y t h :

> *The best way to avoid being robbed is to keep*
> *to yourself and never look up at strangers*
> *when walking down the street.*

R E A L I T Y :

> **A MAJOR WAY TO AVOID BEING ROBBED IS TO**
> **LOOK PEOPLE DIRECTLY IN THE EYE IF YOU**
> **THINK THEY ARE FOLLOWING YOU.**

OF ALL THE CRIMES THAT OCCUR IN A GIVEN YEAR, NONE CAN be more terrifying than being mugged or robbed on the street. Over the years, when we have given crime prevention seminars and block watches, invariably the issue of how to avoid being robbed came up. In addition, the issue of how to avoid being injured in such situations also arose with regularity.

In this chapter, in addition to providing a statistical overview of robbery, we also hear from one of the most dangerous robbers ever to walk the streets of New York City. Finally, we provide an extensive list of empowerment strategies to help you avoid this frightening, but preventable, crime. As always, the theme underlying all robbery prevention strategies is the path of least resistance. Like burglars and auto thieves, robbers are looking for the easiest victim. The trick is learning how to avoid appearing to be an easy target.

THE TRUTH ABOUT ROBBERY

Robbery is defined as: taking anything of value from a person, in the person's presence, by force or intimidation.

Robbery victimization rates, like auto theft and burglary, are different depending on where you live. Below are those regional differences:

ROBBERY RATES BY LOCATION—1992		
Location	% Victimized	% Not Victimized
Urban	1.08%	98.98%
Suburban	.44%	99.54%
Rural	.27%	99.73%
All Areas	.59%	99.41%

Source: *Criminal Victimization in the U.S.*, Table 18, page 38.

It is important once again to note that even though 99.41 percent of the public is never robbed, there were 1.2 million robberies in 1992. This means that while the rates might be low, over 1 million people were victimized by this type of crime and it is important to understand how it works and how to avoid it.

Where do robberies most often occur? To follow are the BJS survey results for 1991.

On street not near your own or a friend's home	39.5%
Parking lot or garage	11.9%
At or in victim's home	9.5%
Near home	5.9%
On the street near home	5.9%
Other commercial building	4.0%
On public transportation or in station	3.8%
At, in, or near friend's, relative's, or neighbor's home	3.7%
In apartment, yard, park or field	3.6%
On street near friend's, relative's, or neighbor's home	2.8%
Inside restaurant	2.0%
Other	7.4%

Source: *1992 Sourcebook of Criminal Justice Statistics*, Table 3.10, page 252.

This information is useful in determining what the most dangerous places are when it comes to being robbed. Clearly, the most common place to be robbed is walking down the street. As we see in the interview with Joseph, our New York City robber, that is precisely where he committed the majority of his robberies.

 **INSIDE THE MIND OF A ROBBER**

"My name is Joseph. I have been a career criminal since I was twelve years old. I am thirty-three years old and I am from Queens, New York. My parents were alcoholics and, from a very young age, I was running on the streets with gangs of other kids who had lost their way.

"My main thing was robbery. I would spend my days drinking and doing drugs. I am going to tell you how I chose my victims and what you can do to avoid people like me on the streets."

On Choosing Victims

"I would always look for the weakest person. Whoever looked the most vulnerable. Like I might find an old man coming down the street with his packages and me and my buddies could go up to him and rob him real quick. The thing is to not look like a victim. It's obvious that you can't run around with a whole bunch of jewelry on and—you know a lot of women will walk around with a lot of pretty jewelry, diamond rings and all that and they in the wrong neighborhood, once these young guys see that, they'll want to rob you because they see you as an easy victim.

"The way you carry yourself is very important. If you're walking down the street and a group of guys is walking behind you and they sense fear on you, they'll try you, but if you pick your head up and walk straight, you might have a better chance of not getting involved.

"Most people are only going to attack people they can intimidate and if they feel they can intimidate you, then it is easier to rob you. If they feel the guy is going to resist and he's not going to give up easily, then they might give a second thought to bothering the guy. Anybody who was walking slumped over with her head down looking weak, I would try her.

"As I got older, I started to get more violent and wanted to impress my buddies, so we started getting guns and robbing people at gunpoint on the streets of New York City. We would wait for someone to come out of a bank and then we would go jump the person. If he came out and looked like the type that had money, we would go rob him.

"Most of the time my motivation was to just get the money, but robbery is a crime that can escalate, and back when I was younger (and stupid) I robbed women because they was easier and one time one of the women resisted and I got turned on during the struggle, so I raped her. It's not a good idea to resist because it makes me mad and I'll hurt you. If a person just gives me the money, I usually didn't hurt her.

"If I was stalking someone, man or woman, and the person all of a sudden turned around and looked me right in the eye, I would usually leave the person alone. My thing was to take the person by surprise. If the person looked at me, I would lose the element of surprise and he would have a better chance to get away and, if he got away, he might go tell someone else. And if I got a weapon on me and I get caught, I'm going to jail. So usually I don't want to take that chance.

"I'm looking to catch you off guard. If I can catch you off guard, usually I try you, right? You are not aware of your surroundings—I'm watching you—you go to your car—I'm watching you—you got your paper and your briefcase, you not even paying attention to anything—I'm watching you—you open your car door, you get in—as soon as you get in, I come down and put the gun to your head and say "shut up"—boom—I'm catching you by total surprise.

"This was kind of my MO. I always liked to wait for someone to get into his car because it's less obvious that I'm robbing him—it looks like I'm just standing over the car talking to the person. Then after I robbed him I would take his car keys so he couldn't go tell someone very fast and I'd leave. I always had my escape route planned in advance.

"It's kind of hard to say where I would like to rob people the most. I would say wherever I could kind of trap the person off in a secluded area where there would be the least chance of being seen, that's where I would do it—and in New York City, there are lots of places like that. I also used to dress up like an office worker and go into buildings at lunch hour and take women's purses from their desks or men's wallets out of their jacket pockets. This was like taking candy from a baby cause people think they're safe once they are in their building at work.

"Another thing we used to do is steal a car and drive around New York City looking for a fancy car like a 5th Avenue or a Mercedes Benz. Then we would pull up behind it and rear-end it. When the car ahead of us would stop, the driver would get out of the car and say, 'Hey you bumped my car' and we would rob him at gunpoint."

On Avoiding Becoming a Robbery Victim

"A lot of women are buying guns nowadays to protect themselves from robbers, but I tell you, if you're a woman and you got a gun, you better know how to use it or I'll use it against you. And another thing—if you're walking around with a gun and it's at the bottom of your purse, what good is it going to do—I come up to you by surprise and ask for your money and you got no time to reach for your gun—besides—I'd probably just steal it.

"No, the best thing you can do is to look like you know where you are going and that you would be a struggle if I was to attack you. I liked to stalk my victims and surprise them. Most people just need to be aware of their surroundings. Things are not always as they seem. Most people they come out and they are in their own little world. They are thinking only about, 'Well, I'm going to the store' and that all they are thinking about whereas if you're more conscious of your surroundings and you try to be cautious and you see a whole group of young guys as you turn the corner, maybe the smart thing would be to turn around and go the other way. But if you're not paying attention, you might walk right down in there.

"Don't have the attitude that it can't happen to you, especially if you're living in a big city. Don't walk somewhere where it's easy for someone to isolate you and rob you without anyone seeing. It's also important to not resist. If you do get into a deal where you're being robbed, give them everything they want or you're going to get hurt.

"I used to rob women a lot and the one thing I'd say about that is that I would always look for a woman walking alone. If there were two women walking together, I would never rob them because it was too risky. One could get away and tell.

"One thing I want to add about looking people dead in the eye. Even though that would make me go away most of the time, it's not a good idea to stare at people or act superior. I can remember some white honky staring at me one time and I got mad and attacked him because I thought he was being disrespectful. Sometimes it would make me mad when I would see a car full of white people driving down the road and they would see me walking down the street and all of a sudden you would hear all the automatic door locks go off—click, click, click. That was like—they think I'm a criminal just cause I'm Black. Of course, I was a criminal, but that's not the point."

ROBBERY VICTIM SCENARIO

Erma was having a pretty good day last year. She had just gotten her paycheck for the month from the small furniture company she worked for. Erma had a pretty set routine. Twice per month on payday she would take her check to the bank and cash it—she didn't have a checkbook because she liked to pay for everything in cash—and this day was no different. She received some $400 in cash and was on her way.

She had come out of the bank and decided to make her usual trek to the grocery store to buy groceries for the week. What she failed to realize was that three robbers had seen her leave the bank clutching her purse and decided to follow her to the store.

When Erma pulled into the parking lot of the grocery store, there were no parking spots available in the main lot near the front so she decided to park along the side of the building where there were no cars and where it would be a shorter walk. Since Erma had a bad leg, she always looked for short cuts to minimize wear and tear on her leg.

She did her shopping and while she was standing in line, she noticed that a woman was looking over her shoulder as she was paying her bill (with cash). She got her groceries and left the store and as she reached for the key to her car, she noticed a man was standing at the front of her car near the hood. Just as she noticed this man, another man came running up to her, grabbed her purse, and left running. The man by the car then took off and she turned around toward the store and saw the woman who had been standing behind her in line staring at her.

She was very shaken by this, but not nearly as shaken as the next week when she went home for lunch at noontime only to find the guy she had seen by her car looking in her apartment window. When he turned around from a distance, she glared at him, looking him directly in the eyes, saying nothing. He then fled quickly.

Moral: There are several things Erma did wrong and several things she did right in this scenario. First, let's discuss what she did right. After being robbed, she immediately called the police and filled out a report, giving them a description of the people involved. Second, she had a locksmith come out to her house and change the locks on her doors since she knew the robber had her house keys, address, and purse contents. She also called her bank and canceled all her bank cards.

What she did wrong was to put herself in that situation to begin with. Whatever one might think about banks and checkbooks, it is never a good idea to cash your paycheck and carry it with you in a one-lump sum. Erma should have put it in a safety deposit box in the bank or deposited part of it in a savings account. Second, she must have communicated through body language to the robbers that she had money in her purse or they would not have followed her.

Third, she showed her cash when she pulled out her wallet to pay her grocery bill which caused the "scout" behind her to signal to her two accomplices that it was a good idea to try to rob her, which they did.

Fourth, she parked in a remote location of the parking lot away from plain view of the store's employees and other customers, which opened her up to being attacked.

ROBBERY PREVENTION
EMPOWERMENT STRATEGIES

Now that you've read real-life scenarios that can clue you in to how to avoid being robbed, review these empowerment strategies for a comprehensive course on safety. Once you implement these simple techniques into your daily routine, you will have a much stronger chance of staying safe in any environment—whether you're at home, at work, commuting, or running errands around town.

➡**EMPOWERMENT STRATEGY #94: It's important to vary your route to and from work.**

It's important to plan a path that generally takes you down safe streets, even if you have to go a little bit out of your way. In other words, don't drive through a hotspot in order to save yourself five minutes off your commuting time. This is especially true for executives and for business people making nightly deposits after work.

➡**EMPOWERMENT STRATEGY #95: If you think you are being followed, don't go home. Home is the worst place to go because you don't want to tell your follower where you live.**

➡**EMPOWERMENT STRATEGY #96: Maintaining your car is an important prevention step. If you break down on a dark street, you are obviously in more danger than if you make it home trouble-free each night.**

➡**EMPOWERMENT STRATEGY #97: Don't drive through hotspots or high crime areas when you commute to work.**

➡**EMPOWERMENT STRATEGY #98: When taking public transportation, be sure to travel during times when there are a large number of other commuters doing likewise.**

One point to remember about taking the bus, train, or other forms of public transportation is that ridership varies widely depending on when you travel. During rush hour, ridership is likely to be business people and relatively safe because it is crowded. But as soon as rush hour is over, within thirty minutes on either side of rush hour, a completely different type of passenger gets on. There can be gang members or people with substance abuse problems who don't work.

➡ *EMPOWERMENT STRATEGY #99: When taking a cab, it is a good idea to travel in pairs, especially for women.*

Taxis are relatively safe, but you want to make sure that the face of the driver on his or her license which must be displayed in most states is the same as the driver in the car. If not, you should get out of the car immediately because you don't know who the driver is.

➡ *EMPOWERMENT STRATEGY #100: When traveling on a subway, travel in pairs.*

Ridership patterns are more difficult to predict on subways, especially in areas like Washington, D.C. The key tip is to travel in pairs and assess what the ridership patterns are in a given area and stick to riding during those times when there is a high volume of passengers who are safe to be around.

➡ *EMPOWERMENT STRATEGY #101: When riding on public transportation, carry yourself confidently, looking around and making firm eye contact with others.*

In terms of how to behave while riding public transportation, it is important to send the nonverbal message that you are strong and confident by looking at new passengers as they enter, but don't stare. You want to send a message that you know who they are and could recognize them if you needed to, but you are not trying to intimidate or threaten them in any way.

Making eye contact with someone who is assessing the chances of committing a crime and getting away with it is a very powerful deterrent, because most criminals want to remain anonymous as much as possible. Looking someone in the eye is a very powerful thing to do and it gives the person the impression that you are self-assured and not someone to mess with.

➡️*EMPOWERMENT STRATEGY #102: While walking down the street, walk with confidence, shoulders back, head up and aware of your surroundings.*

If you are walking down the street with your head down and your shoulders hunched over, you send one kind of message, called the "wounded deer" look. If, on the other hand, you walk down the street with your shoulders back and your head up and your eyes moving around looking in different directions, that is a sign of confidence and power.

➡️*EMPOWERMENT STRATEGY #103: Walk briskly with determination in order to show that you know exactly where you are going.*

It is important to walk briskly—not fast, but with a constant step—it shows that you know what you are doing, that things are under control and you know where you are going. These types of movements are a very strong deterrent to the rapist who is not looking for someone who will challenge him, but someone who will be submissive and give in relatively easily. Therefore, it is important to look as though you are someone who will not give in and who will in fact put up one heck of a fight.

➡️*EMPOWERMENT STRATEGY #104: When someone comes up to you and asks you for money, look the person dead in the eye, say no, and walk away.*

Once again, looking the person straight in the eye (without staring) is a powerful move and it sends a powerful message to the person that you are not someone to mess with.

With regard to people who come up to you and ask you for directions, if you don't feel comfortable striking up a conversation, just look them in the eye, tell them you don't know where the location is, and move on. A lot of people will avoid eye contact and follow them down and continue to pursue the people until they get an answer.

➡️*EMPOWERMENT STRATEGY #105: If you are walking down the street and you think someone is following you, change directions and look for a well-lit area.*

Looking alert is the key to being empowered. You want to do everything you can to avoid looking like a wounded animal or the path of least resistance.

If you are walking down the street and you discover that someone is following you, what should you do? It depends on who you are. One of our off-duty police women was walking down the street in Seattle one day and felt someone was following her, so when she got to a busy street corner, she turned around, looked him in the eye and said in a really loud voice, "Are you following me?" The guy just melted and faded away.

She could pull this off, but the textbook advice is to first change directions and look for a well-lit, safe place to stand. Sometimes, people who are timid have trouble looking others in the eye and so they need to work on their own personal power. This is where a self-defense or martial arts course can be really helpful, not to learn how to overpower an attack, but rather to give the person enough self-confidence to send signals that the person is strong.

➡ *EMPOWERMENT STRATEGY #106: When you are walking in public, carry only the amount of cash you need during the day and no more.*

You always want to limit your losses. So you should assess how much cash you are going to spend in a day and carry enough to accommodate that. If you're carrying $200 and you know you are only going to spend $10, that is foolish. Also, when you go into a convenience store, don't flash how much money you have to the clerk. If you are buying a slurpy for eighty-nine cents, don't take out three $20 bills and wave them around.

Often people will carry every credit card they own, every identification they own, and huge amounts of cash in order to be prepared for any emergency. Some people carry a folded up $50 or $100 bill in a secret compartment of the purse or wallet, one credit card, and minimal cash. This way, if you did have an emergency, you would be ready for it and, if you get robbed, you may lose $50 or $100 but that is all. Under federal law, if your credit card is stolen and you report it within twenty-four hours, you don't lose anything regardless of how much was charged on it by the thief.

➡️*EMPOWERMENT STRATEGY #107: If someone comes up to you and says, "Give me your money," give it to him—period!*

Recall Joseph, the robbery "expert" we interviewed who robbed hundreds of people at knifepoint in New York City, who says the best thing to do when confronted with a robber is, "Do what he wants." Joseph didn't hesitate to hit, shoot or even stab people who resisted him, but those who didn't resist usually got away shaken, but unharmed.

There is no reason why you should endanger your life in order to safe the money and credit cards in your purse or wallet. It is a good idea to have written down the credit card numbers and phone numbers to call if they are lost or stolen and have those separate from your cards so you can report them immediately. So many people have been injured or killed by trying to resist a robbery attempt. It just isn't worth it.

A key difference between being empowered and being afraid is the empowered person knows what he or she is doing and has thought of almost everything that can happen in advance of it happening and the best response to minimize victimization. The fearful person reacts to situations as they arise and doesn't think about them ahead of time.

➡️*EMPOWERMENT STRATEGY #108: Buy a cellular phone to keep in your car at all times for emergencies.*

Having a cellular phone can empower you to call 911 if you break down in a bad neighborhood or anywhere else for that matter. They are generally cheap to purchase and for a minimum amount per month, you can have access to help anytime you need it while driving in your car. It is also a good thing to take hiking or boating to the extent you remain within range of the cellular system in your area.

➡️*EMPOWERMENT STRATEGY #109: Vary where you park each day when you go to work.*

It's a good idea to not be predictable, by parking in different spots each day. This makes it hard for someone to plan an attack. You also want to avoid being in a parking garage alone at night. It is especially good for female employees to travel in pairs down to their car at night after work. It is important to think about when deciding where you are going to park. Look for garages which have a lot of people around.

➡*EMPOWERMENT STRATEGY #110: DON'T GET ON AN ELEVATOR IF YOU ARE UNCOMFORTABLE WITH THE PERSON WHO IS IN IT.*

An elevator is a closed-in environment which can cause problems if you get on with the likes of Joseph, who described his experience robbing a woman in the elevator of a big building in New York City. If a shady character gets on while you are already on the elevator, stand near the buttons so you can press the alarm if something happens or press another floor to stop the elevator at the next floor.

➡*EMPOWERMENT STRATEGY #111: If you are attacked, it is important to make noise and try to draw attention to the situation.*

It is also important to remember, whether you are a man or a woman, that if you are attacked to make a lot of noise. The best deterrent to an attacker is noise. The attacker doesn't want to be discovered committing his crime. There are several different noisemaker products on the market that emit a high frequency, deafening sound when a button is pushed. Whiles these devices are effective when the person can get to them in time, it is not a panacea and the easiest thing to do is scream.

➡*EMPOWERMENT STRATEGY #112: When you go to work in the morning, if you are the first person in the office, you should walk all the way through the office and determine whether anyone is in the office.*

If you are the first person in the office in the morning, it is really important to walk all the way through the office and call out to see if anyone else is present. It will make you feel more comfortable but also ensures that no one is in the office hiding.

If you can lock the door in your work space, that is a positive thing to do too if you are working in the office late at night, early in the morning, or on the weekends. It is another barrier that gives you some warning. Think about the

911 option at work. A lot of people don't make the connection that 911 is for any emergency anywhere—and not just at home.

➡ *EMPOWERMENT STRATEGY #113: When at work, lock your purse or wallet in your desk or a file cabinet.*

The most common crime at work is wallet and purse theft. It is usually done by people who are able to pose as electricians, computer repair people, or copy machine workers, or devise some other way to get past the reception area and then look for purses that are out on top of desks or in a jacket pocket that is easily accessible. These people will dress up like clients or other workers (if it is a big firm) and just try to blend in as much as possible.

There are gangs who go around big office buildings dressed up as maintenance type workers and they have said they take in between $1,000 and $6,000 per day stealing checks, credit cards, cash in purses, and laptop computers.

➡ *EMPOWERMENT STRATEGY #114: If someone is in your office space and you do not know the person, go up and ask him who he is in a nice way.*

The first thing to do is control your space. If someone is in your space, do something about it. You go up to the person in a nice way and say, "Can I help you find someone or something?" Remember to look the person in the eye when you do it. This will end a couple of important signals. First it says I am territorial and I don't want strangers in my space. Second, once again the eye contact is a control element that sends the message that you will recognize the person later, and that you are a powerful person.

If the intruder is a thief, he will give you a reason he is there and then go on to the next office. He doesn't want any hassles.

Women should keep their purses locked up in a desk or a file cabinet. Ideally, it is good to keep your cash and credit cards separate from your purse and carry your purse with you at all times. Most people feel the office is a safe place—an extension of your house, so it is as safe as their homes.

➡ *EMPOWERMENT STRATEGY #115: If you see a maintenance person installing a new light or doing some other kind of maintenance, go up to the*

person and talk to him, with something like, "How is the weather up there?" or other light conversation.

This lets the person know you know who he is. This will also enable you to recognize the person the next time he comes in because typically it is the same person every time working on a building.

This kind of thing is important because, especially in big office buildings, there are so many different kinds of office workers that could plausibly be in the building that it would be easy for an impostor to walk in and go unnoticed.

There are some rings of thieves that are particularly organized that will come in and steal letterhead stationary and envelopes, go home and write up a bunch of invoices and come and take your whole office out. An example is they could write a letter by a fictitious moving company saying they needed to move a bunch of office furniture and then go and take it out. It's farfetched, but it does happen.

➡ *EMPOWERMENT STRATEGY #116: Keep your car in good working condition.*

If you were to break down at night, you might have problems. Also, you should have a contingency plan for what to do if you break down. Have a safety kit in your car.

➡ *EMPOWERMENT STRATEGY #117: Don't leave your purse in your shopping cart when you go to the grocery store.*

Purses in supermarket shopping carts are an open invitation to be stolen. You should always be with the cart if you put your purse in it or, better still, don't put the purse in the cart at all. Also, if you are taking your groceries out to the car and the purse is in the cart, take it out of the cart first and then load the groceries. There have been instances where the woman is loading groceries into her car and has a baby in the infant seat and someone grabs the purse.

➡ *EMPOWERMENT STRATEGY #118: If you go out dancing with friends, make sure at least one of you stays behind to watch the purses of the others.*

If you go dancing at a bar and you have a purse, don't leave it at the table. When you come back, your purse might be gone. Some people case cocktail lounges with the express purpose of stealing purses.

➡EMPOWERMENT STRATEGY #119: While walking home from work, walk with your purse in your hands, and don't rely on the shoulder strap.

This will prevent a robber from running by you and grabbing the purse and running away without your having any recourse and with some risk of injury. Some people suggest that you hold the purse upside down so that if someone comes along to grab it, you can release it and everything will spill out, creating a lot of noise and commotion.

➡EMPOWERMENT STRATEGY #120: As you approach your car, look for signs that someone has been in your car.

Also, look for signs of anyone suspicious around your car. If you notice signs of breaking, go right back to the office and file a police report. Don't wait until you get home because your residence might be in a different police jurisdiction.

➡EMPOWERMENT STRATEGY #121: Women should avoid placing ads in the newspaper.

The risk of a woman putting a personal ad in the paper is that she has a harrasser follow her all over town. Many people think they can screen the person over the phone, but the Ted Bundys of the world are masterful at pretending to be legitimate in order to allay a person's fears.

If you are interested in doing something like that, select a reputable dating service. Whether you use personal ads or are using a dating service, it's a good idea to have the first meeting be with a friend of yours in a neutral location like a public restaurant.

➡EMPOWERMENT STRATEGY #122: If you need to work late or report in early, try to arrange your schedule to work with another employee. When you are leaving after hours, ask a security guard to escort you to the parking lot.

➡EMPOWERMENT STRATEGY #123: If you work in a large office block, find out which elevators shut down after a specified time and which elevators are still operable after normal business hours.

➡*EMPOWERMENT STRATEGY #124: When walking, choose busy streets and avoid passing vacant lots, alleys, or deserted construction sites. At night, walk only in well-lighted areas and try to avoid walking or jogging alone.*

➡*EMPOWERMENT STRATEGY #125: Have your social security check direct deposited into your bank account. Often criminals will steal social security checks out of the mail.*

➡*EMPOWERMENT STRATEGY #126: Carry mace or other personal protection devices in your hand when walking; it does no good at the bottom of your purse.*

➡*EMPOWERMENT STRATEGY #127: Stay away from convenience stores at night.*

➡*EMPOWERMENT STRATEGY #128: Do not walk alone in the evening when it is raining and/or foggy: this provides cover for muggers.*

➡*EMPOWERMENT STRATEGY #129: Don't wear a lot of expensive jewelry that might attract thieves.*

➡*EMPOWERMENT STRATEGY #130: Don't show your wallet or the contents of it when you are in a store buying something.*

➡*EMPOWERMENT STRATEGY #131: When you leave a bank, be alert and don't clutch your purse tightly to your chest as though you have a lot of money. Robbers look for this. Don't look leery, worried.*

➡*EMPOWERMENT STRATEGY #132: When you are buying something in a grocery store, don't show cash in your wallet other than that which you need to make the purchase.*

➥*EMPOWERMENT STRATEGY #133: Don't allow what you see on television and in the newspaper intimidate you into avoiding normal activities.*

➥*EMPOWERMENT STRATEGY #134: When you are traveling and staying in a hotel room, be sure to lock the hotel room door even when you are in it.*

➥*EMPOWERMENT STRATEGY #135: When staying in a hotel, never leave valuables in your room. If you have tickets or cash or traveler's checks, consider storing them in the hotel's safe. Ask the front desk for information about such services.*

➥*EMPOWERMENT STRATEGY #136: When walking in an unfamiliar city, ask someone who lives there for an indication of where the safe places are to walk and where the unsafe places are. Be sure to avoid the unsafe areas, especially if you are traveling alone.*

➥*EMPOWERMENT STRATEGY #137: Do not use a cash machine at nighttime.*

➥*EMPOWERMENT STRATEGY #138: Whenever you use a cash machine, be cautious about who is behind you—you do not want anyone to see you entering your secret code.*

ROBBERY PREVENTION

Rate your level of knowledge when it comes to robbery prevention. Answer yes or no to the following questions.

In the Home

	YES	NO
1.	___	___	Do you keep doors and windows locked at all times?
2.	___	___	Do you have a peephole so that you can see who is outside without having to open the door?
3.	___	___	Do you always verify a person's identification before opening your door?
4.	___	___	If a stranger asks to use your phone, do you refuse to let him into your home and offer to make the call yourself?
5.	___	___	Do you as a woman living alone use your first initials only in telephone directories, on mailboxes, etc.?
6.	___	___	Do you refuse to reveal personal information to anyone on the phone or at your door?
7.	___	___	Do you always have your keys ready when approaching your home?
8.	___	___	If you return home to find windows and doors tampered with, would you avoid entering and go to a neighbor's house to call the police?

Telephone Answering

	YES	NO
9.	___	___	Do you teach family members not to give personal or family information to strangers over the phone?
10.	___	___	Do you record only nonspecific messages on your answering machine and avoid

messages like, "We'll be back at 7:00 P.M. on Sunday?"

11. ____ ____ If you receive an obscene or crank call, would you hang up immediately, saying nothing?

On the Go

YES **NO**

12. ____ ____ Do you plan in advance to use the safest route to your destination?
13. ____ ____ Do you choose routes that pass by high-risk areas, such as vacant lots, alleys?
14. ____ ____ Do you avoid isolated bus stops?
15. ____ ____ Do you walk facing traffic so you can see approaching cars?
16. ____ ____ Do you walk near the curb to avoid the element of surprise or someone hiding between shrubs or in a doorway?
17. ____ ____ Do you stay out of reach if someone in a vehicle stops to ask directions?
18. ____ ____ Are you wary of approaching strangers?
 ____ ____ If you continue to be followed, do you flee to the nearest safe place?
19. ____ ____ Do you try to get a description of the person and/or vehicle following you?
20. ____ ____ Do you avoid hitchhiking?

21. ____ ____ Do you avoid carrying large sums of money in your purse or wallet?
22. ____ ____ Do you carry your purse close to your body, without wrapping the straps around your arm or hand?
23. ____ ____ Do you avoid leaving a purse unattended, even for a moment?
24. ____ ____ Do you avoid displaying large amounts of cash in public?

In Your Car

YES **NO**

25. ____ ____ Do you always lock your car doors while driving?
26. ____ ____ Do you keep windows rolled up whenever possible?
27. ____ ____ Do you avoid picking up hitchhikers?
28. ____ ____ Do you keep your car in good running order to avoid breakdowns in dangerous areas?

29.	___	___	Do you look for well-lit areas to park your car?
30.	___	___	Do you always lock your car when it is parked?
31.	___	___	Do you look around the car before you get out, especially at night or in deserted areas such as underground parking lots?
32.	___	___	When returning to your car, do you have your keys in hand?
33.	___	___	Do you look in the back seat before getting into the car?
34.	___	___	If you are being followed, do you avoid going home and go to the nearest place of safety instead?

• • • • • • • • • • • • •

Count the number of yes answers that you gave to these questions. If you answered no to any of these questions, consider a change in behavior to increase your security. Review the scale below to assess your vulnerability to robbery.

30-34 YES answers—This score indicates you are a fully empowered citizen who has a minimal risk of becoming a robbery victim.

20-29 YES answers—This indicates you have an average understanding of crime prevention principles, but could benefit by rereading the statement from convicted robber Joseph and the empowerment strategies.

10-19 YES answers—This indicates you are vulnerable to being robbed and you should reread the whole chapter on robbery prevention.

0-9 YES answers—If a robber runs across you on the street, you should just hand over your money to them or, alternatively, reread the chapter and retake the test.

The primary key to remember about robbery and robbery prevention is that robbers are looking for the easiest target they can find. Most of the material in this chapter focuses on ways you can appear to look strong and empowered, so you are not an easy target for a would-be robber. Simple body language such as looking around alertly, walking briskly and with a purpose, keeping your shoulders back, and looking people directly in the eye are all ways to avoid looking like an easy victim, which inevitably makes you more vulnerable to *becoming* a victim.

CHAPTER 5

OUTSMARTING CRIME IN THE WORKPLACE

M y t h :

> *The biggest crime threat to my business is shoplifting and armed robbery.*

R E A L I T Y :

> BY FAR THE BIGGEST THREAT TO AMERICAN BUSINESS IS INTERNAL THEFT: EMPLOYEES WHO STEAL FROM THEIR EMPLOYER'S ACCOUNT FOR NEARLY 30 PERCENT OF ALL LOSSES TO AMERICAN BUSINESS EACH YEAR.

THERE IS NOT MUCH CRIME LITERATURE THAT FOCUSES ON embezzlement, crime against business, and employee dishonesty. It seems that this subject would rather be discussed in generalities, and few media personalities and professionals want to focus on the specifics. This is partly due to the fact that not many concrete statistics exist; partly due to the fact that *personal* injury and abuse seems more timely and relevant to American citizens today than crime against business. However, with *internal* theft being a very real threat to American businesses today, we think this topic is more than worthy of discussion.

THE TRUTH ABOUT CRIME
IN THE WORKPLACE

Most of the data that is used in this book comes from data collected by the Bureau of Justice Statistics during their semi-annual national crime victimization survey. Unfortunately, that survey is focused on individual crimes and therefore doesn't look at corporate America or even the vast part of our lives that is taken up in the workplace.

Data that focuses on crime in the workplace is nearly nonexistent. There are a number of reasons for this. One is that owners and managers of businesses are often in denial about the extent to which crime is impacting their bottom line; another is that many business owners simply don't know the extent of their losses due to crime. Finally, very few organizations and/or government agencies collect data on such crimes.

Therefore what we must rely on is a vast array of studies, articles, and "best guesses" on the part of people who look at crimes in the workplace in order to pinpoint the biggest threat to business and how to avoid them.

In order to evaluate the risks of various types of crime to your business, it is important to define the terms used in this chapter.

Robbery: Robbery of a business is similar to robbery of an individual: the victim must be present at the time of the crime and force or threat of force must be used. The term armed robbery describes the kind of force used (i.e., a weapon) and is typically what business owners fear the most. Although armed robbery is not the biggest threat to a business, because the media and popular films often portray this type of violence, business owners often indicate that they are afraid they will be held up at gunpoint.

Burglary: Burglary in a business context is a crime that must happen in a building and, more than that, the suspect must have had no right to be in the building at the time the burglary occurs. Many burglars are the type we see in the movies, where they pry a lock or break a window to gain access to something of value. In addition, however, burglars often hide in a building until after it closes and, when everyone leaves, commit the crime. This means that they have a much easier time, since they don't have to worry about breaking in, and breaking out usually involves simply opening a door.

Theft: Theft is the largest of the three categories. It involves taking something that doesn't belong to you. This can be done by someone who is a customer, an employee, or even the boss. There are very elaborate schemes that are used to steal today. Many involve stealth, some involve slight of hand, and others involve manipulation of records. Irrespective of how the theft is committed, it is a major threat to many businesses.

There are many ways that crime can impact the bottom line of a company. First, it can affect profits directly through losses in products (known as shrinkage), time, cash, or services. Many studies in the past few years have spoken to more subtle, but nevertheless direct, losses such as theft of time or of "unwritten company benefits" such as use of long distance phone services, company vehicles, and company discounts.

In addition to direct losses, there are also indirect losses. If an employee is injured on the job due to crime, that is an indirect loss, since the company may have to reimburse the person in the form of sick leave, medical expenses, and so on to get him or her back to functioning as he or she once had. The company may also have to hire an additional person to fill in for that person while the injured party is recovering. In addition, a customer or employee may sue the company if he or she is injured and feels that the company was negligent in providing a safe environment to work or shop.

Finally, some state and/or communities have passed legislation requiring a business take certain precautions to protect employees that are extremely vulnerable to crime. Many jurisdictions have regulations that require employers to train employees who work after a certain time in the evening in procedures to make them less likely to be robbed or to be injured if a robbery occurs.

In some cases, security itself may become an indirect cost of crime. Guard forces are not cheap, but if they are well trained they may blend in well into the workings of the company. Poorly trained guards are more of a liability than an asset to a company. It is well worth the additional cost to maintain minimum standards that are higher than the norm for security officers. Unfortunately, many businesses hire contract guards the way they do many other things, seeking the lowest bidder. If you know what quality you want and all companies are equal, the lowest bidder may be a good way to go. Unfortunately, there are many different qualities of guard companies. Lowest bid usually means greater liability in the long run.

OUTSMARTING THEFT

How does all this involve a business and its employees and customers? First of all, a business that loses too much through any crime will simply not be in business long, unless it's able to pass the losses onto someone else. One example of the enormity of losses is shown by Safeware Insurance Agency Inc. of Columbus, Ohio, that reported that in 1992, 62 percent of computer losses amongst its insured were from theft (731,000 incidents). The only incidence that caused more of a loss to insured computers were power surges (1,100,000 incidents).

Depending on which "authority" you believe, it is estimated that between 40 and 60 percent of businesses that fail each year do so as a direct result of theft. Many times losses are passed on to an insurance company, but today's theft policies are extremely costly and if they are used too often, the insured soon finds him- or herself without a policy or with extremely high premiums.

How then does a business that is careless with theft absorb the losses without going out of business? By passing them on to their customers. We have been duped in the past few years into thinking that relaxing security at a business provides greater customer service. What it actually does is raises the amount each good customer pays for the goods and services he or she receives.

According to a *U.S. News and World Report* article "about 69 percent of after-tax corporate profits in America" is lost to crime. This amounts to a "crime tax" of about $1,376 per year for each household in the United States!

It makes one rethink what customer service should entail. This is especially true when we deal with check fraud which is becoming the crime of choice for many as we relax our policies in retail business regarding the acceptance of checks (see Inside the Mind of a Check Frauder).

Customers need to get angry about this. We need to send a strong message to the owners and managers of large corporations that tells them we as individual consumers are willing to be slowed down in a check out line to show proper identification to prove that we are the ones who should be passing the check. We need to assure them that protecting our money is good customer service and it is being protected by asking for a person's identification. We need to further give them the message that we are willing to move our business to those businesses who take security seriously if they aren't.

What Good Security Looks Like

What is good security? We have been sold a bill of goods that security is bars, locks, alarm systems, and security officers. These may indicate good security, but often they exist in the wrong combinations or there isn't coordination among everyone involved to see that everything works as it should. Many business managers see security as purely a drain on the bottom line.

In some cases they may be right. But in others, good security planning can not only be an asset, but can turn losses directly into profits. Many also feel that security is always intrusive and unwelcome, however a pharmacy in the Midwest learned that the opposite may be true. The pharmacy was in a hotspot neighborhood and was being victimized by a great deal of shoplifting. They saw their only recourse to be installing a hidden camera, but they felt that cameras would turn away customers.

Eventually they were forced to install the cameras or face bankruptcy. To their amazement, their customer count actually went up and so did their profits. When surveying new customers, they discovered that the area had had such a negative feeling to it that the customers welcomed the cameras—they actually felt safer knowing someone was watching.

According to a study conducted by Dr. Steven Albrecht of Brigham Young University, "Thirty percent of the public will steal or be dishonest on a regular basis, another 30 percent will be dishonest depending upon the situation, and 40 percent will never steal or be dishonest regardless of the situation."

Many businesses in turning over security to a special group of people not only shirk their corporate responsibility, but also make a statement to employees that it isn't important enough for them to be concerned about.

When Al Ward was touring Disney World's Magic Kingdom as part of a crime prevention through environmental design training last spring, he saw the best example of security you can imagine. There were about thirty security and law enforcement professionals being given a tour by the security director of the complex and, of course, we all wanted pictures of the tunnels that are so important to the security of the magic kingdom.

When the first person raised his camera to take a photo, a cast member (not a security person) walked right up to him and said, "I'm sorry sir, but photography is not allowed in the tunnels." Al was very impressed. Obviously the ownership of the security program rested with employees—where it belongs.

In order for employees to "own" the security program, they must be fully aware of the part they play in the overall security plan. They must know that what they are doing is having an impact. And they must know that their part is valuable to the organization. These indicators are from the top down but must be reinforced by each level of management to the lowest level of employee.

This takes written policies and procedures which are the statements from the corporation regarding expected behavior of all levels of employees. In addition, it requires training on a regular basis regarding different ways to implement the policy. Finally, it takes recognition of employees who are successful in implementing the policy.

What topics should these policies include? A policy is a statement of the company's position on theft. A prudent policy will indicate that theft will not be tolerated and that it is everyone's job to reduce theft in his or her sphere of influence to the lowest possible amount. The policy statement should also indicate that people caught stealing will be terminated as well as prosecuted.

The company must also have procedures that spell out how the policy is to be followed by each employee. Procedures must be developed for each part of the company which spell out how employees deal with crime when they identify it. Examples of such procedures that should be incorporated and the crimes they might encounter include:

- ❏ Opening and closing procedures (robbery and burglary)
- ❏ Cash control (robbery, theft, and personal safety)
- ❏ Banking procedures (robbery, theft, personal safety)
- ❏ Loading dock procedures (theft and workplace violence)
- ❏ Hiring policies (theft)
- ❏ Use of exit interviews (theft)
- ❏ Bomb threat policies (personal safety, theft)
- ❏ Executive protection (robbery, personal safety)
- ❏ Security of stationary, forms, and checks (theft, burglary)
- ❏ Employee parking (theft, personal safety)
- ❏ Shoplifting (theft)
- ❏ Cash refund (theft)
- ❏ Armed robbery (robbery, theft, personal safety)
- ❏ Dealing with irate customers (personal safety, theft)
- ❏ Use of company phone/equipment (theft)

Giving employees guidance in the form of procedures regarding things they can do to reduce the company losses and keep themselves safe reinforces the fact that the company is both concerned with their welfare and about loss or improper use of company resources. The more effort that is put into hiring practices and training, the more dividends the company will reap in the form of lower losses which translates directly into increased profits.

The Role of Employees and Customers

What can an employee or customer do about theft? Be present and observe what is going on. If an employee thinks a shopper is stealing or attempting to steal, the best thing he or she can do is provide good customer service. A person can't steal if he or she is being watched. That's why thieves go to fitting rooms or areas that are difficult to see into.

Customers can put pressure on people who are attempting to steal as well. If a shoplifter is being watched by a customer, he or she is likely to think the customer is an undercover security person and, again, the thief will move on. A customer can also alert store employees to suspicious behavior of other customers that might indicate shoplifting.

It is important to note here that shoplifting accounts for some theft losses, but employees account for a larger percentage on average. Some experts estimate that up to 60 percent of business theft losses today are the result of internal theft. A study that was conducted by Sears Roebuck and Co. showed that average losses per shoplifter caught accounted for $80 whereas average losses due to employee theft cost the company about $780.

Each year the Food Marketing Institute in conjunction with London House testing organization studies supermarket chains and their employees. In 1990, the study showed that the stores surveyed had an average of three incidents of employee theft per store. The average known loss was $104. By 1993, the number had increased to 3.6 incidents per store and the losses to $127.66. In 1990, the survey estimated that theft among employees averaged from $6,708 to $181,350 per store annually. One can easily see that employee theft losses can account for a big chunk of corporate profits.

Check and Credit Card Fraud

Check and credit card fraud are sources of big losses to companies. The tab for check fraud is usually passed on to the retail business that accepted the check who in turn passes it on to the consumer. How big is the tab? A New York study of 501 firms released in 1994 estimates that credit card fraud costs New Yorkers an average of $367,000 and check fraud an average of $360,000.

Employees can play a big role in reducing internal theft by letting employees who are attempting to steal know that it is noted and not appreciated by another employee. Peer pressure can work to reduce theft in the workplace. If good screening is done so that the only employees hired are not in the category of the 30 percent who will steal no matter what, the 40 percent of honest employees can keep the 30 percent who are waiting for the opportunity honest.

Employees and customers can have an impact on check forgery if the company supports them with a good company policy and training on its implementation. Employees can follow company policy to the letter on every customer who wants to pay with a check. This doesn't have to be negative. Most of the negativity comes with a negative attitude on the part of the employee or the customer. A clerk with a positive attitude can make even an identification check pleasant.

As a customer, you too can help to reduce this high-loss crime. The easiest way for you to do this is to praise clerks/stores that have and follow good check acceptance policies. If a store doesn't have and follow a prudent policy, ask them why they don't and point out to them that you feel they are jeopardizing your account by not doing so. If they persist, take your business elsewhere. It is important to note here that shoplifters account for some of the theft losses that stores are victimized by, but that of employees can account for a larger percentage.

Embezzlement

Embezzlement is another type of theft that is taking its toll these days. This is a type of theft that involves a person in a position of trust who steals money from the company. The company itself can be protected from this by screening these special employees, bonding them where prudent and carefully crafting a system of regular and impromptu audits that are independently conducted to assure honesty.

Most people who have become bookkeepers or accountants will be very careful not to jeopardize their career. If, however, the company appears to be an easy mark, they may try small thefts to see if they will be caught. If they are caught, the person will have a good explanation. If not, they will continue with larger and larger thefts. The main reason embezzlers get caught is that they become greedy and keep stealing until it is painfully obvious and often too late.

A customer can help reduce embezzlement by noting suspicious behavior on the part of a cashier or accountant. A person who doesn't place money in the till after a transaction is certainly suspect. Another employee may also be of assistance if he or she sees that the company is paying bills to a company it doesn't do business with. This should immediately be pointed out to a manager.

OUTSMARTING BURGLARY

Unlike theft, burglary normally takes place when no one is around. This makes it even more difficult to stop. One thing that is prudent is to check with your local police department to find out what the burglary trend data is for you business neighborhood. Next you should check with your insurance carrier to determine 1) if they require any special security for your area or 2) if they give any cost breaks for special security measures. These are the best places to begin.

Next, it is important to develop good opening and closing procedures. These should alert the business to a break in when the first employees enter the store. The last employee at night (or designated employee) should check to see that everyone is gone from the premises before it is secured for the night. This will lessen the risk of someone hiding after hours in the business.

In addition, it is important to assure that cleaning companies or guard services screen their employees well and are bonded, which will help insure that anyone who has access to your business is honest.

	Total Business	Night	Day	Unknown Time
Average Dollar Loss	$1,400	$1,153	$1,827	$1,420
Burglary Rate (%)	33.8% of Total	15.8% of Total	8.7% of Total	9.3% of Total

Source: *1993 Sourcebook of Criminal Justice Statistics*, Table 3.116, page 375.

There should also be procedures set up that assure that when people leave the buildings to dump garbage or go on rounds that the doors are immediately secured and not simply left unlocked and unattended.

Security systems, plastic coating for window glass, and good locking systems with special attention to good key control also make a business less of a target to burglary.

OUTSMARTING ARMED ROBBERY

Most likely the scariest event that can happen in a business is armed robbery. Robbers, whether or not they are armed, present a very real danger to employees and customers. Many of the lawsuits that have nearly leveled giant corporations in the past few years have involved injuries of employees or customers during an armed robbery. According to a study conducted by the Center for Disease Control and reported in the early 1990s, 87 percent of people who were murdered in the workplace were killed during an armed robbery or a robbery attempt. This makes it very clear that robbery can present a very real threat to employees and companies.

Institution	Commercial House	Service Station	Conven. Store	Bank/Financial
Average Loss	$1,380	$513	$402	3,325
Robbery Rate (%)	11.9% of Total	2.5% of Total	5.3% of Total	1.7% of Total

Source: 1993 Sourcebook of Criminal Justice Statistics, Table 3.116, page 375.

It is important to have good policies and procedures regarding armed robbery and cash control. Setting up any type of pattern for banking may indeed get the unfortunate person carrying the money robbed. Whoever takes money to a bank should be especially trustworthy and should know what to do if things don't seem right at the drop site or bank or if approached by a robber. All policies regarding armed robbery should reinforce that the safety of the employee is more important than the loss of the money.

Much legislation in the past few years has aimed at safety of employees and customers during armed robberies. The Gainesville, Florida, study and ordinance indicated that certain design criteria can be used to better design a convenience store to lessen its attractiveness to robbery. In addition, the addition of one clerk during the graveyard shift can make a difference in the incidence of robberies. Training is also an important part of the ordinance. This ordinance was picked up statewide in Florida and has become a model that many local cities have looked at adopting to avert crime.

In Washington State, a similar though slightly less rigid law was adopted. It requires employees of late night retail businesses to be trained in what to do before, during, and after an armed robbery to reduce the risk of occurrence in the first place and to limit injuries during such an event should it occur. Many in Washington State ignore the legislation because it is not uniformly being enforced. The problem for those people will come in the event of a robbery with injury. Absent any effort by the business to comply with the law, an attorney may be able to prove negligence and win a cash settlement for the injured employee or customer.

As a customer, it is important to be especially watchful after dark when entering a business that has a high potential for robbery. Many times you can see what is going on from outside. Such things as the wrong person behind the counter can indicate trouble before you ever enter a business. Many businesses provide uniforms or smocks for their employees.

If you approach such a business and see the person in the smock standing nervously away from the cash register while a person not wearing the proper smock is behind the counter, go to a phone that is outside the line of sight of the store and dial 911. If the phone is in an adjacent business and you can keep an eye on the parking lot that might be helpful, but don't try to be a hero—your own safety should be a top priority.

OUTSMARTING DRUGS

Many crimes can be linked directly to the use of drugs and the need for money to buy more drugs. Many workplaces seem to be a haven for drug abusers and even drug sales. This usually occurs as a result of either a naive owner/manager or possibly one that is also involved in the abuse. Here's what the Florida Department of Health and Rehabilitative Services has to say about drugs in their manual *Building a Drug-Free Workplace*:

> *The use of drugs is no longer considered a harmless*
> *pastime as drug use is directly related to the impairment*
> *of 16 to 21 million workers per year. This translates into*

an estimated 10 to 30 percent of the American work force
that live a drug-oriented lifestyle . . . The U.S. Chamber
of Commerce reports an estimated $60 billion is lost by
businesses and government due to the increased
absenteeism, higher accident rates, and the reduced
productivity caused by substance abuse.

There has been a great move in the past few years to create businesses that advertise themselves to be drug free. This only works of course if the business has made an effort to learn what that means and to upgrade its policies, management and employee training to assure that it happens. Some companies are laughing stocks because everyone knows that drug abuse is rampant and they naively waive the banner of a drug-free workplace.

The benefits of a drug-free workplace include fewer on the job accidents, lower crime rates and lower insurance rates. It is important to seek out programs that will help businesses become drug free.

As an individual, you also have a role in assuring that a workplace is drug free. A customer seeing an employee operating equipment while high on alcohol or other drugs should consider at least an anonymous report to a company official. A number of years ago, a person who I knew had her husband killed by a drunk driver. When the investigation proceeded, it was learned that the person was driving a company truck and that the company not only knew that the person was suspended, but that he had a drinking problem and had been suspended twice before. The result was a multimillion dollar lawsuit that was easily won by the wife of the victim.

The least a company should do is to set up and adhere to a company policy on drug abuse. This policy should include the following:

- Position on drug use in the workplace
- Consequences for employees using, selling or possessing drugs in the workplace
- Position on workplace safety as it relates to drug use

❑ Position on treatment and rehabilitation services provided to an employee found to be using drugs

❑ Position on drug testing for the detection of drug use

❑ Position on employee educational programs regarding the addictive nature of drugs (including alcohol)

OUTSMARTING VIOLENCE

Workplace violence is something that has gotten a lot of press lately. It is obviously news when a person walks into a corporation with automatic weapons and begins shooting people. The truth is that a company has very little chance of this type of violence occurring. The chance is not zero, however, and this makes it important to address the potential for its occurrence.

Most violence of this type happens as a result of a disgruntled former employee. According to a 1992 study conducted by the National Center for Disease Control entitled Homicide in the U.S. Workplace: A Strategy for Prevention and Research:

❑ Homicide was the third leading cause of occupational injury death in the U.S. for the period from 1980 through 1985, accounting for nearly 13 percent of the nation's total deaths from trauma in the workplace. Homicide was the manner of death for 12 percent of the men and 42 percent of the women who died from injuries sustained in the U.S. workplace during the six-year period for which data were available.

❑ National Traumatic Occupational Fatalities data also indicate that 73 percent of workplace homicide victims died from gunshot wounds.

❑ At the industry division level, 33 percent of workplace homicide victims were employed in retail trade, 19 percent in service industries, and 11 percent in public administration. Law enforcement officers constituted 83 percent of this (public administration) category.

❑ Analysis by more detailed industry sectors indicates that local passenger transportation was one of the most hazardous in terms of workplace homicide. Taxi cab drivers accounted for 47 percent of the deaths in this industrial group.

According to an article in the August 1994 issue of *Beretta USA Leadership Bulletin*, there are five major types of workplace violence:

1] Robbery and other crimes directed at commercial establishments

2] Violence by one employee against another

3] Domestic violence and cases of misdirected affection

4] Violence in schools

5] Crime by terrorists, arsonists, or political activists against business

This violence can take many forms: arson, bombing, bomb threats, kidnapping/extortion, and shooting assaults. Employee screening is in defense against such acts. Obviously people change over time and some people can slip through the best screening endeavors. Two other things that will reduce the odds a bit are managers that create a good work environment for employees and sensitive termination practices.

Many disgruntled employees were upset not by being terminated but by the way it happened. They were embarrassed in front of co-workers, terminated prior to a holiday, terminated as a result of downsizing without adequate lead time to help find another job. Some of these things can't be helped, but if a company is concerned enough about these things *in advance*, they may find fewer disgruntled people coming back to seek revenge with the company.

Bomb threats are a common way that a disgruntled employee (whether past or present) can get back at the company with great feelings of anonymity and safety from being caught. Procedures should be developed that give all people who receive calls training and a form to take down as much information from the caller as possible. A person needs this information to evaluate the need to search or evacuate the building. Some of the information can assist in determining where the most likely areas would be for a search team to begin looking. This training can be sought through the Bureau of Alcohol, Tobacco and Firearms.

Extortion/kidnapping is a very frightening event that can occur if a person is desperate enough. Protection against this involves good personal safety training for managers and their families, home security, codes for children and assurances that their schools will not release them to adults other than parents without express permission from the parent.

Domestic violence accounts for some of the injuries and deaths in the workplace (5 percent of the women victimized at work were attacked by a husband, ex-husband, boyfriend, or ex-boyfriend according to the Bureau of Justice Statistics). No workplace is a good place for an ongoing domestic violence episode to happen. Many workplaces have provided additional support for DV victims in the form of special leave authorized to be involved in court processes in addition to any sick leave that is necessary.

The formulation of company policies can outline ways to exclude the suspect from the premises (usually in conjunction with any court order the victim has). In addition, companies can support the victim with escorts to and from a vehicle/parking lot or garage. They can also transport the suspect from their premises in addition to enforcing the court order. If there are annoying calls from a determined suspect, arrangements can be made to route the victim's calls through a receptionist rather than directly to their work phone.

According to *Beretta USA Leadership Bulletin* and the National Center for the Analysis of Violent Crime (NCAVC) at the FBI Academy, there are some early warning signs to look for to anticipate potential trouble. The signs give managers an indication as to when it is time to intervene by providing the employee with assistance in overcoming his or her problem. The signs are as follows:

1] The employee has a history of violent behavior.

2] The employee has an obsession with weapons, gun magazines, or the discussion of weapons.

3] The individual carries a concealed weapon.

4] The employee uses various forms of intimidation on fellow employees.

5] The employee has an obsession with the job but has little if any involvement with co-workers.

6] The individual makes unwanted romantic advances toward another employee.

7] The employee exhibits paranoid behavior.

8] The employee is incapable of accepting criticism.

9] The employee holds grudges for a long time.

10] The employee has a family, financial, or custodial problem.

11] The employee has exhibited an undo interest in recent violent acts in the workplace.

12] The employee has a history of testing the limits of rules, regulations, and social norms.

13] There is a high level of stress in the job caused by labor problems, reductions in force (RIF), or the introduction of high technology.

14] The individual has exhibited extreme changes in behavior and/or political or religious beliefs.

The primary point is that when an employee begins to exhibit one or more of these signs, a manager needs to intervene with proper management skills and the full array of employee benefits and services to deal with the problem. Violent outbursts from employees usually are the result of a build up. An alert, well-trained, and supportive manager is the best defense against a life-threatening event. One additional thought is that workplace violence often goes hand-in-hand with alcohol or other substance abuse.

What Businesses Can Do to Prevent Violence

The best way for a business to develop good security is from the ground up. When a business is on the drawing board, someone should be assigned or engaged to check what the crime rate is in the area where the business is opening. An assessment of the levels of security being provided in like businesses in the area is also important in determining how best to secure the new one, always keeping in mind that it is prudent to be above the norm in security measures.

There is a concept called Crime Prevention through Environmental Design (CPTED) that can be very important to a new business. The idea is that built space gives off cues to people that make them feel safe or unsafe. CPTED states that there are three different groups of people that are attracted to space: normal users, the people the space was designed for; abnormal users, those who the business would like to keep away; and observers, those who are present because of their daily routine (employees, traffic, people transiting the areas).

If the space is properly designed, it will attract the normal users and observers and repel the abnormal users. The goal is to make the space as productive as possible in a way that it was designed for. The two questions a CPTED planner asks the businessperson are 1) What is it you are trying to do? and 2) How can we help you do it better? This is certainly different from earlier concepts of security. The main reason is that this has little to do directly with security—security is merely a side benefit of successful implementation of CPTED principles.

It is very important, as this chapter attempts to show, that every business develop comprehensive policies and procedures that describe what the company stand is on a certain issue and what is expected for employees to do in certain situations.

One way to develop tight security measures with the full cooperation and approval of staff is to put together an employee committee that represents each division and all levels of employees. The best idea is to consult with an attorney who is well versed in labor law, management issues, and business liability who can both give a set of parameters and review the final product to ensure legal protection.

Such legal advice is important given the growing number of lawsuits brought on behalf of employees injured by violence in the workplace. It is extremely important for employers to know their rights and responsibilities and to make sure they do the best they can to define their workplace to defend against all possible contingencies.

A survey by Northwestern National Life Insurance entitled Fear and Violence in the Workplace gave these suggestions for coping with workplace violence:

1] Implement effective grievance machinery.

2] Maintain good security and crisis management programs.

3] Establish strong, written anti-harassment policies.

4] Foster a supportive work environment.

5] Give employees control over their work.

6] Communicate openly.

7] Resolve conflict through negotiation.

8] Provide counseling for employees fired or laid off.

9] Train supervisors to recognize troubled employees.

If you have a large business or complex, the next phase is to consider the use of security officers. The planning for this phase is essential. It is especially important to design what you want them to do before you begin trying to find a company to do it. Security officers can be a presence that may have a deterrent effect on crime. They can be there to respond to incidents, direct people, set up traffic patterns and restricted parking areas, and manage opening and closing. They shouldn't double as maintenance personnel.

One really important question that a large company needs to make a decision about is, "Should I contract for guard service or set up my own proprietary security department?" There are benefits on both sides and it is important that you check out the best and worst of both before you decide. You should also check to see what state laws are in effect regarding training of security officers. Finally, it is essential that you realize that hiring a company to furnish guards does not necessarily relieve you of civil or criminal responsibility for their actions.

 # INSIDE THE MIND OF A CHECK FRAUDER

Check fraud is a $10 to $20 billion dollar per year industry in the United States according to some estimates and close to 90 percent of the losses come at the hands of retailers. The growth in computer technologies such as scanners and color laser printers has made it dangerously easy not just to steal checks but to manufacture them as well. So if you are a business person who accepts checks on a regular basis as a method of payment, pay special attention to this section.

The following is an interview with a person who was a professional passer of bad checks. Linda was involved in a criminal ring of check frauders in Seattle for a period of three years by her own admission and she estimates that at the peak of activity, she was writing $100,000 per year worth of bad checks—and not getting caught.

In this interview, she talks about how she got the checks, what she looked for in merchants to pass bad checks and what kind of retailers and employees she would stay away from for fear of getting caught.

"My name is Linda. I spent four years making my living writing bad checks. I learned how to do this when I was in high school. Me and some of my friends were just hanging around trying to figure out how to make some money. Then one day, one of my friends said her mom had just gotten out of prison and had learned a new way to make a little income on the side—writing checks. Her mom taught us all how to do it."

On How to Get the Checks in the First Place

"There are many ways to do it. We had a whole group of people who would do it together. It would usually start with some guys breaking into cars and stealing checkbooks. They would also steal checkbooks from mailboxes or from people's homes—I don't know exactly how all they did it 'cause the men would do that. We was in the business of running the checks.

"I did hear about one guy who would get himself a fake ID at one of those passport ID places and then go into a bank and start up different checking accounts. He would give them $50 or something and tell the lady that he wanted to start with a high check number—you know like 450 or 500—he would say it was cause his old account left off at 450 and he wanted to keep his records straight.

"Then a week later, they would mail him pre-printed checks in the mail with a fake address and a fake name like the one on his fake ID and he would just go out and write checks all day long—he would go buy a leather jacket at a department store and then two hours later take it back to another branch of the same store and say it was a gift and that it didn't fit and get a cash refund.

"He would take orders for people—like go write a bad check for a washer and drier for $1,000 and then have it delivered to a guy who gave him $200 cash in advance."

"Sometimes I would get checkbooks from guys like this or from drug houses. You know, a burglar would find somebody's check in a house they was hitting and then they would take it to a fence who happened to also be a drug dealer. The fence would give the burglar say $25 for a box of checks and then we would buy it from him and go have a big time.

"Other times the checks were stolen out of cars and we would buy them the same way as the ones that came from burglaries."

On How We Selected a Business to Hit

"When I first got a checkbook, if nobody else had used it yet, I could go to any store—it didn't matter. I would just go buy stuff anywhere. After a couple of hours or not more than a day, I would only go to stores that didn't have those check machines—you know those stickers that say "SCAN" on them. Cause I know that if a store has that on it, they are going to check to see if the checks are stolen or if somebody had written a bad check on that account already.

"The best stores to hit are the ones that are real busy. This is because they are in such a hurry to get customers through that they don't check very carefully what the driver's license looks like or what the check looks like. Sometimes they don't even ask to see a driver's license."

On How to Get Identification

"Oh that's another thing. We used to make driver's licenses with a board in the background and so on but then we figured out that we could scan a real driver's license into a computer and then change the information around to match the checks we had and then print it out on a color computer. You just laminate your picture on there and you have what looks like a perfect driver's license.

"Another thing was to just go to the Department of Licensing and get a Washington state ID card. This is easier to get than a driver's license and I would just go there and say I lost my license and I needed to get an ID card. I usually did like my friend and would get a passport ID made up before going there so that I had something to show them with the name and address I wanted to use and my picture on it. Then I would just pay my fifteen dollars and walk out with a real state ID.

"The thing about IDs is that even if I didn't look exactly like the person in the picture—say I got someone else's ID which we did a lot, you know trading IDs around—I could always make up my hair to look like hers or put on some different make-up. The only thing I had trouble with is if the ID I had was of a white girl—I am Black and so it was hard to look white, you know?"

On How to Identify a Check Frauder in Your Store

"The thing is, I always tried to be cool when I was inside a store, but now that I think about it, I did fall into a pattern. I would go into a store either when it was real busy or when they were just about to close. The reason I went in just at closing time was cause I was hoping the clerks would be in a hurry to go home and so they wouldn't check my ID or my check too carefully.

"I would also just grab stuff off of the shelf—you know, it didn't really matter too much what I was getting since I wasn't paying for it anyway. So if you see someone come into your store right around closing time, you should be suspicious. Also, if they just start grabbing stuff off of the counter without looking at the price or anything, that should make you wonder too.

"I also want to say that just cause I did this and I am Black, there are plenty of white girls—all types of girls—doing this. So don't just be looking at skin color when you're trying to figure out who's legit or not."

On How Check Frauders Select the Check-Out Person

"I would always be very selective about which checker's line I would go through. I had a very specific kind of person I was looking for. First, I looked for someone who had a big line. This did several things. First it made it likely that the checker would go fast in accepting checks to avoid people having to wait longer in line. Second, it gave me a chance to see how careful they were at looking at checks and IDs.

"I would definitely prefer a checker who was checking groceries real fast and who appeared to be in a hurry. I also would always look for a younger checker as opposed to an older one. This is because the older checkers were more likely to follow the procedures the store had exactly. The younger ones tended to be more carefree and were more likely to skip over things.

"But the best checker of all was a young girl who was on the phone talking to her boyfriend or to one of her girlfriends. I would wait twice as long in line just to go to that person. Once I saw this girl talking to her boyfriend while she was checking and when I wrote my check she looked at my ID and accepted the check even though the driver's license was out of state and had a white girl's picture on it."

On How to Avoid Check Fraud

"I think that the key thing is for the business to set up procedures so that every checker looks at the ID and matches it up with the name on the check. It's also important to look at the check and see what the check number is. If it's low, it could be bad. On the other hand, lots of times we had checks with high numbers on it cause they were stolen, you know? Not new accounts.

"Another thing is to get them stickers that say SCAN on them. That would scare me off after awhile. Cause they have some way of knowing if I had written a bad check or something. Another thing is look for ID cards. If I am writing a check and all I had is a Washington State ID card and no driver's license, you gotta wonder what's going on—especially if I drove in to your store.

"Yeah, doing checks was easy and I never felt too guilty about it 'cause I figure they all had insurance to cover bad checks and stuff like that, so all I was hurting was the insurance company."

$ $ $

There are two things about Linda's story that need clarification. First, the SCAN stickers she referred to are part of a check authorization service provided by a company called Electronic Transaction Corporation. They have most of the major retail chains as clients and any store in their massive network that gets a bad check reports it to SCAN and the check number is subsequently placed into a data base of other bad checks.

Every time one of the SCAN customers accepts a check, they enter the check number and compare it against the millions of bad checks that are already in the data base. If no match is found, the check is considered "authorized" and accepted. The reason people like Linda fear those SCAN stickers is that if they have already written a couple of bad checks off of an account, when they go to write the next check at a store that is on the data base service, it will likely come up as bad.

ETC and the SCAN service is not the only check authorization service in the country, but it is the largest. Such a service can be a useful deterrent to bad check writers like Linda, as can establishing and following a few simple procedures which have been outlined.

The second thing is that while Linda may have had little or no guilt about passing bad checks because it "only hurts insurance companies," she should have because most bad check losses are absorbed by the retail merchant, not big banks or insurance companies. While there are some firms which specialize in insuring checks, those are limited to a small number of purchases and usually only checks written for large amounts. The majority of the $10 to $20 billion lost annually to check frauders is paid out of what would otherwise be business profit.

CRIME AGAINST BUSINESS SCENARIO

Often businesses are too busy to pay attention to details that may cost them large losses. An upscale restaurant is the scene of this particular breach of security in the name of convenience. John was hired as a cook for this business. Unfortunately for the restaurant, John's hero was a con artist who had written a book that detailed many different ways that a bright individual could steal from others.

When John began work in the restaurant, he noticed immediately that he had access to a checking account in addition to cash from the register to pay for different deliveries that were made routinely to the kitchen. It took him a very short time to visit an office supply store and bank in a nearby city. When he returned, he had a rubber stamp in the name of a fictitious business that he had opened a bank account for in a neighboring city. He was ready to go.

A few months later, one of the other employees discovered a receipt on the manager's desk to the business in the neighboring city. He brought it to the attention of the manager with the curt statement, "What's this? We've never done business with this company." The manager then looked into the business (called the phone number on the receipt—discovered the number was to a residence and the person who answered knew nothing about the company). The manager then called the police.

By this time, the business had lost several thousand dollars in checks to the fictitious business. The cook was arrested and many items that were seized in a search warrant of his house indicated he was not a new hand at theft by deception and/or embezzlement.

The Moral: The moral of the story is you can't be too careful regarding who you trust to sign checks in your business. The dummy account is one of the oldest embezzlement tricks in the book. It is obviously important that management maintain a list of those companies the business actually does business with. That should routinely be checked *before* checks are issued.

Any business should have a double check system on delivery of goods anyway—it only makes sense that the same double check should precede a new employee writing checks. It is also important for management to conduct spot audits on the business account on a periodic basis. This will deter most embezzlement attempts as the embezzler will not know when an audit is going to be done and will have to be accountable for checks written that aren't authorized.

CORPORATE CRIME PREVENTION EMPOWERMENT STRATEGIES

Although many of the strategies to avoid business crime have been addressed thus far in this chapter, we list individual empowerment strategies for those who inevitably wish to skip the narrative portions and get right to the tips. Also, here's a handy list to refer to again and again when it comes to safeguarding your business.

➡️*EMPOWERMENT STRATEGY #139: Know your business goals and objectives.*

➡️*EMPOWERMENT STRATEGY #140: Before moving into a building, make sure the requirements of the business are adequately addressed by the space it is being moved into.*

➡️*EMPOWERMENT STRATEGY #141: Make sure to visit to your local law enforcement agency prior to signing any contract for a location for your business. The purpose of the visit is to find out what types of crime are common to the neighborhood you are moving your business into.*

➡️*EMPOWERMENT STRATEGY #142: Talk to the crime prevention unit of the law enforcement agency in which your business will be located to ascertain what types of employee training they will conduct for you at your business location.*

Also ask them if they are aware of any legislation that requires certain businesses to improve security by conducting employee training or conduct security audits and comply with prudent security measures.

➡️*EMPOWERMENT STRATEGY #143: Visit businesses similar to your own and check out what security measures they have taken. (It is wise to exceed the average level of security you see in other businesses.)*

➡*EMPOWERMENT STRATEGY #144: Hire a security consultant that has special training in Crime Prevention through Environmental Design to evaluate your security needs while you are in the design phase.*

➡*EMPOWERMENT STRATEGY #145: Develop written policies and procedures concerning theft (internal and external) plus other policies regarding crime that are dictated either by your location or the nature of your business.*

➡*EMPOWERMENT STRATEGY #146: Make sure your employment application has specific questions regarding criminal convictions as well as background information required for the specific jobs you will be filling.*

➡*EMPOWERMENT STRATEGY #147: Carefully screen new employees before hiring. It is your best defense against dishonest employees.*

➡*EMPOWERMENT STRATEGY #148: Check out such things as gaps in employment in the application process.*

➡*EMPOWERMENT STRATEGY #149: Make telephone calls to verify training, education or certifications, or previous employment. Always try to talk with direct supervisors if possible and always ask if they would rehire the person for the same job.*

➡*EMPOWERMENT STRATEGY #150: Verify home address and telephone numbers of your employees.*

➡*EMPOWERMENT STRATEGY #151: Consider paper and pencil honesty testing. Some methods have been developed recently that also determine tendency toward violence.*

➡*EMPOWERMENT STRATEGY #152: Provide your employees with a copy of company policies and procedures and keep a form signed by them indicating they have read and understand the policies (especially the policy on theft).*

➡*EMPOWERMENT STRATEGY #153: Apply the same standards you would use to hire an employee to select a custodial company or security company.*

➡*EMPOWERMENT STRATEGY #154: Managers should always set a good example for honesty with employees.*

➡*EMPOWERMENT STRATEGY #155: Managers should strictly adhere to company policies and insist that employees do the same.*

➡*EMPOWERMENT STRATEGY #156: Managers should be aware of problems that employees may have in their private lives such as marital problems or money problems; offer assistance within the company's medical, overtime, or leave policies.*

➡*EMPOWERMENT STRATEGY #157: Keep a running accounting of gross sales per shift per day.*

This may give insight into which shifts may be losing money. Consistent, unusually high, gross sales in an area in which it wouldn't be expected might indicate that an employee is bringing family and friends in to make purchases that might be fraudulently discounted.

➡*EMPOWERMENT STRATEGY #158: Keep a record of cash register audits and investigate overages as well as shortages.*

➡*EMPOWERMENT STRATEGY #159: Keep an eye open for an employee that is obviously living beyond his or her income.*

➡*EMPOWERMENT STRATEGY #160: Train employees in till tapping, quick change artists, and shoplifting.*

➡*EMPOWERMENT STRATEGY #161: Use multi-copy numbered receipts and computerize the data so that if a receipt is missing, it is caught quickly.*

➡*EMPOWERMENT STRATEGY #162: Set up good receiving policies (especially if you have a loading dock).*

Assure that at least two people always check deliveries and time and initial receipts or that one person does it with a second person conducting impromptu audits on a regular basis.

➡*EMPOWERMENT STRATEGY #163: Require two pieces of identification on checks.*

Be familiar with what checks look like and what are indicators that they might be counterfeit. The same applies to credit cards. Be sure the company has good check and credit card policies and that they are adhered to.

➡*EMPOWERMENT STRATEGY #164: Check cash register records to determine if you have people using receipts over again to cash refund the same item.*

➡*EMPOWERMENT STRATEGY #165: Have a stringent return policy—the best is to never give a cash refund. Refund by check or only allow exchanges for other merchandise. A good policy is NO RETURN without a receipt.*

➡*EMPOWERMENT STRATEGY #166: Consider mirrors: one-way glass from offices or closed circuit cameras to monitor problem areas.*

➡*EMPOWERMENT STRATEGY #167: Make sure the company has good opening and closing procedures to assure that a burglar would be caught at closing if they were hiding inside the building or that a burglary would be noticed as soon as the first person came to work.*

➡*EMPOWERMENT STRATEGY #168: If a burglary is discovered, protect the scene until the police arrive. This means keeping the people out of the area and not cleaning anything.*

➡*EMPOWERMENT STRATEGY #169: If there is an alarm system, be sure that everyone who must use it knows exactly how to use it.*

If you don't have a security system and you are in a hotspot you might check with your insurance carrier to determine if it might not be a smart move to install one. (Sometimes insurance companies give premium breaks for security measures; sometimes they require security measures in order to collect on existing policies.)

➡*EMPOWERMENT STRATEGY #170: Use a money chest (drop safe) to store any money on the premises.*

Make sure that it is rated by UL for security, not fire. If you need to store documents to protect them from fire, do that in a fire safe. They are not the same and a fire safe is not secure enough to keep money in, especially overnight.

➡*EMPOWERMENT STRATEGY #171: Make sure there is a policy regarding who is responsible for locking up at night.*

➡*EMPOWERMENT STRATEGY #172: Specify a person to walk around the building on a regular basis (at least once per week, preferably after dark), to check for lights out or trees obscuring the light, pry marks on doors or windows, or signs of loitering in the parking lot or parking garages.*

➡*EMPOWERMENT STRATEGY #173: Never mark parking stalls with employee names or assign the same spot to one person if you can possibly avoid it.*

➡*EMPOWERMENT STRATEGY #174: Don't obstruct windows into the business (especially retail) so that people outside can't see the clerk and cash register area from outside.*

➡*EMPOWERMENT STRATEGY #175: Some businesses might need an alarm system with a duress code built in.*

➡*EMPOWERMENT STRATEGY #176: Robbery alarms should always be silent.*

➤*EMPOWERMENT STRATEGY #177: Institute good cash controls in your business.*

Don't deposit at the same time every day or advertise a deposit by carrying a readily identifiable bank bag or prepare a deposit in an unsecured room, or count the till at the register while business is open or leave a deposit on or in an unsecured desk/office prior to banking it.

➤*EMPOWERMENT STRATEGY #178: Make sure that lighting is good inside and out of your business.*

➤*EMPOWERMENT STRATEGY #179: Consider uniforms or smocks that are readily identifiable for your employees where appropriate.*

➤*EMPOWERMENT STRATEGY #180: Train employees in prudent policies to follow before, during, and after a robbery or a robbery attempt.*

➤*EMPOWERMENT STRATEGY #181: Write down what should be done after a robbery and keep it on a laminated sheet near the cash register or in the office to be ready should a robbery occur.*

➤*EMPOWERMENT STRATEGY #182: Since observation and descriptive skills are important, role playing situations at various training events might be worthwhile.*

Many police departments will help managers conduct "mock robberies" to give real-life training without real robberies. It should be emphasized with the law enforcement agency that low-key robberies are what you want and to refuse to participate in high-stress mock robberies.

➤*EMPOWERMENT STRATEGY #183: Develop a strong policy on drugs (including alcohol use) in the workplace. This policy definitely needs to be reviewed by an attorney who specializes in labor law.*

➤*EMPOWERMENT STRATEGY #184: All levels of management need in-depth training in identifying the problem, whether it be an employee selling drugs in the facility or a person who is under the influence of alcoholic or other drugs during the course of the work day.*

In addition, identifying alcoholics is another management task. Once identified, the manager must have the tools to deal with the problem or to send it to someone else who does. Any management/employee interface along these lines must be confidential.

➡*EMPOWERMENT STRATEGY #185: Use and abuse of alcohol or other drugs at company functions should be weighed against company policy and the message such use gives to employees, especially employees who may have a problem with substance abuse.*

➡*EMPOWERMENT STRATEGY #186: Drug or alcohol use should be considered when evaluating on-the-job accidents.*

➡*EMPOWERMENT STRATEGY #187: Company policies, procedures, hiring, evaluation, training, and retention should all reflect the most up-to-date information regarding violence in the workplace, its causes, contributing factors, and signs.*

➡*EMPOWERMENT STRATEGY #188: Special company policies need to address how the company can help protect an employee who is being stalked, the subject of kidnap/extortion (including, but not limited to corporate executives), or the victim of domestic violence.*

These policies and procedures must be in place and managers trained in identifying the threats and implementing the procedures to safeguard the potential victim.

➡*EMPOWERMENT STRATEGY #189: Companies should have counseling for stress, family problems, or anger management as part of their employee insurance plan.*

Counseling and skilled debriefing sessions conducted by someone with the documented skills should follow any traumatic situation that occurs in the workplace. This could include assault, robbery, death of co-worker, prolonged domestic violence incident, etc.

➡️*EMPOWERMENT STRATEGY #190: Company training should include such issues as ethnicity, religious freedom, and sexual harassment.*

➡️*EMPOWERMENT STRATEGY #191: When downsizing, a prudent company will sponsor job training for employees to move into other jobs within the company or a program to help other employees find employment elsewhere.*

➡️*EMPOWERMENT STRATEGY #192: The company should set up a crisis action team that would be designed to help cope with any workplace violence related problem.*

CRIME IN THE WORKPLACE QUIZ

Answer yes or no to the following questions to determine how many procedures in this chapter you have implemented in your workplace environment.

I have the following policies and procedures in my business:

	YES	NO	
1.	___	___	Opening and closing procedures (robbery and burglary)
2.	___	___	Cash control (robbery, theft, and personal safety)
3.	___	___	Banking procedures (robbery, theft, personal safety)
4.	___	___	Loading dock procedures (theft and workplace violence)
5.	___	___	Hiring policies (theft)
6.	___	___	Use of exit interviews (theft)
7.	___	___	Bomb threat policies (personal safety, theft)
8.	___	___	Executive protection (robbery, personal safety)
9.	___	___	Security of stationery, forms and checks (theft, burglary)
10.	___	___	Employee parking (theft, personal safety)
11.	___	___	Shoplifting (theft)
12.	___	___	Cash refund (theft)
13.	___	___	Armed robbery (robbery, theft, personal safety)
14.	___	___	Dealing with irate customers (personal safety, theft)
15.	___	___	Use of company phone/equipment (theft)

• • • • • • • • • • • • •

Count the number of yes answers you gave to these questions, then refer to the scale below to rate your vulnerability to business crime.

12-15 YES ANSWERS—You are a proactive owner/manager who is very security conscious.

8-11 YES ANSWERS—You have a strong working knowledge of crime prevention and have put that knowledge to work for them most part. Consider expanding your procedures as have been discussed in this chapter.

4-7 YES ANSWERS—You should consider adopting some or all of the policies and procedures outlined in this chapter.

0-3 YES ANSWERS—You are vulnerable to becoming victimized by either internal or external theft and should adopt a firm set of policies and procedures as have been outlined herein to outsmart crime.

The underlying message of this chapter is you should treat your business like you treat your family and home—that is, be aware of the crime risks that exist. The primary types of crime that can threaten your business—whether they be internal or external—are preventable if you take a proactive approach to crime. So many businesses are in such denial about crime and that their own employees might steal from them that they never confront the issue until it becomes a crisis. Don't make that mistake: start implementing procedures today that can avert losses in the future.

OUTSMARTING CRIME AGAINST WOMEN

Myth:

> *The biggest threat to a woman's safety is the stranger on the street.*

REALITY:

> **OVER TWO-THIRDS OF THE ASSAULTS AND OVER 70 PERCENT OF ALL RAPES AGAINST WOMEN ARE COMMITTED BY RELATIVES OR ACQUAINTANCES OF THE VICTIM.**

PERHAPS NO SINGLE CATEGORY OF CITIZEN FEELS MORE threatened by crime than women. There is much debate over whether women should carry guns, take self-defense classes, or just lock themselves up in their homes in order to avoid the horrible prospect of being attacked by a stranger. But there are some simple things women can do to avoid both the fear and the reality of crime.

This chapter seeks to debunk several myths of the female crime issue, most notably the idea that the biggest threat is a stranger. We have chosen to focus on the issue of domestic violence and its prevention because close to 70 percent of the violence committed against women is at the hands of someone they know. The gripping statement by a confessed batterer provides the clearest picture we have ever seen of the cycle of violence that can be perpetuated, and the underlying psychological illness which causes it. We conclude the chapter with a number of more generic tips on how to avoid threats from strangers.

THE TRUTH ABOUT CRIME AGAINST WOMEN

Assault is defined as: an unlawful physical attack or threat of attack. Assaults can range from simple (minor threat) to aggravated (serious, nearly fatal).

While the empowerment strategies listed throughout this book apply to men and women, we feel it's important to say some special things about women and crime. The reason for focusing on women is because if the goal is empowerment through reducing fear and increasing understanding of crime, women in today's culture have the most fear of anyone and therefore stand to gain tremendous confidence by learning about crime.

The two crimes women fear the most are assault and rape. In this chapter we focus on domestic violence, which encompasses both rape and assault, but first let's look at the data to assess what the rates of victimization look like.

Below are the victimization rates by location.

ASSAULT RATES BY LOCATION—1992		
Location	% Victimized	% Not Victimized
Urban	3.15%	96.85%
Suburban	2.31%	97.69%
Rural	2.21%	97.79%
All Areas	2.55%	97.45%

Source: *Criminal Victimization in the U.S.*, Table 18, page 38.

The total number of assaults in 1992 totaled over 5.2 million. Total assaults against women in 1992 were 2.2 million.

When it comes to rape, the chances are even less of becoming a victim. The breakdown of rape rates by location are as follows:

RAPE RATES BY LOCATION—1992

Location	% Victimized	% Not Victimized
Urban	.09%	99.91%
Suburban	.07%	99.93%
Rural	.04%	99.96%
Overall	.07%	99.93%

Source: *Criminal Victimization in the U.S.*, Table 18, page 38.

This means that less than one-tenth of 1 percent (less than one in one thousand) women are raped each year. This should be of comfort to women who watch nightly news casts of women crime victims and project themselves into those situations. The total number of rapes that occurred in 1992 were 140,930, of which 83,080 were women.

When it comes to overall rates of violent crime victimization for women, the most startling data relates to the identity of the offender. Below is a chart which describes who is doing these crimes: it may not be who you think.

VICTIM/OFFENDER RELATIONSHIP	% OF SINGLE-OFFENDER VIOLENT VICTIMIZATIONS (1987-1991)	
	Female	Male
Total	100%	100%
Relative/Intimate	33%	5%
Spouse	9.6%	.5%
Ex-spouse	4.0%	.4%
Boyfriend/girlfriend	14%	1.0%
Parent	.8%	.6%
Child	1.3%	.3%
Brother/sister	1.6%	.9%
Other relative	2.0%	1.2%
Acquaintance	35%	50%
Stranger	31%	44%
Unknown Relationship	1%	1%

Source: *Women and Violence*, published by the Bureau of Justice Statistics, 1994, Table 10, page 6.

The startling reality is that 68 percent of the violence committed against women is done by either a family member or an acquaintance, not a stranger. It is for this reason that we have chosen to examine the area of domestic violence, specifically spousal abuse, in order to provide women who find themselves in this desperate situation strategies for avoiding more violence.

One point about personal safety for women vis a vis strangers; most of the robbery prevention empowerment strategies address ways to avoid assault by a stranger and you should follow those whenever possible. We also provide additional personal safety empowerment strategies at the end of this chapter.

DOMESTIC VIOLENCE

This topic has come to the forefront ever since the O. J. Simpson case hit the news in the summer of 1994. After years of toiling in anonymity, domestic violence hotlines and nonprofit groups were suddenly deluged with inquiries for information, especially from the press. The National Coalition Against Domestic Violence (NCADC) estimates that they received over four hundred calls in a two-week period, an unprecedented level of interest.

NCADC has a publication which lists five predictors for whether your mate is at risk of becoming violent:

QUESTION 1:
Did he grow up in a violent family?

According to NCADC, people who grow up in families where they have been abused as children, or where one parent—usually the father—beats the other, are likely to become wife beaters or child beaters, or both. They have grown up learning that violence is normal behavior.

QUESTION 2:
Does he tend to use force or violence to "solve" his problem?

A young man who has a criminal record for violence, who gets into fights, or who likes to act tough is likely to act the same way with his wife and children. Danger signs: Does he overreact to little problems and frustrations, such as not finding a parking space or having a bad seat at the movies? Is he destructive when he's angry? Does he punch walls or throw things when he is upset? Any of these behaviors may be a sign of a person who will work out bad feelings with violence.

QUESTION 3:
Does he abuse alcohol or other drugs?

There is a strong link between violence and problems with drugs and alcohol. Be alert to his possible drinking problems, particularly if he refuses to admit that he has a problem or refuses to get help. Do not think that you can change him.

QUESTION 4:
Does he think poorly of himself?

Does he guard his masculinity by trying to act tough? He may think he's acting like a man, but in fact he may be acting like a future batterer.

QUESTION 5:
Does he have strong traditional ideas about what a man should be and what a woman should be?

Does he think a woman should stay at home, take care of her husband, and follow his wishes and orders? In other words, does he act like women are second-class citizens?

In this section we reveal the statement by an admitted wife beater, Jeff, who tells his story with painful honesty. As you read through his statement, think about the five predictors of domestic violence listed above and see if Jeff fits them. Also, NCADV has identified seventeen behaviors which they list in asking the question, "How many of these things has your partner done to you?" Has he ever. . .

1] Ignored your feelings?

2] Ridiculed or insulted women as a group?

3] Ridiculed or insulted your most valued beliefs, your religion, race, heritage, or class?

4] Withheld approval, appreciation, or affection as punishment?

5] Continually criticized you, called you names, shouted at you?

6] Humiliated you in private or public?

7] Refused to socialize with you?

8] Kept you from working, controlled your money, made all decisions?

9] Refused to work or share money?

10] Took all car keys or money away from you?

11] Regularly threatened to leave you or told you to leave?

12] Threatened to hurt you or your family?

13] Abused, tortured, killed pets to hurt you?

14] Harassed you about affairs your partner imagined you were having?

15] Manipulated you with lies and contradictions?

16] Destroyed furniture, punched holes in the walls, broke appliances?

17] Wielded a gun in a threatening way?

 INSIDE THE MIND OF A BATTERER

"My name is Jeff. I am thirty-two years old and I was a batterer. I abused women not only physically but emotionally and psychologically and thought it was perfectly normal. I had a lot of anger inside of me ever since I was a little kid. My mom and dad they seemed normal enough, but I will say my dad was never around too much. He was not physically violent, but I used to get a lot of lectures from him when I would do something wrong. I also found out recently that he sexually abused my two older sisters when they were young.

"When I grew up what I got was lectures—hours and hours of lectures. There was no physical stuff, it was mostly psychological abuse—it was one of those households where it was very difficult to express yourself. There was a lot of putdowns but I don't blame them for the way I turned out.

"My modeling came from my friends. My father did shift work and so I didn't have a father figure. My models when I was growing up were the outlaws, misfits, standouts: the person who didn't take any crap. At least that was my perception. I hung out with the kids who partied. I hung out with kids who could steal booze from their parents. We were sort of each other's role models.

"My dad had his own private hell going on. In retrospect, he was battling the fact that he was molesting his own two daughters—he didn't have time to deal with me."

On Anger

"For as long as I can remember I was angry. Even when I was a little kid, I was always angry. I can remember my mom saying, "Gee why are you so angry all the time?" I can remember the first relationship I had with a girl, I was always angry. I played the perpetual victim—I looked at the world like everybody was out to get me and I would say things like, 'How come I don't have a girlfriend like the other guys?' and never took responsibility for my own stuff.

"I was seventeen years old and I can remember some of my first conversations with my girlfriend were angry. I didn't view women as people—I thought they were objects. I believed then that if they got out of line, slap them. Don't take any lip from them. That was normal thinking and I had no other reasons in my head or in my belief system that said there was anything wrong with that—none.

"Women were easy to take the violence out on because they don't fight back. I wasn't an idiot—you do that to a guy and they will kick you senseless.

The amazing thing is the women stayed with me. With the relationships I've had, all of the women came from an abusive family. They were either sexually abused, emotionally abused, and typically the father was an alcoholic. So I played the role of 'Daddy' or the brother and nothing was any different from what they had experienced growing up so they didn't think anything was wrong.

"My pattern was the same every time. You see a pretty girl—young—always about four years younger than me. I would start going out with them—it goes really well for awhile until they start to get on your nerves. In my case, that was after about two months—after the physical attraction has worn off and it gets real. I would get annoyed, and say things like, 'Can you turn the damn TV down?!'

"When we talked, I would talk and they would listen. That's another danger sign. If the man doesn't listen to the woman and won't shut up long enough to pay attention to what she wants to talk about, that's part of the pattern. The guy's a victim and he blames everyone for his own problems. So if the guy won't shut up and listen, that's a sign of future abuse.

"It always starts with verbal abuse and disrespect. Things start to get physical: slamming doors, breaking things, especially if you break their things because that hurts them and it shows them who's boss. I would continually threaten women with statements like, 'Mess with me and I'll break your stuff' or 'Mess with me harder and I'll break you. I'll shove you around. I'll rip your clothes up. I'll tell you hell no you're not going out.'

"But I can go out. It's okay if I go out. It's okay if I spend the money. It's okay if we do what I want to do. But it's not okay to talk about how you feel, it's not okay to talk about what you want to do, it's not okay if you leave, it's not okay if you spend money, in fact it's not okay if you do anything unless I tell you to.

"I needed total control. See, 'cause if my life is out of control and I'm a piece of junk and I'm not worthy and I have no respect for myself and I don't give a damn about anything, I'm certainly not going to care about you. But if I can control you and keep that in order then I can at least control something. Extreme remorse follows the abuse, with promises like, 'Oh baby, I'm sorry—I didn't mean it' and 'I'll never do it again—I promise.'

"The man will say or do anything to avoid her leaving. I would send her flowers at work or chocolates. I was afraid if she left, then I wouldn't have anyone to blame for my problems. Plus, I had a terrible fear of abandonment. If I can make my life your responsibility, then I can make it your fault. I can make it your fault if the money is gone, I can make it your fault if I don't get that job promotion, I can make it your fault if the kids go hungry.

"I don't have kids but I'm glad I don't because I am convinced that if I had had kids, I would have abused them. Because I would have taken out my anger on anyone who was around me."

On the Cycle of Violence

"The cycle of violence happened with me over and over again. This is how it happens:

"First there is the badmouthing, the psychological abuse where you tell her she is no good and everything about her sucks. Then the violence kicks in where you start slamming doors and breaking stuff. Then you start to slap her around and hit her. Then you have remorse and you tell her anything you need to say to keep her from leaving. Then there is the honeymoon period where everything is okay.

"Then the resentments and the annoyances begin to build which cause you to start badmouthing her and the whole pattern is repeated. And the thing that I have learned from the group sessions is that the time period between stages of the cycle gets shorter and shorter and the peaks get higher and higher, the severity of the violence escalates and if the two people stay in the relationship, the woman will end up dead. They may both end up dead.

"This happened to me. I got more violent. It went from the disrespect to the verbal abuse to the emotional abuse to breaking things to physically beating to kicking to punching, open fist to closed fist to where it didn't matter anymore to rage blackouts and then there was the guilt and the remorse and the cycle repeated itself.

"Oh, and another thing. I have never been arrested for rape, but when I look back on my time with my first wife, I definitely raped her—there is no other word for it—violence.

"If you keep people down and they are pinned down for so long, you strip them of their soul. A lot of people wonder why women stay in these relationships, but in my case I had my wife to the point where she would say, 'It's okay to call me names, just don't call me a bitch.' They get to the point that they just want to survive and they don't have it in them to leave. They say to themselves, 'Maybe today he won't hit me.'

"Every one of the relationships I have had, there was the cycle of violence. Eight years ago, it was another typical day in my life. I came home from the bar and I was out with my buddies. I came home when I said I would and my girlfriend accused me of doing cocaine. Well, that day I didn't do cocaine and within thirty seconds I was throwing her into the wall. I pulled the phone out of the wall so she couldn't call anybody and I told her, 'How dare you question my integrity? I was home when I said I would be home! I'm getting sick of you nagging me' and I went into rage just that quick.

"And when we were done, she had gotten to the phone and she had called the Bellevue Police Department and they took me off to jail. And as they were taking me, she was saying, 'No, don't, I'm sorry.' And I turned around to her and said, 'You're dead.' I bruised her pretty bad. But I had done it before and this was the first time she had called the police. She was afraid.

"This was how I got introduced to my own recovery: by getting arrested and sent to a diversion program. They said if I went to this group they called the 'responsibility group' every week, I wouldn't go to jail. That was eight years ago, and I went to the group every week for two years. I also stopped the drug and alcohol abuse and am still in therapy today.

"I believe I am still the same person today that I was back then. But I am better able to control my anger and I don't act out in violent ways toward other people. My relationship with my girlfriend continued after my arrest. I blamed her for turning me in even though she never pressed charges. The state pressed charges. But my behavior continued—I slept with her best friend—and the relationship eventually ended. I was still violent for years even after I stopped drinking. Drinking is a symptom of the problem, never the root cause.

"I just got a call from my ex-wife—the first time I had talked to her in ten years. She is now involved with a twenty-seven-year-old man who is violent, who likes to get into fights and hurt people and has a track record of cheating on the women he has gone out with. And I'm on the phone with her and she is telling me this and also telling me that he isn't going to do that to her.

"She also told me that if there is one thing she had learned by being married to me it was to stand up for herself. And I told her if there is anything I wish you had learned from being with me is to stay the heck away from people like me. I have come to find out that a lot of my anger is fear."

On How to Recognize a Batterer

"The number one thing to look for is the pattern. If the man has a record of violence or not being faithful or if he is disrespectful of the woman or of others, that is a signal. If you are out on a date with the guy and he is bad mouthing everyone you come into contact with, then you know he has a lot of anger and that anger could escalate. I used to say things like: 'Geez, are you going to wear that ugly dress again?,' 'I told you I wanted my dinner at five o'clock,' 'Why do you always have to pick on me?,' 'I left her because she was a tramp,' and 'Her dad was a jerk. I don't need that.'

"If you hear comments like this, turn on your heels and leave. I used to sit on bar stools at night with other guys and they would all be saying the same things I was: 'I can't stand my old lady—she's always nagging at me,' 'She won't keep the kids' stuff cleaned up,' 'She doesn't keep the house picked up,' and 'She won't let me do what I want.'

"I couldn't understand sitting next to a loving husband and father. I didn't believe it was possible. Someone would say, 'I love my wife' and I would say, 'Yeah, right, I'm sure you do you wimp.'

"I used to just slam everybody. You slam the entire class of humans connected with your wife. I did that—the other person's stuff isn't important. It was bringing someone else down so you could feel better. My wife would say, 'Can I have a hug?' I would say, 'No way. Get away from me.' Or she would come home and say, 'I got a promotion Honey, isn't that great?' and I would say, 'So? So you got a promotion for doing your job? Am I supposed to be impressed? You've been working there for three years.'

"I used to publicly humiliate my wife and I had no emotion except rage, followed by numbness—even if I made her cry, I didn't feel anything. If a man can't feel, then he is dangerous and women should stay away from them.

"I would feel remorse after hitting her and I would say to myself, 'I can't believe I did it again.' I could see the pattern and I asked myself why I did it. The sad truth is because I wanted to. Why does a guy beat up his wife? Because he wants to. Why is he mean to her? Because it's what he wants to do. The question is why can't he stop it. Why is he not willing to do something about his behavior.

"I didn't want to have anything to do with her friends. I never felt worthy to socialize. I had a terrible self-image. I always felt that if anyone knew who I was they would hate me. So everything had to be on my terms or not at all.

"I once beat a pregnant dog so hard that it killed the puppies because it killed her. It was her dog. I was very physically abusive toward animals. I was physically abusive toward anything I could be physically abusive toward, but especially toward her because it was a way of emotionally and psychologically abusing her.

"When I was sleeping around with other women, I would come home and accuse her of cheating which was nothing more than a projection of my own guilt and poor self-image. I lived in an apartment where every wall had a hole in it that I had punched in it."

On How to Get Out of an Abusive Situation

"To women who find themselves in this situation, they should get out before the escalation takes place or risk death. Because the violence escalates— it always escalates, so if you think its going to get better, you're wrong. One of the best things to do is when the guy is gone, leave him with no forwarding address. If you are at the beginning of the relationship and you try to leave, the guy is going to get whiny on you and he'll say anything to get you to stay. Things like, 'Why are you leaving? I haven't done anything to you yet,' 'I'm sorry I said that about your mother,' 'If you want your friends to come over, that's okay, I can leave when they come over,' 'You are the world to me—I'll buy you a new TV.'

"And if he is cracking a beer while he's saying it—leave. Alcoholism is a problem in itself but the combination of alcoholism and violence is deadly. And the thing is that if there are just words and no action, don't put up with it. If the man isn't taking action to confront what is going on in his life, its not the woman's responsibility to stay.

"To the men out there who might be reading this and wonder what they should be doing, I say get help. As far as the violence goes, take responsibility for your life. Join a group. The responsibility group I was in was great because it was a group of violent men. I would come in and say, 'My wife is nagging on me and she is a pain in the . . . ,' and they would stop me and say, 'We don't care what you think she is doing, what is your role in all of this? Take responsibility for your life. Don't blame everyone else.'

"It's not right to hurt your wife, it's not right to beat up your fiance, it's not right to put down her children, it's not right to disrespect her feelings, it's not right not to be respectful. And if you can't respect others, then you can't respect yourself and you deserve more than that.

"It's not courageous to be mean and to be a bully. It takes a lot more courage and strength and intelligence to stop being violent than to continue. If you've got a big ego and you're proud of yourself and you think you're a strong man because you can control other people, find out how strong you really are—stop it. Do something about it—seek some behavioral change—that's what takes real guts."

DOMESTIC VIOLENCE VICTIM SCENARIO

Jane was very much in love with her husband John. They had met in the usual way (for the 1970s) in a bar. They had dated for about six months and had a kind of whirlwind romance, with John pulling out all the stops to make sure she fell madly in love with him almost from the word go. After their first date, he had sent a dozen long-stemmed roses to her office along with an expensive box of fine candy.

This process was repeated after every date for almost the entire six months until he finally popped the question and, after getting the royal treatment and having had no reason to think it would not continue, Jane said yes. Jane had simply been bowled over by John's romantic ways, something she had never seen in her family which had been full of anger and divorce and alcoholism. And while she knew that John drank and occasionally took drugs, it seemed to be no more so than any other friends of hers.

After about two months of marriage, John seemed to change. He started complaining to Jane that she wasn't keeping the house clean enough or that she made too much noise. After about three months, he was going out to bars every night with his buddies and, because of some lipstick marks she found on a shirt collar, Jane suspected he might be cheating on her.

John also started to show his anger, something that was never apparent during their courtship. He would get angry, always for something she had done wrong or not done correctly, and he started to break things—small things at first, but then it began to escalate. Jane started to get worried when one night, in a fit of rage, John slapped her for not having dinner ready on time.

Jane felt like the man she married had transformed into someone else, someone who might even become violent. But she was too afraid and embarrassed to tell anyone and she was afraid if she protested to John that he would either become enraged and hit her or, worse still, leave her.

John's temper tantrums got worse and worse until one night, in a fit of absolute rage, he threw her out of a moving car onto the sidewalk and sped off. That night, when he saw that he had caused severe bruises, he was a different man. He was showering her with love and in a deep state of remorse, he went out and bought her a new TV. The gifts kept coming for a period of days until Jane finally forgave him in the now desperate hope that he would be able to control his anger—unfortunately John's anger got worse, not better.

The event that caused Jane to finally leave the relationship and get help was when John came home one night after drinking at the bar with his buddies and flew into a violent rage. He started kicking their dog violently with Jane pleading for him to stop, to no avail. That night she walked out and never went back.

The Moral: This scenario is very typical of relationships which end either tragically or near tragically. Jane was lured to John by his romantic overtures, but also, she said later, because he reminded her of the good side of her father. She realized in retrospect that she was chasing the fantasy that she could find a man who had all her father's good traits and none of the bad. She realizes now that she was kidding herself.

She also realizes now that she should have identified the danger signs early on in the relationship: the heavy drinking, the drug use, the temper flare-ups, the badmouthing, but she didn't know any better. Now that she has studied the cycle of abuse and violence and attended support groups, she realizes how obvious the signs were.

As is often true in domestic violence cases, Jane did not have an easy time walking away from John. He followed her to work, he parked in front of her apartment, he called her on the phone begging her to come back. It finally got to the point where she had to get a restraining order from the court to get him to leave her alone—and sometimes even that did not work. She knows it was the right thing to do however and her message is that if you are in that situation, even though there is a lot of pain at the time, it is important to get out—the pain of leaving such a relationship is always less than if you stay in it.

CRIME AGAINST WOMEN
EMPOWERMENT STRATEGIES

There are over two thousand different programs around the United States that deal with domestic violence. If you need help finding one, contact the National Coalition Against Domestic Violence at (303) 839-1852 or write to:

National Coalition Against Domestic Violence
P.O. Box 18749
Denver, Colorado 80218

Because domestic violence is a complex and sensitive subject, we feel it is important to leave prevention advice to the experts, such as psychotherapists, counselors, and trained domestic violence professionals. We would simply remind you of the predictors of domestic violence listed earlier in this chapter and the seventeen items which the National Coalition Against Domestic Violence list as behaviors which can lead to violence (see page 147).

If you are involved with a man who comes from a background that is conducive to violence or if you have observed behavior like that described by Jeff and/or the NCADV list, then our advice to you is to get help immediately before the situation escalates.

The empowerment strategies listed below address general personal safety strategies for women, especially as they relate to feeling and acting safe from strangers. For while two-thirds of violence against women are from people they know, one-third is from strangers. These strategies are designed to help you avoid that small percentage of stranger danger that does exist out there.

➡ *EMPOWERMENT STRATEGY #193: If you work in a large office building, find out which elevators shut down after a specified time and which elevators are still operable after normal business hours.*

➡ *EMPOWERMENT STRATEGY #194: Check the identification of any stranger who asks for confidential information, or any delivery or repair person who wants to enter a restricted area or remove equipment.*

➡*EMPOWERMENT STRATEGY #195: Keep your purse or wallet locked in a drawer or cabinet at all times.*

➡*EMPOWERMENT STRATEGY #196: Post emergency numbers for security, police, and fire assistance near every phone.*

➡*EMPOWERMENT STRATEGY #197: If you notice any suspicious persons or vehicles, call security or the police.*

➡*EMPOWERMENT STRATEGY #198: Be alert when you go home. It is the hardest time to be alert because you're tired. Try to see if people are around.*

➡*EMPOWERMENT STRATEGY #199: Keep doors and windows locked at all times. On a warm weather day, don't leave a side door open.*

➡*EMPOWERMENT STRATEGY #200: Have keys ready when approaching your home.*

➡*EMPOWERMENT STRATEGY #201: If you arrive home to find that windows or doors have been tampered with, don't go inside but, instead, call the police from a neighbor's house.*

➡*EMPOWERMENT STRATEGY #202: If someone arrives unexpectedly at your house, find out who it is before opening the door. Install a peephole in the door.*

➡*EMPOWERMENT STRATEGY #203: Record only nonspecific messages on your answering machine and avoid messages like, "We'll be back at seven o'clock on Sunday."*

➡*EMPOWERMENT STRATEGY #204: Don't give personal information to unknown callers. If you receive an obscene or crank call, hang up immediately, saying nothing.*

➡*EMPOWERMENT STRATEGY #205: When walking, choose busy streets and avoid passing vacant lots, alleys, or deserted construction sites. At night, walk only in well-lighted areas and try to avoid walking or jogging alone.*

➡*EMPOWERMENT STRATEGY #206: Don't list your full name in the phone book. You should use a first initial only, your husband's name (especially if widowed), or not be listed at all. Such listings have the potential to invite prank calls.*

➡*EMPOWERMENT STRATEGY #207: Don't leave your purse in your shopping cart when you go to the grocery store.*

➡*EMPOWERMENT STRATEGY #208: If you go out dancing with friends, make sure at least one of you stays behind to watch the purses of the others.*

➡*EMPOWERMENT STRATEGY #209: While walking on the street, clutch your purse in hand, and do not rely on a shoulder strap for carrying purposes.*

➡*EMPOWERMENT STRATEGY #210: Avoid placing personal ads in the newspaper.*

➡*EMPOWERMENT STRATEGY #211: Consider carrying a fanny pack instead of a purse or some kind of bag that can wrap around your body.*

➡*EMPOWERMENT STRATEGY #212: If you carry a purse, consider carrying your wallet in an inside coat pocket.*

➡*EMPOWERMENT STRATEGY #213: If you get an obscene phone caller, consider getting a whistle and blowing the whistle into the phone as loud as you can.*

➡*EMPOWERMENT STRATEGY #214: If you get an obscene phone caller, another strategy is to click on the receiver and then say, "Operator this is the call I would like you to trace for me," and then hang up.*

DOMESTIC VIOLENCE PREVENTION QUIZ

By answering the following questions you can help determine if you are at risk of being battered by your mate. Remember, oftentimes abusive behavior or language is the precursor to actual fits of violence, so look for subtle signs that indicate you might be in a relationship with a violent partner.

Does your mate ever. . .

	YES	NO	
1.	___	___	Ignore your feelings?
2.	___	___	Ridicule or insult women as a group?
3.	___	___	Ridicule or insult your most valued beliefs, religion, race, heritage, or class?
4.	___	___	Withhold approval, appreciation, or affection as punishment?
5.	___	___	Continually criticize you, call you names, shout at you?
6.	___	___	Humiliate you in private or public?
7.	___	___	Refuse to socialize with you?
8.	___	___	Keep you from working, control your money, make all decisions?
9.	___	___	Refuse to work or share money?
10.	___	___	Take all car keys or money away from you?
11.	___	___	Regularly threaten to leave you or tell you to leave?
12.	___	___	Threaten to hurt you or your family?
13.	___	___	Abuse, torture, or kill pets to hurt you?
14.	___	___	Harass you about affairs your partner imagined you were having?
15.	___	___	Manipulate you with lies and contradictions?

16. ____ ____ Destroy furniture, punch holes in the walls, break appliances?
17. ____ ____ Wield a gun in a threatening way?

• • • • • • • • • • • •

Tally the number of yes answers. If your partner exhibits any of these characteristics, it is important to get some professional advice, assistance, or counseling with regard to the issues of personal violence. The existence of any one of these behaviors does not necessarily mean that your partner is a batterer, but may be an early warning sign of behavior to come.

――――――――

Our strong advice to anyone who finds herself in this situation is to *get help right away*. There are women's shelters in most communities throughout the United States and if you are unsure who to call, call the National Coalition Against Domestic Violence; they can refer you to services in your community. Like every crime described in this book, domestic violence is a preventable crime. Even for those who seem to feel they have nowhere to turn, it is important to remember there are always safe places to contact. And if you know a woman who is suffering at the hands of a batterer, intervene. It is a crime that frequently escalates and, if left to go on unabated, could result in death.

CHAPTER 7

OUTSMARTING YOUTH VIOLENCE AND GANGS

Myth:

> *Most of the violence committed by gang members is against innocent kids who are not involved in gang activity.*

REALITY:

> ALTHOUGH THERE ARE EXCEPTIONS, THE MAJORITY OF VIOLENCE PERPETRATED BY SO CALLED "GANG BANGERS" IS WITHIN THE GANG CULTURE, MOST OFTEN BETWEEN ONE GANG MEMBER AND ANOTHER.

THE ONE AREA OF CRIME WHERE VIOLENCE HAS IN FACT RISEN IS in the area of youth violence. Yet even though there have been increases in the number of kids involved in gang violence, misperceptions persist about the extent of this violence and the threat such violence poses for other age categories in our society.

In this chapter we evaluate the data on rates of youth violence and we hear from all of our criminal "experts," most notably from a career gang banger named Sad Cat who paints a picture for us of why gangs do what they do and what kind of a threat they pose to our kids, our society, and our future.

THE TRUTH ABOUT YOUTH VIOLENCE AND GANGS

If you have a teenager in school, what are the chances that he or she will become the victim of a violent crime like rape, robbery, or assault? This is an area that needs to be looked at carefully given all of the news reports of gang activity and violence in schools, especially inner city schools. It is also important to understand whether the risk of being the victim of violence has increased in the past twenty years.

The chart below evaluates victimization rates for kids age twelve to nineteen. Since the BJS focuses on the population over twelve, we are not going to evaluate data for those under twelve years of age.

VIOLENT VICTIMIZATION RATES BY AGE (RAPE, ROBBERY, ASSAULT)

FOR 1988		
Age	**% Victimized**	**% Not Victimized**
12-15	5.69%	94.31%
16-19	7.2%	92.8%
20-24	5.89%	94.11%

FOR 1992		
Age	**% Victimized**	**% Not Victimized**
12-15	7.57%	92.43%
16-19	7.79%	92.21%
20-24	7.01%	92.99%

Source: *Violent Crime*, published by the Bureau of Justice Statistics, 1994, page 4.

While these rates have risen dramatically during the past five years for the twelve to twenty-four age group, they have remained relatively stable or have gone down for older people. And because there are more and more Americans in the older age categories, the overall rates of violent crime have remained stable.

Even more disturbing is the amount of violent crime that involved the use of handguns. Between 1980 and 1992, the number of aggravated assaults involving a firearm increased 77.2 percent. The total number of violent crimes involving handguns increased 44.2 percent. The biggest victims of this increase were Black teenagers.

AVERAGE ANNUAL RATE OF CRIMES COMMITTED WITH HANDGUNS—1992

ALL MALE VICTIMS

Age of Victim	% Victimized	% Not Victimized
12-15	.50%	99.50%
16-19	1.42%	98.58%
20-24	1.18%	98.82%

BLACK MALE VICTIMS

Age of Victim	% Victimized	% Not Victimized
12-15	1.41%	98.59%
16-19	3.97%	96.03%
20-24	2.94%	97.06%

WHITE MALE VICTIMS

Age of Victim	% Victimized	% Not Victimized
12-15	.31%	99.69%
16-19	.95%	99.05%
20-24	.92%	99.08%
All Ages	.46%	99.54%

Source: Selected findings, *Handgun Violence*, Bureau of Justice Statistics, 1993, page 3.

Clearly the most at risk here are Blacks between the ages of sixteen and twenty-four years of age. In the male sixteen- to nineteen-year-old category alone, the Black victimization rate is four times higher than the white rate.

Another disturbing sign of the times is the percentage of kids carrying weapons to school. According to the BJS, the following high school students reporting carrying weapon to school:

	Carried a weapon 1990	1991	Carried a handgun most often 1991
Total	20%	26%	11%
Male	32%	41%	12%
Female	8%	11%	7%

Source: *1992 Sourcebook of Criminal Justice Statistics*, Table 3.73, page 319.

In addition, the BJS asks high school seniors every year a series of questions about things which have happened to them during the past twelve months. The following are the questions and how the class of 1992 answered:

QUESTION 1:
Has someone injured you with a weapon (like a knife, gun, or club)?

Not at all	94.9%
Once	3.2%
Twice	1.0%
3 or 4 times	0.3%
5 or more times	0.5%

QUESTION 2:

Has someone threatened you with a weapon but not actually injured you?

Not at all	86.0%
Once	8.6%
Twice	2.8%
3 or 4 times	1.7%
5 or more times	0.9%

QUESTION 3:

Has someone injured you on purpose without using a weapon?

Not at all	87.2%
Once	7.4%
Twice	3.2%
3 or 4 times	1.1%
5 or more times	1.1%

QUESTION 4:

Has an unarmed person threatened you with injury but not actually injured you?

Not at all	75.4%
Once	13.5%
Twice	3.8%
3 or 4 times	3.8%
5 or more times	3.4%

QUESTION 5:

How often have you gotten into a serious fight at school or at work?

Not at all	81.1%
Once	11.5%
Twice	4.0%
3 or 4 times	1.8%
5 or more times	1.7%

QUESTION 6:

How often have you taken part in a fight where a group of your friends were against another group?

Not at all	78.7%
Once	11.5%
Twice	4.4%
3 or 4 times	3.2%
5 or more times	2.2%

QUESTION 7:

How often have you hurt someone badly enough
to need a bandage or a doctor?

Not at all	87.2%
Once	7.3%
Twice	2.9%
3 or 4 times	1.6%
5 or more times	1.1%

In 1989, the BJS asked about the presence of gang activity in schools. The percentages of students reporting gang activity varied depending on location:

STUDENTS REPORTING GANG ACTIVITY—1989

Central city	25%
Suburbs	14%
Nonmetropolitan	8%

Source: 1992 *Sourcebook of Criminal Justice Statistics,* Table 3.70, page 308.

What do all of these statistics mean? One thing is for certain. There is a growing presence of crime, guns, and fear among teenagers in America, especially in urban areas and especially among the Black population. This brings us back to the vulnerability continuum which has been mentioned again and again in this book. If we were to draw the continuum to reflect 1992 rates of violent crime victimization involving the use of firearms, we would put Black teenagers between sixteen and nineteen on one end and white women age sixty-five or older on the other end. The rate of victimization for Black males sixteen to nineteen is 3.97; for white females over sixty-five it is .02. This means the Black male rate is two hundred times greater!

Another indicator of the presence of violence in schools is the extent to which students avoided certain places in school or have ever feared attack.

Students by Age	Avoided Places	Fearing an Attack	
	At School	At School	Going to School
12 years	8%	27%	18%
13 years	7%	27%	17%
14 years	7%	24%	15%
15 years	6%	21%	13%
16 years	5%	20%	14%
17 years	4%	17%	12%
18 years	4%	13%	10%
19 years	8%	20%	15%

Source: *1992 Sourcebook of Criminal Justice Statistics,* Table 3.63, page 295.

One final point about violence: There is a widespread perception that having one's child abducted is a very real threat. For years, the pictures of missing children on the backs of milk cartons and in mailers that come to homes made many Americans worry that their children would be abducted by a stranger. But this type of threat is a myth similar to the myth of a stranger being the primary risk to a woman's safety. While it is certainly important to be aware of your child's safety and take precautionary measures to insure safety, a fear of having your child abducted need not pervade your life. Consider the following quotation:

> *Up to 98 percent of all missing children are teenage runaways—of the remaining 2 percent, virtually all are abducted wrongfully by a parent. That leaves fewer than two hundred to three hundred children abducted by strangers annually.*
>
> ***—Bill Treanor, Director of the***
> ***American Youth Center, Washington, D.C.***

HOW KIDS ARE DRAWN TO CRIME

Many people wonder what makes a gang member tick, and what it is exactly that makes an adolescent turn to violence and crime. In this section, we explore what it is like to be a gang member by intcrviewing several former members of gangs who are currently in prison in Washington State.

The interviews with prisoners which we conducted reveal some common themes about how and why kids are drawn to crime. In addition to the excerpts we have already included in this book, the criminals focus on telling us what they know and what their advice would be to avoid crime. But they also have a lot to say about why they turned out the way they did.

Of the nine criminals we interviewed, six of them indicated they came from violent homes and all of them came from homes where the parents had lost touch with their needs and were poor communicators.

The following are excerpts from each interview where childhood and parenting were discussed:

Joe: "I came from a very dysfunctional family. My stepfather was an alcoholic and he used to beat up my mother. I used to run away from that because I didn't know how to deal with that, so I was on the street at a very young age. So I was running around stealing things out of stores, you know, when you're out all day as a little kid you get a little hungry, steal a couple of cakes and eventually I got into more serious crimes. . . . My stepfather, you know, he beat me for no reason and I couldn't change it, so I just grew up with a lot of fear, so that played a big role in my personality."

Christopher: "My dad's been in and out of prison for about twenty years. I was in school up until the eighth grade. My mom was pretty cool, then she got a divorce and married this other guy. Life wasn't too good, so I ran away from home and school. I was running—I guess that's one of the things that I liked about the crowd that I hung around—we pretty much all had the same background, you know what I'm saying? Either somebody in their family had been in prison or the parents are alcoholics or drunks or drug addicts, irresponsible, self-centered. . . . Yeah, I have had my ass whipped in the morning and was told that's for when you mess up later . . . lots of drinking. Lots of drugs. You gotta remember, my mom was eighteen years old and in her second marriage. That's a lot. She was just a kid having a kid." (Christopher's mom was fourteen when he was born and she and his real father never married. Now, she is thirty-eight and has been married four times.)

Nova: "I am originally from Alabama. I came to Long Island, New York, when I was four years old. In my past, in the outlook of how people views things, as a child—compassion—people to listen to—I didn't have that. . . . You know, when you're a child, a child goes to a grown up about something, but the grown up don't listen—put 'em off and put 'em off. So the child become real mean . . . I grew up in a violent household. Mainly, I just wanted someone to listen to me. About six months ago I wrote a letter to my mamma for the first time and in it I said, 'You know Momma, you always made sure I had everything I needed; a shirt on my back, food in my stomach—you was willing to give me anything I needed . . . except you.' "

Roger: "Well, when my parents divorced, my mother moved in with him (Manuel, who turned out to be a drug kingpin in Miami)—he had a real beautiful home on the water there—he had the Jaguar, the Lincoln Continental—I moved from basically the middle-class area to this upper-class area—my mother married him and we moved in. It was just really something I had never had before and he gave me anything that I asked for. I wanted a motorcycle—he would get it for me. The one thing neither he nor my mother would give me was the one thing I needed the most—time."

Ed: "My father drank and was abusive, but that wasn't all the time. But even when everything was good, we still didn't talk. If you had a problem you kept them to yourself. I didn't go to my father, I didn't talk to him. I didn't talk to my mother, so I always felt like I was separate from the family, so I would act out in ways to get attention: 'Oh, you messed up again' and I would get a yelling, but at least they would be talking to me. So it was good enough for me. I just carried that on in later life. . . . When I was growing up, I was suicidal most of the time. It wasn't that I wanted to die, but I got attention from it."

Drew: "I always felt unique when I was a kid—I always felt that the feelings I felt nobody else felt and if I tried to express these feelings to my mother and father, they wouldn't listen. They had me at a late age, so they were kind of pushing me to the side—when I thought about expressing feelings to them, I knew they would get down on me—I didn't feel normal, so to speak, so if I said something to my family, I would feel degraded or judged and I didn't want to do that. . . . I kept everything in—I just wanted to be accepted and I felt that I really wasn't accepted by my family—I was never abused, sexually abused, never hit as a kid. . . . I didn't have any responsibilities, I didn't have to take out the garbage, I didn't have any responsibilities at all—that was another thing—my mother showed me her love by giving me money. So I was given money all my life and she saw how happy it made me when she would give me money to go to the mall and play Pacman and stuff like that. She saw that I was happy and she felt that was love . . . but it wasn't."

As you can tell, each of these men felt that they were different and were estranged from their families. When asked what they felt could be done by parents to keep kids from doing what they did, all of them said parents need to truly listen to their kids—pay attention and have time for them. At least half of these men were from middle-class homes where money was in abundant supply, which dispels the myth that all criminals are from financially impoverished families. They are all from families who lacked love, however.

WHAT IS THE ATTRACTION OF STREET GANGS?

All of these men began their careers as criminals with other kids who were either the same age or older who had similar backgrounds, felt disenfranchised, and were either looking for something to do to make money, kill time, or be accepted. One of the things parents fear most today is that their child will be forced into participating in gang activity. According to the street gang manual prepared by the Los Angeles County Sheriff's Department:

> *Few youths are forced into gangs, as is popularly believed, but seek out membership in an attempt to associate with other youth who have similar background deficiencies. . . . Street gangs begin due to a myriad of social and economic reasons. Two of the most common reasons for youth joining gangs are the breakdown of the*

family as a cohesive unit and desperate poverty. . . .
Some join gangs because of peer group pressure, or
because it is just the popular thing to do. Oftentimes, a
person joins a gang for protection against rival gangs.

Kids have formed gangs to hang out with probably as long as there have been kids. There are differences between cliques and gangs, primarily revolving around the focus the group has. The following is an extended statement from a former Samoan Crips member named Sad Cat. This statement will give you a clear sense of why some kids decide to join gangs.

INSIDE THE MIND OF A GANG MEMBER

"My name is Sad Cat and ever since I was eight years old, I have been a member of the Samoan Crips gang. I started out joining the peewees version of the Samoan Crips called the "Little Rascals" when I lived in Long Beach, California. My two older brothers were Crips and I didn't know any better and so when I saw them gang banging and didn't have no other role models, I decided I needed to be a Crips member too.

"My pops he was trying to get his own life together because my mother died when I was real young and so he spent most of his time trying to find himself a new wife. I started off in crime by stealing lunch money from other kids. We would hide in the bushes and jump them and get maybe fifty cents. When we had saved up enough, then we would go ask one of the older gang members to buy us beer. There was always someone who would buy us beer and cigarettes.

"Then when I got a little older, I officially became a Crips member at age twelve. I joined by walking the line. This meant there were about fifteen gang bangers on one side and fifteen on the other side about two feet apart. I had to walk through the line with all thirty of them punching me, kicking me and just trying to take me down. If you made it to the end of the line without passing out, you were a Crips. You gotta show heart, that you can take it and you gotta punch back—ain't no way to make it through without punching back. Luckily I made it.

"My dad discovered that I was getting involved in gangs and so he moved the family up to Seattle, Washington, thinking there would be less crime and gang activity—he was wrong. I immediately hooked up with some Samoan Crips up there in Washington and started smoking weed and dealing crack cocaine. I tried to start my own gang but it was kind of difficult because I had trouble meeting new people. So I joined a gang that was already going. A lot of times people ask me why do kids join a gang. Well there are lots of reasons, but I'll tell you the main ones."

On the Need for Role Models

"It's messed up, but a lot of kids who join the gangs like me they just want to fit in somewhere and they ain't getting no love from home. The gang give you protection and they treat you like you family, you know. If I need something, one of my homeboys will give it to me.

"In my case, my pops was a great guy and everything but he never around—he didn't discipline me and those few times he tried, I rebelled because I had already gotten so into gang banging. My role models were my older brothers who were Crips and it was like monkey see, monkey do, you know? They be dealing rock and carrying guns around and so I thought well if my brothers are Crips I guess I must be too."

On the Importance of Money

"I learned pretty quick that the gangs they into making money—big money. You know, I see all these guys making money and I want to make it too. It was weird—the older gang members they didn't want us to be dealing 'cause they didn't want us to turn out bad, you know? But they did it and we saw how much money they making, so what am I supposed to do?

"Back when I was small, we used to hold for the older gang members. We'd hold the crack in case they got busted 'cause young guys never go to jail, you know? So we would always shave off just enough to go sell it and make a little something for ourselves without the older gang members knowing about it and that's how I got started dealing drugs.

"When I first came to Seattle, I started selling Sherm to kids. Sherm is like elephant tranquilizer and you dip cigarettes in it and sell the cigarettes.

Nobody in Seattle had ever heard of that and I was responsible for bringing it up from California.

"I didn't really try to recruit other kids into the gang, but I didn't need to cause they saw the money we was making. I mean, if I had a pair of shoes on me and you were going to school and your parents live well off and my parents—we stay in the housing authority—and I see your pair of shoes—you're getting a new pair of shoes every month and you see my shoes—I'm getting a new pair of shoes every day, you know what I mean? I'm getting a new pair of shoes every day because I am selling crack, robbing people, but I'm making a grand, two grand a week."

On the Need to Prove You're a Man

"A lot of what a gang is about is proving how tough you are and for teenagers that is an important thing. So say your little brother wanted to join my gang. I would tell him to go down the street and rob that little old lady who lives there and then go beat up her son. If he does that and even if he gets the living daylight kicked out of him by the son, I would still let him join the gang because he had the heart to try. That is why there is so much violence among the gangs— you got a lot of kids who are trying to find themselves and all their role models are people who deal drugs, drink and fight and so they act just like them.

"Most of the violence is between gang members. You know, if someone is against my color of bandanna or if they crossed out my gang sign on the wall, then I gotta do something to them. Sometimes innocent people can get caught in the middle of a gang fight. I remember one time we was having a break dancing contest between me and my cousins and this other gang—you know popping? and it was a little contest, no money involved, and there was some bystanders standing around checking out the scene and the other gang members lost and the ones I was with we had won—so then somebody said something and a fight broke out and we thought the bystanders were with the other gang so we beat them up too. They were just in the wrong place at the wrong time.

"It always ended up that way. In every group there is a bad apple. Whether they started it or we started it, whether I said something or they said something—it can even happen over crazy looks—if you are staring at somebody real crazy or just staring to be staring, the other guy can take that wrong. It always starts off crazy.

Most of the time, we didn't mess with civilians, you know people who weren't in gangs—but we would sell drugs to them—I would sell drugs to anyone."

On the Role of Drugs and Alcohol in Street Violence

"What makes gang members that way is alcohol. I was drunk all the time since the age of eight and that gave me the balls to do some of the things I did—it also made me stupid—I did a lot of stupid things. I started getting arrested for assaults, robbery, burglary—there wasn't nothing I wouldn't do and when gangs break out and start fighting a lot of it is 'cause they're messed up on alcohol or drugs—you take that away, a lot of the problems go away.

"I'd say the main way for people to stay cool and keep away from the gang scene is—if you are a parent, watch your kid close, give him something to do that is positive like sports or something and pay attention to them. Pops, he was cool but he was never there—I was raised by my grandmother and she couldn't control me. You gotta be there for your kids or else they go looking for someone else. It isn't real complicated—all kids want is someone to copy how to act—if that person is a gang banger, you got a problem, if it's a basketball coach or a parent who's together, then there's no problem—it's as simple as that."

X   X   X

Sad Cat was the only one of the people interviewed who indicated "gang" affiliation, most of them talked about hanging out with other kids when they began their criminal activity. Joe spoke to hanging out and about violence associated with his group. "We was just a group a young guys, punks hanging out together. . . . If I do something with someone else as opposed to by myself, I am more susceptible to being violent because I am trying to impress the other guy. If I was alone, I had no one to impress. By myself, I didn't have the heart to do half the things I was able to do in front of others. . . . it's just the mentality of young kids."

Drew talked about committing his first burglary with another kid he hung out with. "My first burglary was done before I got involved in cocaine. I was hanging out with a kid who was obsessed with marijuana and alcohol and he was very bad, this kid that I was hanging out with, he went all the way over the edge and committed a rape and went to jail and I was hanging out with this kid. I was about fifteen and he was about twenty . . . it was definitely his idea—he was like my idol so to speak and he definitely had an influence over me. I don't know if it was out of fear or if I just wanted to hang out with him—I think it was both."

Christopher speaks of hanging out as a kid. "I got with a couple of my friends and we went to a park and ride where you go for the buses and we had some Ford keys we had gotten out of a junk yard and we were waiting for a bus. . . .One of my friends who was a little older than me had done it before so instead of waiting for the bus, we tried the keys in the car in the park and ride and we ended up getting the car. . . .There was a bunch of kids in the neighborhood that started doing this stuff and it was like a competition thing, you know? I knew other kids by going to green Hill and Maple Lane (Washington State juvenile detention facilities) who were doing the same thing in different neighborhoods, different cities and stuff."

Sad Cat's gang was initially his older brothers, but soon became other kids who lived in the neighborhood. "The first I can remember getting involved in it was everyday I watched my older brothers go to school—'cause they were gang members back then . . . they were Samoan Crips. So every day I be watching them going to school and I would be watching cartoons cause you know I'm not even old enough to go to school yet, but I am being spoiled running around the house, being spoiled doing the things young kids do and I see my brothers coming home and I'd be around them a lot and I hear the things they says like, "Oh man, I just beat down this Bloods member and they beat down their rivals and all that and I get used to hearing that for so many years that. . . .I'm like uh automatically thinking, okay, I guess if my brothers are Crips, then I'm a Crips member myself and so the older I got the more adapted I got to listening to their stories, the next thing you know, I just fell into that pattern you know what I mean—the way they dress—monkey see, monkey do."

All of the criminals we interviewed were members of a street gang in one way or another, whether they knew it or not. According to the L.A. Sheriff's Department, the definition of a street gang is:

> *A group of people who form an allegiance for a common*
> *purpose and engage in acts injurious to public health*
> *and morals, who pervert or obstruct justice or the due*

administration of laws, or individually or collectively,
who create an atmosphere of fear and intimidation within
the community.

If we accept this definition, most of the criminals we talked to, even if they didn't truly organize in the fashion of a street gang, met the definition by hanging out with others with a common purpose to engage in antisocial acts.

The mentality of such a group is what makes youth gangs of any type frightening to the community. Add to that the fact that weapons are increasingly involved and people get downright paranoid. We all remember "West Side Story" and the gangs of the 1950s, but there is a big difference when you compare zip guns and chains with automatic weapons. When we look at kids in the past, we see kids who got into fist fights, got bloody or bloodied someone else, but survived. Today, survival is not a given. As Sad Cat remembers one of his friends:

"Yeah, I had a friend of mine, he couldn't fight, but he had a gun . . . it was a little .25—I think it was his mother's. He brought it over to this little hang out we got. We hung out at this little garage—my friend's room was this garage—so we would all meet up over there and drink . . . on the way to the store, he had met up with some other guy and they got into a verbal confrontation and the guy swung at my friend and my friend dropped and got back up and pulled out this gun and shot him. He's probably locked up somewhere now."

He also talks about himself. "Yeah, I was gang banging at the time and I met this girl—she doesn't gang bang, but she sells crack too and the little spot where I was selling was kind of dry. There was hardly any money coming through and so she came by and told me about another spot where she said I could sell a whole bag of crack and so I said let's go and she took me over to a spot where my rivals, the Bloods, hung out. I didn't know they were there at the time, but I took a gun with me anyways.

"The clientele was going up to the other Bloods gang members and their crack rocks were smaller and mine was pretty big, so they started coming to me and I sold out real quick—and the next thing I know I'm at the bus stop—and I'm drunk at the time—real drunk. These two gang members were real hot about me taking their clients and being on their turf, so I'm assuming they're going to rob me of everything I got just for being on their turf. Next thing you know, one of them asks me if I have change for a hundred. I guess their plan was for me to reach into my pocket and pull out all my money and then he and his partner would rob me.

"I told him I didn't and his partner walked to the side of me and right before he was getting ready to swing at me, I hit the other guy and he backed up and reached for something in his stomach and he was ready to come at me and so I hit him on the side of the head with the gun and the gun went off. His partner just took off.

"The broad who was with me was stuck, she was stunned that the guy dropped, you know? This went on for like ten minutes and there was no cops. I stood there for awhile and then left in a cab. The witnesses turned me in. Now I'm doing fifteen to life for attempted murder."

The disturbing thing about these stories is the detached way the shootings are described. In the last case, Sad Cat just hung around for ten minutes in the middle of downtown Seattle and then left in a cab. Usually we think of people shooting others, realizing what they have done, panicking and then leaving immediately. The violence seems to be much more accepted and those involved don't even think of the shooting victim as a victim.

One big difference between the Los Angeles style street gangs and the kids hanging together and getting into trouble is the initiation process. Recall Sad Cat's description of being "jumped in" by walking a line of gang members on either side, kicking and punching at the candidate. "I didn't get hurt that bad—just a bloody nose, cut eyebrow, fat lip . . . and you hit back, you better hit back . . . cause there are fists coming from everywhere—from the back of your head, from the side, under, even on top."

In most gangs, once you're in, it is considered a life-long commitment. Some gangs consider a person who moves away from the area to be out of the gang. In other cases, a person who leaves to go to prison may not be considered a gang member when he comes back. Most, however, consider a gang member one until he is either dead or "jumped out," a process a gang member undergoes similar to the "jumping in" ceremony—only worse. A Tacoma gang unit described the original Bloods gang in Tacoma today: all but one of them are either dead or crippled or in prison.

HOW DO WE REACH KIDS?

So what can you do to avoid your child becoming a gang member or the victim of violence? One strategy is to listen to the voices of gang members who have been down the drugs and violence road. The following is an open letter written by another gang member housed at the Clallum Bay Correctional Facility in Washington State. He is writing this to the children of America who are at risk of joining gangs. If you find it to be as powerful as we did, we suggest you read it to your child or to someone you know who you think might be at risk of joining a gang.

To my Young Asian Brothers:

Listen to me now or listen to me later. I'm Andres Pacificar #977107. I'm an ex-Asian gang member, and I live among tons of steel and concrete. I would like to convince you my young Asian brothers that gangs and violence are a one way road to my world. My world is a place you never think of before you make the mistake of picking up a gun. You see, young brothers, you don't find respect from a bullet, and you don't bring your homeys when you travel my road. There is an old cliché that rings oh so true—but it says ALL the tough guys are dead or in prison. But prison is also the home of the misguided and the confused, the liar, and the perverted, and the murderer, all call prison home.

Prison is the reality of violence—a place where time doesn't matter, and pure loneliness is your true companion. And death is final. Right now brothers, you have the riches of youth and the opportunity to make a choice away from gangs and violence, the chance to show your brothers that you made a choice not to become part of my world, but to lead others away from it. So earn the respect of many by hearing my message NOW, or don't listen and hear my message when you enter my world.

—Andres Pacificar, #977107

The violence is here. The gangs are here. The first thing we must do is acknowledge that there is a problem. Denial will allow more time for problems to get worse and worse. The next thing we have to do is understand what draws kids to violent behavior and gangs. We need to first of all pay attention to our very young. We need to listen to them, really listen. Finally, we need to give up some of our precious time.

Drew discusses what parents should do. "I would say just keep the kid active. Make sure he's in school, ask questions: Where is he going? Why he's going there? If he is staying overnight at another kid's house, make sure you call the other parent and make sure there is going to be another adult there. It's when kids start getting room to do things that they want and they're not questioned. That's when they get into trouble."

Christopher speaks on the subject of what we can do. "One thing I would like to add is if we were to give kids more positive outlooks and if counselors in school notice kids that are missing days of school or notice kids with misty eyes like they've been smoking pot—show those kids positive influences like music or sports or art or whatever the kids seem to have a little bit of interest in—they can pull it out of them—maybe people, if they read this book they can prevent their stuff from being stolen and help their kids from becoming one of these criminals like me."

Drew best sums up why paying attention to the kind of friends your kids hang out with is so important. "Yeah, I always hung out with the older kids and I looked at them as role models. The problem is the responsible older kids aren't available to hang out with because they have a job or they are studying. The kids I hung out with were deadbeats and they were the only ones around to hang out with."

Youth Programs

Many programs are being looked at to change violent behavior. In Washington State for instance, police agencies are involved in several programs that seem to be making an impact. Bellingham, Washington, has been involved in a program called SHOCAP (Serious Habitual Offender Citizen Action Program) which initially identifies the most violent kids in the community, follows their activity, and either forces them to change their behavior or warehouses them in state institutions.

While this is a very narrowly focused program, it offers several benefits other programs don't have. First, by focusing on the worst problem kids and calling them on their behavior, it sends a zero-tolerance message to those they hang out with. If they are removed, it removes a powerful negative mentor from the community who may impact other kids.

Second, the program involves the whole community. In order for it to work, law enforcement, courts, corrections, schools, and social service agencies must constantly interact and communicate with each other. The long-term prospects for such a program are very good. Allowing the community to identify these kids (who are extremely at-risk at an early age) and get help to their families or remove the kids to a better home gives them a chance in life.

The Bellevue Police Department has begun a program in which an officer is responsible for four Housing and Urban Development (HUD) apartments in the city. The officer has focused attention on prevention in these neighborhoods and found that the residents are as interested in preventing crime as anyone else in the community. He has helped engineer some physical changes that will be beneficial in terms of security, worked with residents who decided to form citizen patrols in the complexes and found support in the community in terms of donations of everything from diapers to sporting event tickets.

The officer lives in one of the complexes with his family and has taken a real personal interest in the complex and the people who live there. This type of program will hopefully take some of the isolation from this community, assure improved community services and provide positive mentoring for the kids who live there.

The Seattle Police Department is working with a community that is fed up with drug dealers selling drugs on their neighborhood streets. What that community has chosen to do is to take back the street corners from drug dealers on Friday and Saturday nights. The way they do that is to take shifts standing on the street corners. They are given some training from the police and police radios. What they have seen is that rather than confront the citizens and be hassled by the police, the drug dealers follow the path of least resistance and relocate to another neighborhood. Unfortunately, this program doesn't get at a solution to the overall program, but it does solve the problem in their community.

Another program which we think is going to be a model for the rest of the nation is in Mountlake Terrace, Washington. They open a school on Friday and Saturday nights specifically to gang members. The program is called the "Neutral Zone." Here the kids are frisked before they are allowed to enter, there are strict behavioral rules that are enforced, but athletic facilities are opened for any kid that is willing to submit to the search and follow the rules. The facility is staffed by volunteers (many of whom are police officers) who see that the environment is safe. The success of this program has been overwhelming. Not only has the Mountlake Terrace Police seen a marked drop in the level of gang activity, but there are hundreds of kids showing up every Friday and Saturday night to play basketball, work out on weights, etc. They are now sponsoring parenting classes at the site, GED courses, and other classes that the kids have shown an interest in.

Innovative programs such as these are not unique to Washington. Some of the areas hardest hit by crime have become laboratories of innovation for crime fighting and are making real progress. Communities differ; gang activity differs; criminal activity differs. One solution won't solve all the problems of every community. It is important to identify programs from other communities that are similar to yours. Innovation is the name of the game. Many times people are surprised by what they can do with little money and a lot of energy.

In addition to these programs, there are many others in communities throughout the U.S. With regard to those kids who join to feel a sense of belonging or family, their are a number of programs which especially single mothers can access for their child who may need a positive male role model. Programs like Big Brothers or Big Sisters are excellent and are present in most communities.

There are also youth services bureaus and churches which have mentoring programs, and youth groups that provide positive programming on a regular basis that not only provide good role models but also keep kids busy doing positive activities. YWCAs have a lot of good programs and cities are starting to be more creative with parks department programs and keeping gyms open twenty-four hours a day or until late in the evening so kids can stay off the streets.

In Seattle, there is a lot of innovation going on with the idea of one-stop shopping youth service bureaus. Working with parks departments, youth bureaus in Seattle have developed the concept of a family support center which has a menu of services and activities which all members of the family can access. For example, a single mother can go to the family support center and take a parenting class or get counseling while her son plays basketball in the gym which is housed in the same building.

Kids are our future. We need to handle them as we would a stock portfolio—carefully, knowledgeably, and with clear goals in mind. The difference is they need a human being who cares watching over them. Most children by nature are kind and loving and more would be if they felt close to their parents or other adult role models. The only thing stopping us from sharply reducing gang activity and violence is the willingness to personally reach out and nurture the generation that follows us. It is a challenge we simply cannot afford to ignore.

KIDS AND VIOLENCE SCENARIO

• •

The group of kids who hung around the high school on Saturday night were not all gang members. Sure there were a few Crips and a few Bloods who decided to have a break-dancing contest, but there were other kids who upon seeing the activity, came over to watch. They spent about an hour taking turns with one team of break dancers (the Crips) performing and then another team (the Bloods) trying to outdo them. There was nothing dangerous about the activity— everything was friendly and peaceful—for awhile.

Ricky and his friend Pete had been walking by the high school when they saw this activity so they stopped by and watched. At the end of the contest, one team declared themselves the winner and the other team did likewise. They started to argue over who had really won the contest and pretty soon they were all fighting. Unfortunately for Ricky and Pete, they were in the vicinity and were mistaken as gang members. Because they were not gang members, they did not want to fight nor were they particularly "tough" guys. The result was that Ricky got severe cuts over his eyes, bruised ribs, and a cut lip.

More significant than his injuries, Ricky is now afraid to go to school for fear that he will encounter the gang members he had mistakenly got mixed up with. Pete is also similarly afraid even though he wasn't injured.

The Moral: As Sad Cat has mentioned and as we saw in the above scenario, the typical way a non-gang member gets involved with gang violence is if he (or she) is hanging around gang members and is mistaken for one. For high school students, it is not always a simple thing to avoid being in close proximity to gang members, but it is definitely to their advantage to be aware of the dangers inherent in such proximity.

YOUTH VIOLENCE PREVENTION EMPOWERMENT STRATEGIES

It is our contention that criminals are grown, not born, and that most victimization, including youth violence, is preventable. The following empowerment strategies are a good place for parents to start to help their children avoid becoming involved in street violence, substance abuse, or gang activity.

➡*EMPOWERMENT STRATEGY #215: Ensure that your child knows his or her full name, address, telephone number, and an emergency contact name and number. Teach your children how to use the telephone and dial 9-1-1, or 0.*

➡*EMPOWERMENT STRATEGY #216: Thoroughly check the background of baby-sitters and day care center personnel.*

➡*EMPOWERMENT STRATEGY #217: Set up procedures with your child's school or day care center as to whom the child will be released to other than yourself, and what notification procedure they are to follow if the child does not show up on time.*

➡*EMPOWERMENT STRATEGY #218: Practice with your child the route he or she should take to walk to school or to friends' homes.*

➡*EMPOWERMENT STRATEGY #219: Show your child safe places he can go in case of an emergency, like a neighbor's house.*

➡*EMPOWERMENT STRATEGY #220: Avoid putting your child's name on clothing, books, hats, bikes, or toys. Children may respond to a stranger who calls them by name.*

➡*EMPOWERMENT STRATEGY #221: Define what a stranger is. Let your children know that just because they see someone every day, for instance the mailman, paperboy, milkman, or neighbor, it does not mean that these people are not strangers. A stranger may be a man or a woman.*

➡*EMPOWERMENT STRATEGY #222: Teach your child that if she is approached by a stranger, not to talk to the person and to run away in the direction of people and light. If your child is grabbed by a stranger, teach her to scream, "Help," kick, and attempt to break loose.*

➡*EMPOWERMENT STRATEGY #223: Never leave a child alone; not at home, in a vehicle, at play, in the toy section of a store, or anywhere. Don't let your child go to a public restroom alone.*

➡*EMPOWERMENT STRATEGY #224: Instruct your child that if he or she is separated from you in a store, not to look for you but instead, go to the nearest check-out stand and ask the person at the register for help.*

➡*EMPOWERMENT STRATEGY #225: Teach your child that no one has a right to touch him or her on any part of the body and that your child should tell you if someone tries to do so.*

➡*EMPOWERMENT STRATEGY #226: If you and your spouse are not living together, make sure your child knows exactly what days he is supposed to be with each parent.*

➡*EMPOWERMENT STRATEGY #227: Evaluate for yourself how much gang activity is present at your child's school and then look for help from the school administration, gang intervention counselors, and the PTA for ways to help your child avoid joining.*

➡*EMPOWERMENT STRATEGY #228: Look into local youth programs available in your community.*

➡*EMPOWERMENT STRATEGY #229: Look for constructive activities to get your kids involved in, like summer employment and/or recreational activity camps.*

➡*EMPOWERMENT STRATEGY #230: Talk to your kids about guns and how to confront the presence of weapons in their school.*

With 200 million handguns on the streets, kids in today's society need to learn about them and how to avoid trouble. As a parent, it is important to talk to your kids about what they would do if a friend presented a weapon to them or was playing with one. It is a good idea to have someone you know who knows about guns (if you don't) teach them about the dangers inherent in them and how they are used in order to prevent problems.

➡ *EMPOWERMENT STRATEGY #231: Consider developing a contract with your child that is jointly developed and signed by both parties regarding issues like drug and alcohol use, driving, and other safety issues.*

One of the core reasons kids go astray is that they have not developed a clear set of rules with which to operate. This is why they often are so easily influenced by their peers and can get into trouble. As a responsible parent, you can encourage the idea of your child sitting down early on and developing some rules of the road or a covenant or a credo or whatever you wish to call it which will help him clarify how he is going to behave. The following is an example of a set of ten principles that you and your child might agree to follow with regard to driving.

1] I will never get into a car where anyone in the car is or has been drinking or is or has been on drugs, even if it means walking home or calling my parents for a ride.

2] I will never get behind the wheel if I have had anything to drink or let anyone ride in my car who has been drinking.

3] I realize that cars can be very dangerous when I am walking and will attempt to spot and know where all cars are within a one-hundred-yard radius when I am walking.

4] I will always obey the speed limit and if I am riding in a car, will encourage the driver to obey the speed limit. If he doesn't, I will ask to leave the car.

5] I will keep the car doors locked while driving and when the car is parked.

6] I will never provoke another driver with hand gestures and if provoked by another driver, will ignore him and continue on my way.

7] I will always cross at a crosswalk and wait for the green light before crossing a street.

8] I will remember to stop, look, and listen for cars before crossing a street that does not have a crosswalk.

9] I will always use a seat-belt whenever I am in an automobile.

10] I will park my car in a safe, well-lit location.

➡️ *EMPOWERMENT STRATEGY #232: It is important to teach your children from an early age on what "good touch" is and what "bad touch" is, which parts of their bodies are private, and which aren't.*

Private parts are generally described as those parts of the body which are covered by a bathing suit. The issue of sexual molestation can be very sensitive and very confusing to a child. The key to minimizing the chances of this happening is to teach your children about boundaries, especially with adults who may or may not be related. It is also important to teach them that once these boundaries are crossed, the child should take decisive action to resist. The three-step rule for avoiding sexual molestation is:

1] Say no.

2] Run away.

3] Tell someone.

In order to ensure that the first step is followed, the child must know what is appropriate and what is inappropriate behavior. There are many organizations which have produced brochures on the issue of avoiding sexual abuse, which can easily be obtained by calling the local organization.

➡️ *EMPOWERMENT STRATEGY #233: An unattended child is a child at risk. Arrange with your child an alternative place to wait if you are delayed, especially in the darker winter evenings. Suggest a well-lit store or inside an arena or school.*

➡️ *EMPOWERMENT STRATEGY #234: Have children walk in pairs or groups.*

➥*EMPOWERMENT STRATEGY #235: Children should always travel the same way home.*

➥*EMPOWERMENT STRATEGY #236: Don't allow your young child to go to a public washroom unattended.*

➥*EMPOWERMENT STRATEGY #237: Check your baby-sitters' credentials thoroughly. In your absence, they are guardians of a priceless treasure.*

➥*EMPOWERMENT STRATEGY #238: Tell your child it is not rude to ignore an adult who is asking directions on the street. Another adult could be asked for more accurate information.*

➥*EMPOWERMENT STRATEGY #239: Tackle the subject of sexual abuse prevention with the same honest matter of fact manner you would attach to road safety.*

Remember, the only time a child will ask you about sexual abuse is after it has happened. Be open to the subject and your child will remember that you are accessible.

➥*EMPOWERMENT STRATEGY #240: Discuss with your child the difference between fact and fiction so that she may understand the nature of taking an oath. (This may be necessary for a court appearance.)*

➥*EMPOWERMENT STRATEGY #241: If you suspect that an abuse has taken place, encourage your child to talk about it.*

- ❏ Establish in the child's mind that he or she is not to blame.
- ❏ Do not correct the child's story; listen to the original words, even those which are babyish or family words.
- ❏ Do not suggest or modify what the child is trying to say. Your ideas might confuse the truth.
- ❏ Do not show horror or anger; however if caught by surprise and unable to control your emotions, be clear that your anger is meant for the offender, not the child.

➡️*EMPOWERMENT STRATEGY #242: When you are aware of an incident of sexual abuse, call the police or the child welfare authorities immediately. Ensure that a social worker, a police officer, and someone supportive to the child is present when evidence is given.*

➡️*EMPOWERMENT STRATEGY #243: Make sure your child knows his or her own address.*

➡️*EMPOWERMENT STRATEGY #244: Make sure your child knows where to go in an emergency.*

➡️*EMPOWERMENT STRATEGY #245: Make sure your child knows never to get into a stranger's car.*

➡️*EMPOWERMENT STRATEGY #246: Learn as much as you can about communicating with children and do it from early ages on.*

➡️*EMPOWERMENT STRATEGY #247: Talk to adolescents about unusual drawings on notebooks, especially if you see similar drawings on walls in the neighborhood.*

Gang and hip-hop graffiti are two types of vandalism that parents should learn about and be aware of. If your child has a lot of spray cans or large magic markers, and spends a lot of time out on the streets at night, it may be time to discuss what is going on.

➡️*EMPOWERMENT STRATEGY #248: Look for changing styles of language in your child. If your child begins to drop specific letters from all words, it may be an indication that he or she is involved with gangs.*

Members of Crips gangs for example will often drop the letter "b" from their vocabulary, especially when they are talking to their homeys (friends). Bloods, on the other hand, will drop the letter "c."

➡️*EMPOWERMENT STRATEGY #249: Learn all you can about gangs and indicators of gang membership. Many police agencies, teen centers, and schools offer classes for parents.*

Wearing oversized sagging pants is not necessarily a sign of gang membership. Kids are often attracted to styles and popular dress. Gangs differ from place to place in name, signs, colors, etc. The only way to keep current is to talk to someone who works with gangs on a daily basis.

➥*EMPOWERMENT STRATEGY #250: The most important way to deter your child from joining a gang is to listen to him and get him involved in positive activities like sports or outdoor activities like 4-H club, Outward Bound, or the Boy and Girl Scouts of America.*

YOUTH VIOLENCE PREVENTION QUIZ
for Parents

In order to safeguard your child from violence, drugs, sexual abuse, and gang activity, you should take the time to teach him or her about these subjects, and the necessary precautions and actions to take should your child encounter an uncomfortable or dangerous situation. In order to assess your level of knowledge, and the extent to which you have discussed various issues with your child, answer the following questions.

	YES	NO	
1.	____	____	Does your child know what to do if lost?
2.	____	____	Have you ever discussed peer pressure with you child?
3.	____	____	Have you ever discussed with your child what abnormal behavior is?
4.	____	____	Have you discussed when your child should get out of a friend's car?
5.	____	____	Have you discussed with your children what should be done if they find themselves at a questionable party?
6.	____	____	Have you ever taken a walking tour of your neighborhood?
7.	____	____	Have you physically checked out the facilities your child attends such as day care or school, sports facilities, or other play areas?
8.	____	____	Does your child know when to reject adult authority?
9.	____	____	Have you ever discussed emergency procedures with your child?
10.	____	____	Does your child carry personal identification and medical information?
11.	____	____	Are both you and your child prompt?
12.	____	____	Do you know if your child is a follower?
13.	____	____	Do you know if your child is a wanderer?

14. ___ ___ Can you account for your child's whereabouts hourly?
15. ___ ___ Have you discussed with your child who might be the best people to approach if he or she needs help?
16. ___ ___ Have you ever done any public transportation training with your child?
17. ___ ___ Do you know specifically how much money your child has to spend?
18. ___ ___ In the presence of your child, do you display a positive attitude toward the police and the law?
19. ___ ___ Is your home a gathering place for kids?
20. ___ ___ Have you thought of why?
21. ___ ___ Do you know whose house is a gathering place for kids?
22. ___ ___ Do you know the telephone numbers and addresses of your child's friends?
23. ___ ___ Have you met the parents of your child's friends?
24. ___ ___ Do you feel you listen to your child?
25. ___ ___ Do you feel you spend enough time with your child?
26. ___ ___ Does your child know how and where to reach you at any time?

• • • • • • • • • • • • •

Count the number of yes answers you gave to these questions. Any question to which you answered no requires a change in behavior to increase your child's security. Review the scale below to rate your empowerment and your child's level of security.

18-26 YES ANSWERS—Indicates you are an empowered and proactive parent who is taking bold action to ensure your child is safe.

10-17 YES ANSWERS—Indicates that you have a solid working knowledge of positive parenting techniques, but you may want to reread the chapter or look for more books on parenting.

0-9 YES ANSWERS—The fact that you are reading this book puts you ahead of many parents, especially younger ones, but you may want to devote some time to taking a parenting class or reading some more books on parenting. You might also find it helpful to join a parents networking group or support group in your area.

Like all crimes, youth violence is not inevitable nor is gang involvement. In order to curb the expansion of these two phenomena, parents must take increased responsibility for their children and, if possible, for the behavior of other children.

As members of society, we must think about ways we can model the way for some of these kids who have no role models. Whether that means becoming a Big Brother or Sister or volunteering to coach a youth basketball team or just being a dedicated parent to your own kids, the increases in crime among youth we have observed will not turn around without a lot of hard work from us all. It is time to get started.

OUTSMARTING 8
CRIME AGAINST
OLDER ADULTS

Myth:

> *The older and weaker you are, the more likely you are to be victimized by crime.*

REALITY:

> AS YOU GET OLDER, YOUR CHANCES OF
> BECOMING A CRIME VICTIM ACTUALLY GO
> DOWN. OLDER ADULTS ENJOY THE LOWEST
> LEVELS OF VICTIMIZATION OF ANY AGE GROUP
> IN THE COUNTRY.

OLDER ADULTS ARE ALSO A GROUP THAT IS PARTICULARLY frightened by what they perceive to be an escalating crime rate and an increasingly unsafe world. The American Association of Retired Persons routinely polls its members and finds that crime is always among the top three concerns they have. In 1994, crime was the number one concern of AARP members.

In this chapter we review the facts about crime victimization among the older population and hear from our inmate crime experts about whether they believed seniors made good targets. We will also hear what they had to say to their grandmothers about how to avoid crime.

THE TRUTH ABOUT CRIME AGAINST OLDER ADULTS

Older adults are in the paradoxical situation: they comprise the group least frequently victimized by crime and, at the same time, the group most frightened by it. Declining physical strength, the media and general common sense would have one believe that older folks would be particularly susceptible to crime.

As a police chief recently was quoted as saying in a major U.S. newspaper, "If you are a gang member, who are you going to rob? A thirty-five-year-old who works out four times per week or a little old lady who is struggling down the street?" The answer is not as simple as one might think. Sad Cat, the Samoan Crips gang member from the last chapter, says, "We didn't never go after no little old ladies, they was fine—they ain't never got nothing I want—no little old men neither. They cool. No we always got after each other—you know other gang bangers—we never thought nothin' about seniors."

So while it makes sense that older folks might be more vulnerable because they are less capable of fighting or running from criminals, at least one reason why they are not as victimized as others is because the gang members like Sad Cat are more interested in fighting each other. Another reason older adults are less victimized is because their lifestyle puts them in less danger than younger people.

"My wife and I just don't go out as much now as we did when we were younger," says an AARP volunteer. "It's not because we are afraid of crime so much, it's just that as you get older, your lifestyle changes and you don't do as much. And that includes going out at night," he says.

In fact, we interviewed dozens of older adults who echoed this sentiment. It is not to say that older adults are totally unconcerned about crime. In fact, they all say they think there are appalling levels of it, especially as depicted on television. But those we interviewed were equally divided on the question of whether crime was actually worse now than it was twenty years ago. The two comments below will describe the split in opinion:

"I think the media is overblowing it and the only reason crime seems worse is because every time something happens anywhere in the country, it shows up on the six o'clock news," said one woman at a senior center.

Another said, "I have lived in the same neighborhood for the past thirty years. We used to never have to lock our doors—or even close the doors in the summertime. Now, there are sirens going by us every hour and if I don't lock my doors when I leave, I'll get burglarized in a heartbeat."

Whatever your view of crime may be, it is important to remember that each year, less than 2 percent of all older adults over sixty-five years of age are ever victimized by crime. This is not to suggest that you need not do anything in the way of crime prevention, but it does mean that you should feel relatively free to live your life without fearing a gang banger's gun will be pointed at you.

According to the Bureau of Justice Statistics, older adults (sixty-five and over) are the least victimized segment of the population. Below is a comparison of crime victims for various age categories:

VIOLENT CRIME		
Age	% Victimized	% Not Victimized
12-24	6.46%	93.54%
25-49	2.72%	97.28%
50-64	.85%	99.15%
65+	.40%	99.60%

PERSONAL THEFT		
Age	% Victimized	% Not Victimized
12-24	11.27%	88.73%
25-49	7.12%	92.88%
50-64	3.8%	96.20%
65+	1.9%	98.10%

Source: *Violent Crime*, April 1994, page 4.

These statistics show that when it comes to violent crime victims, the crime rate for those under twenty-five are sixteen times higher than for those over sixty-five (6.46 percent versus .4 percent). Notwithstanding this difference, think about how small .4 percent is. This means that in 1992, 99.6 percent of all people sixty-five and older in the United States were not victimized by violent crime.

When it comes to victimization rates depending on where you live, consider the following:

VIOLENT VICTIMIZATION RATE BY LOCATION 65+ POPULATION (1992)

Location	% Victimized	% Not Victimized
Urban	.71%	99.29%
Suburban	.29%	99.71%
Rural	.22%	99.78%

THEFT VICTIMIZATION RATE BY LOCATION 65+ POPULATION (1992)

Location	% Victimized	% Not Victimized
Urban	2.64%	97.36%
Suburban	1.9%	98.1%
Rural	1.14%	98.86%

Source: *Elderly Crime Victims*, published by the Bureau of Justice Statistics, March 1994, page 2.

Once again, it is important to understand what these statistics mean. Take the data regarding violent crime victimization for urban, suburban, and rural seniors. The data suggest that .71 percent of all older adults living in an urban area were victimized by violence in 1992. That means that 99.29 percent of all seniors were not victimized by violence.

With regard to household crime such as theft for urban dwellers, the rates are higher: 11.2 percent. This means that 11.25 percent of all older adults living in the city were the victims of a household crime such as theft in 1992. But stated positively, 89.8 percent of them were not victimized. The rate is cut in half for those who live in rural areas (6.4 percent).

While these low rates of victimization for seniors are good news, the bad news is that unprecedented numbers of seniors do not feel safe in their communities. The Bureau of Justice Statistics each year asks those they interview about crime whether they feel safe. The answers are broken down by age group and vary depending on the cities in which one lives. But the percentage of older adults who feel unsafe routinely runs between 25 to 60 percent of the population depending on the city, far higher than their actual rate of victimization. Whether this is due to the media's preoccupation and fascination with reporting gruesome crimes every night on the news is unclear, although we suspect this to be the case.

The problem is that the perceived threat of becoming a crime victim is so real to many older Americans that in some respects they become the victims of fear more than the crimes themselves. There is a sort of "bunkering down" mentality that is sweeping across the nation especially among older adults whose declining physical strength makes the fear of violence and their inability to defend against it even greater.

Purse Snatchers and Pickpockets

The two types of crime other than violence which older adults fear the most are purse snatching and getting their pocket's picked. Therefore we will address these two crimes a bit more in depth.

In 1992, there were 152,300 purse snatchings in the United States. The rate of victimization for this type of crime based on where you live is as follows:

Location	% Victimized	% Not Victimized
Urban	.11%	99.89%
Suburban	.04%	99.96%
Rural	n/a	n/a
Overall	.07%	99.93%

Source: *Criminal Victimization in the U.S.*, Table 18, page 39.

When it comes to older adults, the rates of victimization for purse snatching are similarly low:

Location	% Victimized	% Not Victimized
50 to 64	.09%	99.91%
65+	.06%	99.94%

Source: *Criminal Victimization in the U.S.*, Table 4, page 23.

Notwithstanding these extremely low rates of victimization, it does not mean that having one's purse snatched is an impossibility. Therefore, there are some simple precautions one can take to virtually eliminate the chances of being victimized by this type of crime.

For women, the basic rule is: Don't dangle your purse away from your body so as to make it easy to snatch. If a thief who is moving quickly toward you can grab onto your strap and keep moving, the chances are good that he will get away. The only way this would not happen is if you were to resist by jerking away the purse, hanging on to it or otherwise trying to fight with the thief. This is a very dangerous thing to do, especially considering that older adults, when they are victimized, are more likely than younger people to be seriously injured. Therefore it is very important to avoid resisting a thief or anyone who is seeking to forcibly take your money. As we say many times in this book, your life is worth more than any money you might happen to have on you.

As we have also mentioned earlier, it is best to carry something other than a purse like a fanny pack that can be tied closely to your waist area. If you must carry a purse, be sure to carry it close to your body so a would-be thief will find it too difficult to surprise you or tear it away. Also, if you carry a purse, don't wrap the strap around your wrist in case someone does grab it and drags you to the ground.

Obviously, the best way to avoid loss as a result of a purse snatch is to carry very little cash on you when you go out. If you do carry money, don't let anyone on the street see it by carrying your purse or wallet open for all to view.

In terms of pickpocketing, there were 332,500 pickpocket victims in 1992. The breakdown by location of such victims is as follows:

Location	% Victimized	% Not Victimized
Urban	.28%	99.72%
Suburban	.14%	99.86%
Rural	.06%	99.94%
All	.16%	99.84%

When it comes to the rates of victimization for older adults, there are similarly low rates of victimization:

Age	% Victimized	% Not Victimized
50 to 64	.10%	99.90%
65+	.14%	99.86%

Source: *Criminal Victimization in the U.S.*, Table 4, page 23.

When it comes to avoiding having you pocket picked, there are some common sense things to remember. When you are walking down the street, be sure that you wallet is not in you back pants pocket, but rather in a jacket inside pocket or in your front pocket with your hand on it. Also, be alert to a stranger bumping you by surprise or someone coming up and talking to you for no apparent reason. These are called "bump and run" scams which are designed to divert your attention toward something while your pocket is being picked. It is especially prevalent in big cities.

Another diversionary tactic is someone falling down in front of you and pretending to be injured. While you attend to the person, an accomplice is lifting you wallet.

Bank Examiner Scam

One of the most time-tested crimes that target seniors is the bank examiner scam. This involves someone posing as an official from your bank calling you up and telling you he would like your assistance in solving a problem he is having at the bank. He explains that there is a teller working for the bank who is exchanging real money with counterfeit and handing the counterfeit money out to customers and pocketing the real money.

He then asks you to go to the bank and withdraw a large sum—usually about $2,000—and then arrange for you to hand it over to him so he can have the "bank examiner" inspect the bills to see if it is counterfeit. He then says he will personally redeposit the money in your account.

This scam seems implausible but every month since we have been involved in law enforcement, we hear about another victim of the bank examiner who lost a significant chunk of his or her savings.

The thing to remember is that no bank would ever involve one of its customers in an internal investigation—in fact, it would never even want to admit that it had such a problem. And bank personnel surely would never ask a customer of the bank to act as a decoy to catch the culprit in the act. So beware!

Pigeon Drop

This is another time-tested street scam that targets seniors and can result in thousands of dollars lost to the victim. It involves two con artists working together who pretend to not know each other. One approaches a senior and claims to have found a large sum of money in a brown paper bag. They show the bag with the money in it and are wondering whose it is and what to do when the con artist's accomplice walks up and asks what they are doing. When they explain that they found the money, the accomplice explains that his brother is a police officer and that the money is probably profits from a drug deal gone bad. He further states that if they hold the money and wait for ten days without anyone claiming it, they can split the money.

At this point they have to decide who will hold the money until the ten days has passed. The con artists agree to let the victim hold the money provided he or she puts up $500 in good faith money. They then follow the victim to the bank, watch her withdraw the money and in the meantime they remove the cash that was in the bag and put cut paper in it instead. The victim gives them each $250 as good faith money and they give her the bag and take off, leaving her with phony telephone numbers and a bag of worthless paper.

This may be where the expression "left holding the bag" came from.

The Danger of Telemarketing Hoaxes

In reality, the greatest crime threat to those sixty-five and older is not violence or burglary or even auto theft. The greatest threat is consumer fraud, especially telemarketing. The FBI in March 1993 ended a three-year investigation into the activities of fraudulent telemarketers with a raid called "Operation Disconnect" in which they raided one hundred boiler rooms and arrested almost five hundred people. They discovered during the course of this investigation that of the one hundred boiler rooms they closed down, thirty-four of them were set up exclusively to target and steal money from older adults.

The American Association of Retired Persons released a study in January, 1994 entitled Older Consumer Behavior in which they concluded that older consumers were much more trusting than younger people and consequently more vulnerable to the swindling techniques of smooth-talking con artists.

The U.S. Senate Select Committee on Aging did a study as far back as 1978 which estimated that older adults, who comprise 12 percent of the U.S. population, were 30 percent of all the victims of consumer fraud in the United States. And with telemarketing fraud alone estimated to take in over $40 billion per year, older adults may be losing as much as $13 billion per year to swindlers.

A good book to look at on this subject is entitled *Schemes & Scams*, written by Doug Shadel and John T., a convicted telemarketing con artist who reveals how he swindled older adults out of their life savings and why they were particularly attractive targets.

Elder Abuse

Another category of crime against older adults which is not discussed much in the media is the whole area of elder abuse. This includes all forms of financial exploitation including fraud from a third party but also exploitation from family members who want to get grandma's money before other relatives do. It also includes neglect issues and physical abuse from caregivers and/or family who are either simply malicious and cruel or who get frustrated from trying to provide for young children and elderly parents and earn a living at the same time.

AARP has a number of useful brochures on the subject of elder abuse. Perhaps the best one is entitled *Domestic Mistreatment of the Elderly*. In addition, every state in the United States has social and health services agencies with trained personnel who work in the area of adult protective services and can intervene if they are made aware of such mistreatment.

INSIDE THE MIND OF A CRIMINAL

It's hard to imagine a criminal who specifically seeks out older adults to take advantage of. But there are criminals who do just that—specifically prey on the older adult because they know that they can employ specific tactics to get what they want. The crimes range from robbery to a variety of specific scams and hoaxes, but no matter what the crime, the hoodlum is looking for some specific traits in his next victim.

On How Older Adults Are Targeted by Criminals

During the course of our extensive interviews with the various inmates in prison, we specifically asked them the extent to which they targeted older adults. The following excerpts are what some of them said:

Drew: "I never targeted seniors. I never targeted any group—I just didn't want to get caught and the key to that was finding empty houses. That was my whole gig. But I'll tell you one thing I observed: a lot of times, older adults will be getting ready to go visit their grandkids or something and they will make a few trips out to the car with some stuff, then they will make a few more trips with some stuff—pretty soon I'm watching them and they are pretty obviously going to be gone for awhile. So I wait for them to drive away in the car and then I hit them. Seniors should be more careful about advertising that they are leaving—so should everyone really."

Joseph: "I would rob anyone who came walking down the street at the wrong time. Yeah, I would rob a little old lady, but no more than I would rob a young lady or an old man or a young man. The victim I looked for was always in the wrong place at the wrong time: at night, in an alley, alone—you stay away from these places, you be alright."

Nova: "Most of the people I victimized lived on the streets and were prostitutes or drug dealers—I think a lot of the crime never reaches regular people, but they think it does 'cause they watch TV."

Roger: "The drug dealers rob each other, the prostitutes rob each other, and some of the time, some criminals rob anyone that happens to be there at the time. Even though I felt when I was using and taking the risk that I would rob anyone, I don't think I could mug a senior citizen—I think they would remind me too much of my own grand mother."

On What Older Adults Should Do to Avoid Crime

We asked these inmates what they would tell their grandmother to do to avoid crime.

Drew: "Well, my mother carries a gun. I don't think it's a good idea for my grandmother to carry a gun though—that would be pretty goofy. Besides, if she carried a gun, she might have to use it and that would ruin her whole day."

Sad Cat: "I'd say don't go out at night—at night is when them crazies come out. I'd also say don't drive at night—and don't drive alone neither."

Joseph: "Somebody weaker than most like old people, they should do their business during the daytime when it's light and there is people around. I can remember robbing an older lady one time and it was at night in a bad part of New York City and I thought, damn, what's this woman doing hobbling down the street just waiting to get nailed?"

Nova: "The first thing I would tell my grandmother is to not wear too much big jewelry—that just attracts the bad element like a fly to flypaper. Another thing is that older people—they walk out of banks holding onto their purse like it was filled with gold or something and it's pretty obvious they just took out some money. The best thing for them to do is to look casual like they ain't got no money when they come out of the bank."

Joseph: "The thing I look for is fear. If a person, old or not, looks like she is afraid, then I'm gonna try to rob her. Unfortunately, I think seniors are afraid more, so they may be robbed more 'cause us robbers, we look for fear."

OLDER ADULT VICTIM SCENARIO
• •

Gladys had a regular routine. Every day at 10:00 A.M. she would go to the store to buy groceries or just to pick up the morning paper and get out of the house. It gave her a purpose each morning and that was important since her husband had died two years ago and she was fighting boredom and depression.

Each day, she would walk the short three blocks from her condo to the mini-mall and she had never had any problems with people bothering her and certainly she never felt in any kind of danger—that is until one spring morning. She had gotten up at 5:00 A.M. as always, fixed herself breakfast, and watched the morning talk shows. She then went out and began the short walk to her store. About halfway to the store, she sensed that someone was following her. Instead of turning around and looking, she began to get frightened and so she put her head down and began to walk more quickly.

As she picked up speed, so did the person she thought was following her. About one block from the store, she finally got up the courage to turn around and quickly glance over her shoulder. Just as she did this, a man came running up to her from the other side and grabbed her purse and attempted to steal it from her. She instinctively grabbed onto the strap with all her might and held on. The robber, who was a short, white man in his late teens, was stronger than she was and he ripped the purse from her, wrenching her arm almost completely out of its socket and causing her to fall down and twist her knee.

The Moral: Gladys lost her purse and the forty-five dollars in it that day. But more importantly, she also dislocated her shoulder and bruised her knee, two injuries which took over a year to heal properly. Also, she was so shaken by the incident that she no longer walks to the store but takes a cab or sometimes has her daughter take her.

Gladys was not wrong to go for a daily walk—exercise is a very positive activity for anyone. The mistake she made was to go for the walk at the same time and in the same place every day. Such a pattern makes it easier for a robber to identify victims. Also, she should have carried little or no money on her and if she did carry any, it should have been in a fanny pack that is hard for a robber to grab and run with. Finally, when she was confronted by the robber, she resisted, causing serious injury to her. Once again, there is no amount of money that is more valuable than your life or your health. So if you are confronted, don't resist. You never know if your assailant is going to be carrying a weapon.

EMPOWERMENT STRATEGIES
FOR OLDER ADULTS

Many of the empowerment strategies discussed throughout this book apply to older adults. However, there are several empowerment strategies which we feel are specific to this population and need to be included here.

➡ *EMPOWERMENT STRATEGY #251: Remember you cannot get something for nothing, no matter what anyone says.*

If you receive something in the mail which says you have won a prize, whether it is cash or merchandise, THROW IT IN THE TRASH. You cannot get something for nothing and if you participate in such promotions, you will be continually harassed by telemarketers until you either die or change your phone number.

➡ *EMPOWERMENT STRATEGY #252: If you think you know someone who is a potential victim of fraud, do something about it.*

If you know someone who lives alone and may be getting phone calls from telemarketers, intervene and make sure the person is not participating in sweepstakes promotions and other kinds of gimmicks designed to steal the victim's money.

➡ *EMPOWERMENT STRATEGY #253: Take what you see on the news with a grain of salt.*

Whenever you see crime reports on the news, remember the statistical chances of you becoming a victim. Also recognize that the media intentionally shows gruesome murders and crimes to enhance their ratings in the ultra-competitive news business and it does not necessarily reflect the risks of crime to you personally.

➡ *EMPOWERMENT STRATEGY #254: Find out what the crime rate is in your community.*

If you are concerned about crime in your neighborhood or in your community, contact your local police department and ask them for a crime report which tells you exactly how many crimes have been committed in your area and what kind of crimes they were. Do not rely on the news media for such information. Make sure to focus on your immediate neighborhood because the threat of crime can vary widely from neighborhood to neighborhood and even from block to block.

➡*EMPOWERMENT STRATEGY #255: Remember that not only are older adults less victimized by crime, but burglars hate neighborhoods that have seniors.*
 Recall that Drew the burglar said he added one point on his risk scale for every senior citizen he observed in a neighborhood. This means older adults are a deterrent to crimes like burglary since they are home during the day and therefore available to watch for suspicious behavior.

➡*EMPOWERMENT STRATEGY #256: Stay sociable as you age; maintain and increase your network of friends and acquaintances.*

➡*EMPOWERMENT STRATEGY #257: Keep in contact with old friends and neighbors if you move in with a relative or change to a new address.*

➡*EMPOWERMENT STRATEGY #258: Develop a "buddy" system with a friend outside the home. Plan for at least a weekly contact and share openly with this person.*

➡*EMPOWERMENT STRATEGY #259: Ask friends to visit you at home; even a brief visit can enhance your well-being.*

➡*EMPOWERMENT STRATEGY #260: Accept new opportunities for activities. They can bring new friends.*

➡*EMPOWERMENT STRATEGY #261: Participate in community activities as long as you are able.*

➡*EMPOWERMENT STRATEGY #262: Volunteer or become a member or officer of an organization.*

➥EMPOWERMENT STRATEGY #263: Be sure that you have someone you are in regular contact with and share your concerns and fears with people and talk it out.

➥EMPOWERMENT STRATEGY #264: Make sure you lock your front door even when you are home, such as out in the back gardening or otherwise working in the yard.

➥EMPOWERMENT STRATEGY #265: When you go to your car in a parking lot, walk past it first to see if anything or anyone is lurking in or around the car.

OLDER ADULTS PERSONAL SAFETY QUIZ

In order to gauge your behavior from a crime prevention standpoint, answer yes or no to the following questions.

	YES	NO	
1.	___	___	I rarely go out at night alone.
2.	___	___	I always lock my car doors whenever I am out driving.
3.	___	___	I almost never use automatic teller machines and, if I do, it is always during the daytime.
4.	___	___	My house is always locked whenever I go out—that includes doors and all windows.
5.	___	___	When I am out walking, I try to walk at a brisk pace, with my head up and I am alert, keeping aware of what is going on around me.
6.	___	___	As an older woman, I try not to wear an excessive amount of jewelry when I go out because I think it is just asking for trouble.
7.	___	___	As an older woman, whenever I go to the bank, I make sure that I am not clutching my purse nervously when I leave. I don't want to give anyone the signal that I might have cash on me.
8.	___	___	When I am out walking, I try to walk with someone else and I listen to my instincts. If a particular street gives me or my friend a strange feeling, we'll turn and go the other way.
9.	___	___	Whenever I am out walking, I walk away from bushes or fences where someone might be hiding. I also stay away from isolated streets and parking lots.
10.	___	___	If someone calls me on the phone or sends me a letter telling me I have won a fabulous prize like a car, I always ignore them, because I know that if it sounds too good to be true it is and that lots of con artists target older people with free-prize promotions.

• • • • • • • • • • • • •

Count your number of yes responses, then compare your score with the scale below. Any question you answered no to should be a signal to review your behavior in that area.

8-10 YES ANSWERS—Indicates a strong understanding of crime prevention principles.

5-7 YES ANSWERS—Indicates a fair knowledge of how to be an empowered older person. You may wish to reread the chapter on robbery prevention.

3-6 YES ANSWERS—Consider reviewing the material in this book again and consider contacting **AARP** or your local police department for additional educational materials on crime prevention.

0-3 YES ANSWERS—Consider getting a big dog, a big husband or a police officer for a neighbor—and start reading up on crime prevention!

While older adults are the least likely victims of violence and other kinds of crime, they are among those Americans who are most fearful of it. Education and information about their real chances of becoming victimized is one way to alleviate fear; action is another. This chapter provides strategies for both in order to free older adults from the growing sense they have that they are not safe in their own homes.

Crime Prevention Resources

The following is a list of agencies and organizations that can be of value to individuals and community groups in learning more about prevention of crime in their homes, neighborhoods, and communities.

In addition to several national organizations, we have listed the state criminal justice agency or program for each state where you can ask for crime prevention resources available in your community. Local agencies that should be considered resources include: police departments, especially community policing and crime prevention units; attorney general offices; state crime prevention programs; state crime prevention associations; local chapters of the American Society for Industrial Security; local rape crisis centers and programs; local domestic violence programs; community crime prevention programs; and chambers of commerce.

The state uniform crime reporting programs are part of a nationwide effort to collect data on the number of reported crimes filed with local law enforcement agencies each year throughout the United States. Each state has established a central location where they collect reports from the hundreds of jurisdictions throughout the state for collating and reporting to the Department of Justice. To find out about reported crime in your state, contact one of the agencies listed in that section.

National Organizations

American Association of Retired Persons
1909 "K" Street NW
Washington, D.C. 20049
(800) 728-4393
Membership organization that represents older adults (50+). This organization has developed many training programs, publications, and brochures geared to reducing crime and fear of crime in the population they serve.

American Society for Industrial Security
1655 North Fort Myer Drive, Suite 1200
Arlington, Virginia 22209
(703) 522-5800

Membership organization of security professionals. Provides training through international programs, international conferences and local chapter training events. Produces security management magazine, a standard for the security community. Certification program for security professionals (Certified Protection Professional) is developed, tracked, and tested through this organization. Prints a newsletter called *Dynamics* to supplement other information. Local chapters are often a good resource for information and training programs.

The Bureau of Justice Statistics
Justice Statistics Clearinghouse
National Criminal Justice Reference Center, Box 6000
Rockville, Maryland 20859
(800) 732-3277
Part of the Department of Justice that collects, organizes, and disseminates data. Prints many publications each year that relate to specific crime topics. Primary documents are the *Sourcebook* and *Criminal Victimization in the U.S.*

Crime Stoppers International
3736 Eubank Boulevard, Suite B-4
Albuquerque, New Mexico 87111
(800) 245-0009
A nonprofit organization that was organized to coordinate efforts in solving crimes that were thought to be unsolvable. Chapters in various cities are organized with a citizen board, law enforcement, and media involvement. The purpose is to show reenactments of crime on television, radio, and in the print media to help encourage people to remember things about the incident that weren't reported and to follow through. Caller is anonymous and may receive a reward upon arrest and charging of the suspect.

International Association of Crime Prevention Practitioners
1696 Connor Drive
Pittsburgh, Pennsylvania 15129
(412) 655-1600
Membership organization open to any person who has an interest in crime prevention. This organization sponsors a national training symposium once a year, provides a newsletter, conducts regional training, offers a basic crime prevention curriculum, a crime prevention specialist exam and offers referral and technical assistance.

Mothers Against Violence in America
901 Fairview Avenue, N, Suite A-170
Seattle, Washington 98109
(206) 343-0476 or (800) 897-7697

MAVIA is a 501(c)(3) nonprofit, nonpartisan, educational organization dedicated to reducing violence in communities and promoting the safety and well-being of children. MAVIA sponsors SAVE (Students Against Violence Everywhere) chapters in elementary, middle, and high schools. Founded in Seattle in 1994, MAVIA is now expanding to other states throughout the country.

National Auto Theft Bureau
10330 South Roberts Road, Suite 3A
Palos Hills, Illinois 60465
(708) 430-2430
The National Auto Theft Bureau formulates and implements policies for the prevention of vehicle theft, vehicle arson, and vehicle fraud. The NATB cooperates with duly constituted public authorities in the prosecution of individuals engaged in vehicle crime and fraud.

National Burglar and Fire Alarm Association
7101 Wisconsin Avenue, Suite 1390
Bethesda, Maryland 20814
(301) 907-3202
Membership organization for alarm dealers. Great source of information regarding how to choose an alarm company and how to reduce false alarms, and is a resource for contacts in chapters throughout the United States.

National Coalition Against Domestic Violence
P.O. Box 18749
Denver, Colorado 80218
(313) 839-1852
National information and referral center for the general public, media, battered women and their children, agencies and organizations, lobbying organization, technical assistance provider, clearing house for model programs and the sponsor of "National Domestic Violence Awareness Month."

National Crime Prevention Council
1700 "K" Street NW, 2nd Floor
Washington, DC 20006
(202) 466-6272
Focal point for crime prevention efforts throughout the U.S. National media campaign sponsored by the Ad Council, outreach training, many programs and resource materials organized and directed by this organization. Sponsor of national crime prevention month activities. Operates a computerized crime prevention database for information regarding most crime prevention topics and programs throughout the country.

National Crime Prevention Institute
School of Justice Administration, University of Louisville
Louisville, Kentucky 40292
(502) 588-6987
Part of the University of Louisville that was formed in the early 1970s. The NCPI has been seen as the cornerstone of law enforcement crime prevention training in crime prevention. Operates a crime prevention library and has labs on alarms, locks, lighting, and design. Conducts outreach training throughout the world.

National Sheriff's Association
1450 Duke Street
Alexandria, Virginia 22314
(703) 836-7827
Membership organization that has been active in many areas in crime prevention including the TRIAD: a partnership between law enforcement and older adults.

National Victim Center
P.O. Box 17150
Fort Worth, Texas 76102
(800) FYI-CALL (394-2255)
The National Victim Center is a nationwide information and referral service which has information on over six thousand local programs througout the nation in seventy-five different criminal justice topics including sexual assault programs for victims of all ages.

Timothy D. Crowe & Associates
14508 Ashmont Place
Louisville, Kentucky 40223
(502) 245-7834
A foremost authority on the concept on "Crime Prevention through Environmental Design," a national trainer for SHOCAP (Serious Habitual Offender Community Action Program), and a resource for police agencies regarding juvenile programs and police management. Crowe is a former director of the National Crime Prevention Institute and has written numerous publications.

ALABAMA
**Alabama Law Enforcement
Planning Agency**
3465 Norman Bridge Road
Montgomery, Alabama 36105-0939
(205) 242-5891

ALASKA
Alaska Department of Public Safety
P.O. Box N
Juneau, Alaska 99807
(907) 465-4322

ARIZONA
Arizona Criminal Justice Commission
1275 W. Washington
Phoenix, Arizona 85007
(602) 255-1928

ARKANSAS
**Arkansas Crime Prevention
Information Center**
One Capitol Mall
Little Rock, Arkansas 72201
(501) 682-2222

CALIFORNIA
California Crime Prevention Center
Office of the Attorney General
1515 "K" Street, Suite 389
Sacramento, California 95814
(916) 324-7863
·················
**California Office of
Criminal Justice Planning**
1130 "K" Street, Suite 300
Sacramento, California 95815
(916) 323-7722

COLORADO
**Colorado Crime Prevention
Resource Center**
690 Kipling, Suite 3000
Denver, Colorado 80215
(303) 239-4442

CONNECTICUT
Office of Policy and Management
Connecticut Management and
Justice Planning Division
80 Washington Street
Hartford, Connecticut 06016
(203) 566-3020

DISTRICT OF COLUMBIA
**District of Columbia Office of
Criminal Justice Plans and Analysis**
1111 "E" Street, NW, Room 500c
Washington, D.C. 20004
(202) 727-6537

DELAWARE
Delaware Criminal Justice Council
820 N. French Street, 4th Floor
Wilmington, Delaware
(302) 577-3430

FLORIDA
**Attorney General's Office of
Crime Prevention and Training**
The Capitol
Tallahassee, Florida 32399-1050
(904) 487-3712
·················
**Florida Crime Prevention
Training Institute**
Attorney General's Office

The Capitol
Tallahassee, Florida 32399-1050
(904) 487-3712

GEORGIA
Georgia Criminal Justice
Coordinating Council
10 Park Place South, Suite 200
Atlanta, Georgia 30303
(404) 656-1721

HAWAII
Department of the
Attorney General
Crime Prevention Division
222 S. Vineyard Street, Suite 703
Honolulu, Hawaii 96813
(808) 586-1416

IDAHO
Idaho Department of
Law Enforcement
Idaho Crime Prevention Office
6081 Clinton Street
Boise, Idaho 83704-60601
(208) 327-7102

ILLINOIS
Illinois Attorney General's
Crime Prevention Bureau
100 West Randolph, 13th Floor
Chicago, Illinois 60601
(312) 814-6128

INDIANA
Indiana Criminal Justice Institute
101 West Ohio Street, Suite 1130
Indianapolis, Indiana 46204
(317) 232-2561

IOWA
Iowa Criminal and
Juvenile Justice Commission
c/o Department of Management
Capitol Building
Des Moines, Iowa 50319
(515) 242-5823

KANSAS
Kansas Bureau of Investigation
1620 SW Tyler
Topeka, Kansas 66612
(913) 232-6000

KENTUCKY
Kentucky Justice Cabinet
Commonwealth Credit Building
417 High Street, 3rd Floor
Frankfort, Kentucky 40601
(502) 564-7554

LOUISIANA
Louisiana Commission on Law
Enforcement and Administration
of Criminal Justice
1885 Wooddale Boulevard, Suite 710
Baton Rouge, Louisiana 70806

MAINE
Maine Criminal Justice Academy
93 Silver Street
Waterville, Maine 04901
(207) 873-2651

MARYLAND
Maryland Police and Correctional
Training Commission
3085 Hernwood Road
Woodstock, Maryland 21163
(301) 442-2700

MASSACHUSETTS
Massachusetts Committee
on Criminal Justice
100 Cambridge Street, Room 2100
Boston, Massachusetts 02202
(617) 727-6300

MICHIGAN
Michigan Office of Criminal Justice
P.O. Box 30026
Lewis Cass Building
Lansing, Michigan 48824
(517) 373-6655
··················
National Center for Community
Policing, Michigan State University
School of Criminal Justice
560 Aker Hall
East Lansing, Michigan 48824-1118
(800) 892-9051

MINNESOTA
Minnesota Crime Watch
Minnesota Bureau of Criminal
Apprehension
1246 University Avenue
Minneapolis, Minnesota 55104
(612) 643-2576

MISSISSIPPI
Mississippi Division of Public Safety
301 West Pearl Street
Jackson, Mississippi 39203-3088
(601) 949-2225

MISSOURI
Missouri Department of Public Safety
Truman Office Building
301 W. High Street, Room 870
Jefferson City, Missouri 65102
(314) 751-4905

MONTANA
Montana Board of Crime Control
303 North Roberts
Helena, Montana 59620
(406) 444-3604

NEBRASKA
Nebraska State Crime Commission
and Criminal Justice
P.O. Box 94946
Lincoln, Nebraska 68509
(402) 471-2194

NEVADA
Nevada Office of the Attorney General
401 South Third Street, Suite 500
Las Vegas, Nevada 89101
(702) 486-3420

NEW HAMPSHIRE
Office of the Attorney General
State Annex
25 Capitol Street
Concord, New Hampshire 03301
(603) 271-3658

NEW JERSEY
New Jersey Department of Law and
Public Safety
Richard J. Hughes Justice Complex
25 Market Street, CN-085—5th Floor,
West Wing
Trenton, New Jersey 08625
(609) 292-4919

NEW MEXICO
ID Resource Center of Albuquerque
2913 San Mateo Boulevard
Albuquerque, New Mexico 87110
(505) 883-0983

NORTH CAROLINA
North Carolina Department
of Crime Control and
Public Safety
P.O. Box 27687
Raleigh, North Carolina 27611
(919) 733-5522

NORTH DAKOTA
Bureau of Criminal Investigation
Attorney General's Office
P.O. Box 1054
Bismarck, North Dakota 58502
(701) 221-6180

OHIO
Ohio Crime Prevention Association
1560 Fishinger Road
Columbus, Ohio 43221
(614) 459-0508

OKLAHOMA
Oklahoma Criminal Justice
Resource Center
P.O. Box 11400
3400 Martin Luther King Avenue
Oklahoma City, Oklahoma 73136-0400
(405) 425-2596

OREGON
Oregon Board on Police and
Standards and Training
Oregon Police Academy
550 N. Monmouth Avenue
Monmouth, Oregon 97631
(503) 378-2100
·················

Educational Systems
and Resources
33 North Central Avenue, Suite 212

Medford, Oregon 97501
(503) 779-0016
·················

Graffiti Is Not Art
East Zone Community Crime
Prevention Program
Gresham Police Department
1333 NW Eastman Parkway
Gresham, Oregon 97030
(503) 667-6029

PENNSYLVANIA
Pennsylvania Commission on
Crime and Delinquency
P.O. Box 1167
Federal Square Station
Harrisburg, Pennsylvania 17108-1167
(717) 787-2040

RHODE ISLAND
Rhode Island Governor's
Justice Commission
222 Quaker Lane, Suite 100
West Warwick, Rhode Island 02893
(401) 277-2620

SOUTH CAROLINA
Division of Public Safety
Governor's Office
1205 Pendleton Street, Room 481
Columbia, South Carolina 29201
(803) 734-0427

SOUTH DAKOTA
Office of the Attorney General
State Capitol
500 E. Capitol Avenue
Pierre, South Dakota 57501
(605) 773-4687

TENNESSEE
Tennessee Governor's
Planning Office
John Sevier Building
500 Charlotte Avenue
Nashville, Tennessee 37243-0001
(615) 741-1676

TEXAS
Texas Governor's Office
Criminal Justice Division
P.O. Box 12428, Capital Station
Austin, Texas 78711
(512) 463-1919

UTAH
Utah Department of
Public Safety
4501 South 2700 West
Salt Lake City, Utah 84119
(801) 965-4062

VERMONT
Vermont State Police
Training Division
103 S. Main Street
Waterbury, Vermont 05676
(802) 244-7357

VIRGINIA
Department of
Criminal Justice Services
805 E. Broad Street, 10th Floor
Richmond, Virginia 23219
(804) 786-4000

WASHINGTON
Washington State Crime
Prevention Association
Highway-Licenses Building, 7th Floor

Olympia, Washington 98504
(206) 753-1883
··················

King County Sexual Assault
Resource Center
P.O. Box 300
Renton, Washington 98057
(206) 226-5062
··················

Mothers Against Violence in America
901 Fairview Avenue, N, Suite A-170
Seattle, Washington 98109
(206) 343-0476
··················

Eastside Domestic Violence Program
P.O. Box 6398
Bellevue, Washington 98008-0398
(206) 562-8840

WEST VIRGINIA
West Virginia Criminal Justice
and Highway Safety Office
5790-A MacCorckle Avenue SE
Charleston, West Virginia 25304
(304) 348-8814

WISCONSIN
Wisconsin Department of
Criminal Justice
23 W. Washington Street, Room 101
Madison, Wisconsin 53707-7857
(608) 266-1221

WYOMING
Division of Criminal Investigation
Office of the Attorney General
316 West 22nd Street
Cheyenne, Wyoming 82002
(307) 777-7181

State Uniform Crime Reporting Programs

ALABAMA
Alabama Criminal Justice
Information Center
770 Washington Avenue, Suite 350
Montgomery, Alabama 36130
(205) 242-4900, ext. 225

ALASKA
Uniform Crime Reporting Section
Department of Public Safety
Information System
5700 East Tudor Road
Anchorage, Alaska
(907) 269-5659

ARIZONA
Uniform Crime Reporting
Arizona Department of Public Safety
Post Office Box 6638
Phoenix, Arizona 85005
(602) 223-2263

ARKANSAS
Arkansas Crime Information Center
One Capitol Mall, 4D-200
Little Rock, Arkansas 72201
(501) 682-2222

CALIFORNIA
Bureau of Criminal Statistics
Department of Justice
Post Office Box 903427
Sacramento, California 94203
(916) 227-3554

COLORADO
Uniform Crime Reporting
Colorado Bureau of Investigation

690 Kipling Street
Denver, Colorado 80215
(303) 239-4300

CONNECTICUT
Uniform Crime Reporting Program
294 Colony Street
Meriden, Connecticut 06450
(203) 238-6653

DELAWARE
State Bureau of Investigation
Post Office Box 430
Dover, Delaware 19903
(302) 739-5875

DISTRICT OF COLUMBIA
Data Processing Division
Metropolitan Police Department
300 Indiana Avenue, Northwest
Washington, D.C. 20001
(202) 727-4301

FLORIDA
Uniform Crime Reports Section
Special Services Bureau
Florida Department of Law Enforcement
Post Office Box 1489
Tallahassee, Florida 32302
(904) 487-1179

GEORGIA
Georgia Crime Information Center
Georgia Bureau of Investigation
Post Office Box 370748
Decatur, Georgia 30037
(404) 244-2614

HAWAII
Uniform Crime Reporting Program
Crime Prevention Program
Department of the Attorney General
Suite 701
810 Richards Street
Honolulu, Hawaii 96813
(808) 586-1416

IDAHO
Criminal Identification Bureau
Department of Law Enforcement
700 South Stratford Drive
Meridian, Idaho 83680
(208) 327-7130

ILLINOIS
Bureau of Identification
Illinois State Police
726 South College Street
Springfield, Illinois 62704
(217) 782-8263

IOWA
Iowa Department of Public Safety
Wallace State Office Building
Des Moines, Iowa 50319
(515) 281-8422

KANSAS
Kansas Bureau of Investigation
1620 Southwest Tyler Street
Topeka, Kansas 66612
(913) 232-6000

KENTUCKY
Kentucky State Police
Information Services Branch
1250 Louisville Road
Frankfort, Kentucky 40601
(502) 227-8783

LOUISIANA
**Louisiana Commission on
Law Enforcement**
1885 Wooddale Boulevard
12th Floor
Baton Rouge, Louisiana 70806
(504) 925-4440

MAINE
Uniform Crime Reporting Division
Maine State Police
Station #42, 36 Hospital Street
Augusta, Maine 04333
(207) 624-7004

MARYLAND
Central Records Division
Maryland State Police
1711 Belmont Avenue
Baltimore, Maryland 21244
(410) 298-3883

MASSACHUSETTS
Uniform Crime Reports
Crime Reporting Unit
Massachusetts State Police
1010 Commonwealth Avenue
CIS Fifth Floor
Boston, Massachusetts 02215
(617) 566-4500

MICHIGAN
Uniform Crime Reporting Section
Michigan State Police
7150 Harris Drive
Lansing, Michigan 48913
(517) 322-5542

MINNESOTA
Office of Information Systems
Minnesota Department of Public Safety

Suite 100-H, Town Square
444 Cedar Street
St. Paul, Minnesota 55101
(612) 296-7589

MONTANA
Montana Board of Crime Control
303 North Roberts
Helena, Montana 59620
(406) 444-3604

NEBRASKA
Uniform Crime Reporting Section
The Nebraska Commission
on Law Enforcement and
Criminal Justice
Post Office Box 94946
Lincoln, Nebraska 68509
(402) 471-3982

NEVADA
Criminal Information Services
Nevada Highway Patrol
555 Wright Way
Carson City, Nevada 89711
(702) 687-5713

NEW HAMPSHIRE
Uniform Crime Report
Division of State Police
10 Hazen Drive
Concord, New Hampshire 03301
(603) 271-2509

NEW JERSEY
Uniform Crime Reporting
Division of State Police
Post Office Box 7068
West Trenton, New Jersey 08628-0068
(609) 882-2000, ext. 2392

NEW YORK
Statistical Services
New York State Division of
Criminal Justice Services
Stuyvesant Plaza
Executive Park Tower Building
8th Floor, Mail Room
Albany, New York 12203
(518) 457-8381

NORTH CAROLINA
Crime Reporting and Field Services
State Bureau of Investigation Division
of Criminal Information
407 North Blount Street
Raleigh, North Carolina 27601
(919) 733-3171

NORTH DAKOTA
Information Services Section
Bureau of Criminal Investigation
Attorney General's Office
Post Office Box 1054
Bismarck, North Dakota 58502
(701) 221-5500

OKLAHOMA
Uniform Crime Reporting Section
Oklahoma State Bureau
of Investigation
6600 North Harvey, Suite 300
Oklahoma City, Oklahoma 73116
(405) 848-6724

OREGON
Law Enforcement Data Systems Division
Oregon Department of State Police
400 Public Service Building
Salem, Oregon 97310
(503) 378-3057

PENNSYLVANIA
Bureau of Research and Development
Pennsylvania State Police
1800 Elmerton Avenue
Harrisburg, Pennsylvania 17110
(717) 783-5536

RHODE ISLAND
Rhode Island State Police
Post Office Box 185
North Scituate, Rhode Island 02857
(401) 647-3311

SOUTH CAROLINA
South Carolina Law
Enforcement Division
Post Office 21398
Columbia, South Carolina 29221-1398
(803) 896-7162

SOUTH DAKOTA
South Dakota Statistical
Analysis Center
c/o 500 East Capitol Avenue
Pierre, South Dakota 57501
(605) 773-6310

TEXAS
Uniform Crime Reporting Bureau
Crime Records Division
Texas Department of Public Safety
Post Office Box 4143
Austin, Texas 78711
(512) 465-2091

UTAH
Uniform Crime Reporting
Utah Department of Public Safety
4501 South 2700 West
Salt Lake City, Utah 84119
(801) 965-4445

VERMONT
Vermont Department of Public Safety
Post Office Box 189
Waterbury, Vermont 05676
(802) 244-8786

VIRGINIA
Records Management Division
Department of State Police
Post Office Box 27472
Richmond, Virginia 23261-7472
(804) 674-2023

WASHINGTON
Uniform Crime Reporting Program
Washington Association of Sheriffs
and Police Chiefs
Post Office Box 826
Olympia, Washington 98507
(206) 586-3221

WEST VIRGINIA
Uniform Crime Reporting Program
725 Jefferson Road
South Charleston, West Virginia 25309
(608) 266-3323

WISCONSIN
Office of Justice Assistance
222 State Street, 2nd Floor
Madison, Wisconsin 53703
(608) 266-3323

WYOMING
Uniform Crime Reporting
Criminal Records Section
Division of Criminal Investigation
316 West 22nd Street
Cheyenne, Wyoming
(307) 777-7625

QUICK REFERENCE

Empowerment Strategies Chart

OUTSMARTING BURGLARY

EMPOWERMENT STRATEGY #1: Be selective about where you live. Before buying a house, investigate the neighborhood you are thinking of moving into.

EMPOWERMENT STRATEGY #2: Rekey your house when you first move into it. Change all the locks.

EMPOWERMENT STRATEGY #3: Make sure that you have a solid core as opposed to a hollow-core door on all exterior doorways. It is possible to break through a hollow-core door with your fist.

EMPOWERMENT STRATEGY #4: Use lighting when you are not home to give the appearance your house is not empty.

EMPOWERMENT STRATEGY #5: Have your neighbor park his/her car in your driveway when you are gone for extended periods of time.

EMPOWERMENT STRATEGY #6: Consider buying an alarm system, especially if you live in an area which has a relatively high crime rate.

EMPOWERMENT STRATEGY #7: In order to determine how easy it is to break into your house, try pretending you are a burglar.

EMPOWERMENT STRATEGY #8: Remember that a house has six sides, not just four, and when you evaluate your security, determine how easy it would be for a burglar to climb in a skylight or a daylight basement.

EMPOWERMENT STRATEGY #9: Lock your windows and doors when you leave your house.

EMPOWERMENT STRATEGY #10: If you are out in your neighborhood and you notice someone who doesn't belong or whom you have never seen before in your neighborhood, strike up a conversation with him or her.

EMPOWERMENT STRATEGY #11: Give people the impression that you care about your house. Mow the lawn, keep the paint up, and do this even if you're out of town.

EMPOWERMENT STRATEGY #12: Fences can be an effective deterrent if they enclose your property and create a psychological barrier, but don't create concealment for a burglar.

EMPOWERMENT STRATEGY #13: Install passive infrared lighting in the front and the back of your house.

EMPOWERMENT STRATEGY #14: Put valuables you rarely use in a safety deposit box at your bank.

EMPOWERMENT STRATEGY #15: When you are on vacation, leave a key with a friend or trusted neighbor and have him or her take in your paper and mail.

EMPOWERMENT STRATEGY #16: Take your camcorder (or rent one) and go from room to room identifying all of your personal belongings. Photograph them and narratively describe when you bought each item, how much you paid, and the approximate value of each item.

EMPOWERMENT STRATEGY #17: Start a block watch in your neighborhood whether or not you have been the victim of a crime.

EMPOWERMENT STRATEGY #18: Always be able to see who is at your door before opening it. If you don't know the person at your door, there's no reason to open the door.

EMPOWERMENT STRATEGY #19: Never leave your garage door open when you leave the house.

EMPOWERMENT STRATEGY #20: If you decide you need an alarm system, apply the rule of three: shop for a system at three different companies.

EMPOWERMENT STRATEGY #21: If you are burglarized, look at your checks to see if any have been stolen.

EMPOWERMENT STRATEGY #22: Use a locking mailbox or a post office box to avoid having mail stolen.

EMPOWERMENT STRATEGY #23: It is a good idea not to have your name on the mailbox or on the outside of your house.

EMPOWERMENT STRATEGY #24: If someone calls you and wants to take a survey of you, generally it is not a good idea to participate.

EMPOWERMENT STRATEGY #25: When you leave a message on voicemail or an answering machine say, "We can't come to the phone right now, but if you leave a message we'll get right back to you."

EMPOWERMENT STRATEGY #26: Post emergency numbers for security, police, and fire assistance near every phone.

EMPOWERMENT STRATEGY #27: If you notice any suspicious persons or vehicles, call security or the police.

EMPOWERMENT STRATEGY #28: Be alert when you go home. It is the hardest time to be alert because you're tired. Try to see if people are around.

EMPOWERMENT STRATEGY #29: Keep doors and windows locked at all times. On a warm weather day, don't leave a side door open.

EMPOWERMENT STRATEGY #30: Have keys ready when approaching your home.

EMPOWERMENT STRATEGY #31: If you arrive home to find that windows or doors have been tampered with, don't go inside but, instead, call the police from a neighbor's house.

EMPOWERMENT STRATEGY #32: Don't give personal information to unknown callers. If you receive an obscene or crank call, hang up immediately, saying nothing.

EMPOWERMENT STRATEGY #33: If you use flood lights on the exterior of you house, make sure they face toward the house, not away from it: the latter can provide cover for a burglar.

EMPOWERMENT STRATEGY #34: Consider installing a Beware of Dog sign in your window.

EMPOWERMENT STRATEGY #35: Hook up a timer not only to lights but to a police scanner or television to better replicate being home.

EMPOWERMENT STRATEGY #36: Beware of people calling unsolicited saying you've won free dinners or show tickets: it might be a burglar seeking to get you out of your house.

EMPOWERMENT STRATEGY #37: Look out for repair men, pizza delivery men, plumbers, or yard workers who are really burglars. If they walk around to the side of a house, call the police.

EMPOWERMENT STRATEGY #38: Never confront a burglar—always call the police.

EMPOWERMENT STRATEGY #39: Lock your garage. Also, lock the door that goes from the garage to the house.

EMPOWERMENT STRATEGY #40: Don't keep valuables in your master bedroom: that is the first place the burglar looks.

EMPOWERMENT STRATEGY #41: Stay away from places where there aren't many people, like isolated parking lots.

EMPOWERMENT STRATEGY #42: If you see someone strange in the neighborhood asking questions about a neighbor, don't tell him anything, especially if the neighbor about whom he is inquiring is out of town.

EMPOWERMENT STRATEGY #43: If you see someone suspicious, make a phone call—make it obvious that you're calling.

EMPOWERMENT STRATEGY #44: Don't make it obvious that you are trying to look like you are not home.

EMPOWERMENT STRATEGY #45: Keep skylights closed and locked wherever possible. It is a common access point for burglars.

EMPOWERMENT STRATEGY #46: Plant prickly shrubbery around you house; burglars won't want to hide in them.

EMPOWERMENT STRATEGY #47: Lighting is especially important for people who live on a golf course or adjacent to a greenbelt since that is perfect access for a burglar to get into the backyard.

EMPOWERMENT STRATEGY #48: Close your blinds when you are at home. That way a peeping tom can't see you.

EMPOWERMENT STRATEGY #49: If you live in an apartment or condominium on the second or third floor, don't forget to lock sliding glass doors that lead to balconies. A burglar could access them with a ladder easily.

EMPOWERMENT STRATEGY #50: Don't leave ladders lying around your house. If you live in a condo or apartment, get the manager to secure ladders in a storage facility.

EMPOWERMENT STRATEGY #51: If you are away from home a lot and you have a big house, consider renting out the downstairs or another part of the house so that there will always be someone home when you are gone.

EMPOWERMENT STRATEGY #52: When you are going on a trip, consider calling the post office and getting them to hold your mail for you while you are gone. This is useful if you do not have a neighbor who can collect it for you.

EMPOWERMENT STRATEGY #53: Be sure there are no large trees with branches overhanging your house that could be used by a burglar to climb onto the roof.

EMPOWERMENT STRATEGY #54: If you decide to build a fence, be sure it is one you can see through. Solid wood fences provide unlimited cover for burglars once they are in your yard.

EMPOWERMENT STRATEGY #55: Make sure gates to your yard are latched securely before leaving.

EMPOWERMENT STRATEGY #56: Consider marking the valuables in your home with your driver's license or your social security number.

OUTSMARTING AUTO THEFT

EMPOWERMENT STRATEGY #57: Lock your car door.

EMPOWERMENT STRATEGY #58: Always have at least a quarter tank of gas in your car to avoid running out in a dangerous place.

EMPOWERMENT STRATEGY #59: Lock your car doors while driving.

EMPOWERMENT STRATEGY #60: Keep your car well-maintained to avoid breakdowns.

EMPOWERMENT STRATEGY #61: Check the back seat before getting into your car.

EMPOWERMENT STRATEGY #62: Have keys ready when approaching your car.

EMPOWERMENT STRATEGY #63: Park your car in well-lighted areas.

EMPOWERMENT STRATEGY #64: Keep area maps in your glove compartment, and always get directions before driving to an unknown location.

EMPOWERMENT STRATEGY #65: NEVER pick up hitchhikers.

EMPOWERMENT STRATEGY #66: Never leave packages or valuables in plain sight. Lock them in the glove box or the trunk.

EMPOWERMENT STRATEGY #67: Never keep personal identification, credit cards, or checks in the car.

EMPOWERMENT STRATEGY #68: Avoid parking lots where a key is left with an attendant or with the vehicle.

EMPOWERMENT STRATEGY #69: At night, park your car in a garage if possible. If you must park in a driveway or a carport, leave an outdoor light on.

EMPOWERMENT STRATEGY #70: Don't leave your car parked at unattended railroad or airport parking lots for long periods of time.

EMPOWERMENT STRATEGY #71: Consider getting a car alarm if you live in a high crime or "hotspot" area.

EMPOWERMENT STRATEGY #72: Consider getting a steering wheel locking device like a heavy-gauge steel bar.

EMPOWERMENT STRATEGY #73: Park your car with the wheels turned toward the curb, making it difficult for a thief to tow your car.

EMPOWERMENT STRATEGY #74: Consider installing a "kill" switch in your car. This is a hidden switch that prevents the car from being started.

EMPOWERMENT STRATEGY #75: Keep a tool kit in the car.

EMPOWERMENT STRATEGY #76: Keep title and registration on you or in a locked compartment in the car.

EMPOWERMENT STRATEGY #77: Keep change in the car for emergency calls.

EMPOWERMENT STRATEGY #78: Never park near a place where someone could be hiding, like the bushes or a dumpster.

EMPOWERMENT STRATEGY #79: Before getting into your car, be sure no one was following you in order to trap you in your car.

EMPOWERMENT STRATEGY #80: Vary your route to work.

EMPOWERMENT STRATEGY #81: Keep doors locked and windows rolled up when driving.

EMPOWERMENT STRATEGY #82: Do not engage in hand gestures or making faces of any kind with other drivers.

EMPOWERMENT STRATEGY #83: Maintain one and one-half to two car lengths between you and the next driver.

EMPOWERMENT STRATEGY #84: Consider getting a cellular phone to keep in your car in the event of emergencies. Take it with you when you park your car.

EMPOWERMENT STRATEGY #85: Keep pen and paper in the car in order to write down suspicious activity and report it to the police. If you are a hit and run victim, be sure to write down the license plate number of the vehicle that hit you.

EMPOWERMENT STRATEGY #86: If you break down or get a flat tire on a major road, wait for a law enforcement official. Never accept a ride from a stranger.

EMPOWERMENT STRATEGY #87: Maintaining your car is an important prevention step. If you break down on a dark street, you are in more danger obviously than if you make it home trouble-free each night.

EMPOWERMENT STRATEGY #88: Don't drive through "hotspots" or high crime areas when you commute to work.

EMPOWERMENT STRATEGY #89: When taking public transportation, be sure to travel during times when there are a large number of other commuters doing likewise.

EMPOWERMENT STRATEGY #90: When taking a cab, it is a good idea to travel in pairs, especially for women.

EMPOWERMENT STRATEGY #91: When traveling on a subway, travel in pairs.

EMPOWERMENT STRATEGY #92: When riding on public transportation, carry yourself confidently, looking around and making firm eye contact with others.

EMPOWERMENT STRATEGY #93: As you approach your car, look for signs that someone has been in your car.

OUTSMARTING ROBBERY

EMPOWERMENT STRATEGY #94: It's important to vary your route to and from work.

EMPOWERMENT STRATEGY #95: If you think you are being followed, don't go home. Home is the worst place to go because you don't want to tell your follower where you live.

EMPOWERMENT STRATEGY #96: Maintaining your car is an important prevention step. If you break down on a dark street, you are obviously in more danger than if you make it home trouble-free each night.

EMPOWERMENT STRATEGY #97: Don't drive through hotspots or high crime areas when you commute to work.

EMPOWERMENT STRATEGY #98: When taking public transportation, be sure to travel during times when there are a large number of other commuters doing likewise.

EMPOWERMENT STRATEGY #99: When taking a cab, it is a good idea to travel in pairs, especially for women.

EMPOWERMENT STRATEGY #100: When traveling on a subway, travel in pairs.

EMPOWERMENT STRATEGY #101: When riding on public transportation, carry yourself confidently, looking around and making firm eye contact with others.

EMPOWERMENT STRATEGY #102: While walking down the street, walk with confidence, shoulders back, head up and aware of your surroundings.

EMPOWERMENT STRATEGY #103: Walk briskly with determination in order to show that you know exactly where you are going.

EMPOWERMENT STRATEGY #104: When someone comes up to you and asks you for money, look the person dead in the eye, say no, and walk away.

EMPOWERMENT STRATEGY #105: If you are walking down the street and you think someone is following you, change directions and look for a well-lit area.

EMPOWERMENT STRATEGY #106: When you are walking in public, carry only the amount of cash you need during the day and no more.

EMPOWERMENT STRATEGY #107: If someone comes up to you and says, "Give me your money," give it to him—period!

EMPOWERMENT STRATEGY #108: Buy a cellular phone to keep in your car at all times for emergencies.

EMPOWERMENT STRATEGY #109: Vary where you park each day when you go to work.

EMPOWERMENT STRATEGY #110: Don't get on an elevator if you are uncomfortable with the person who is in it.

EMPOWERMENT STRATEGY #111: If you are attacked, it is important to make noise and try to draw attention to the situation.

EMPOWERMENT STRATEGY #112: When you go to work in the morning, if you are the first person in the office, you should walk all the way through the office and determine whether anyone is in the office.

EMPOWERMENT STRATEGY #113: When at work, lock your purse or wallet in your desk or a file cabinet.

EMPOWERMENT STRATEGY #114: If someone is in your office space and you do not know the person, go up and ask him who he is in a nice way.

EMPOWERMENT STRATEGY #115: If you see a maintenance person installing a new light or doing some other kind of maintenance, go up to the person and talk to him, with something like, "How is the weather up there?" or other light conversation.

EMPOWERMENT STRATEGY #116: Keep your car in good working condition.

EMPOWERMENT STRATEGY #117: Don't leave your purse in your shopping cart when you go to the grocery store.

EMPOWERMENT STRATEGY #118: If you go out dancing with friends, make sure at least one of you stays behind to watch the purses of the others.

EMPOWERMENT STRATEGY #119: While walking home from work, walk with your purse in your hands, and don't rely on the shoulder strap.

EMPOWERMENT STRATEGY #120: As you approach your car, look for signs that someone has been in your car.

EMPOWERMENT STRATEGY #121: Women should avoid placing ads in the newspaper.

EMPOWERMENT STRATEGY #122: If you need to work late or report in early, try to arrange your schedule to work with another employee. When you are leaving after hours, ask a security guard to escort you to the parking lot.

EMPOWERMENT STRATEGY #123: If you work in a large office block, find out which elevators shut down after a specified time and which elevators are still operable after normal business hours.

EMPOWERMENT STRATEGY #124: When walking, choose busy streets and avoid passing vacant lots, alleys, or deserted construction sites. At night, walk only in well-lighted areas and try to avoid walking or jogging alone.

EMPOWERMENT STRATEGY #125: Have your social security check direct deposited into your bank account. Often criminals will lurk out in front of the social security office.

EMPOWERMENT STRATEGY #126: Carry mace or other personal protection devices in your hand when walking; it does no good at the bottom of your purse.

EMPOWERMENT STRATEGY #127: Stay away from convenience stores at night.

EMPOWERMENT STRATEGY #128: Do not walk alone in the evening when it is raining and/or foggy: this provides cover for muggers.

EMPOWERMENT STRATEGY #129: Don't wear a lot of expensive jewelry that might attract burglars.

EMPOWERMENT STRATEGY #130: Don't show your wallet or the contents of it when you are in a store buying something.

EMPOWERMENT STRATEGY #131: When you leave a bank, be alert and don't clutch your purse tightly to your chest as though you have a lot of money. Robbers look for this. Don't look leery, worried.

EMPOWERMENT STRATEGY #132: When you are buying something in a grocery store, don't show cash in your wallet other than that which you need to make the purchase.

EMPOWERMENT STRATEGY #133: Don't allow what you see on television and in the newspaper intimidate you into avoiding normal activities.

EMPOWERMENT STRATEGY #134: When you are traveling and staying in a hotel room, be sure to lock the hotel room door even when you are in it.

EMPOWERMENT STRATEGY #135: When staying in a hotel, never leave valuables in your room. If you have tickets or cash or traveler's checks, consider storing them in the hotel's safe. Ask the front desk for information about such services.

EMPOWERMENT STRATEGY #136: When walking in an unfamiliar city, ask someone who lives there for an indication of where the safe places are to walk and where the unsafe places are. Be sure to avoid the unsafe areas, especially if you are traveling alone.

EMPOWERMENT STRATEGY #137: Do not use a cash machine at nighttime.

EMPOWERMENT STRATEGY #138: Whenever you use a cash machine, be cautious about who is behind you—you do not want anyone to see you entering your secret code.

OUTSMARTING CRIME IN THE WORKPLACE

EMPOWERMENT STRATEGY #139: Know what your business goals and objectives are.

EMPOWERMENT STRATEGY #140: Before moving into a building, make sure the requirements of the business are adequately addressed by the space it is being moved into.

EMPOWERMENT STRATEGY #141: Make sure to visit to your local law enforcement agency prior to signing any contract for a location for your business. The purpose of the visit is to find out what types of crime are common to the neighborhood you are moving your business into.

EMPOWERMENT STRATEGY #142: Talk to the crime prevention unit of the law enforcement agency in which your business will be located to ascertain what types of employee training they will conduct for you at your business location.

EMPOWERMENT STRATEGY #143: Visit businesses similar to your own and check out what security measures they have taken. (It is wise to exceed the average level of security you see in other businesses.)

EMPOWERMENT STRATEGY #144: Hire a security consultant that has special training in Crime Prevention through Environmental Design to evaluate your security needs while you are in the design phase.

EMPOWERMENT STRATEGY #145: Develop written policies and procedures concerning theft (internal and external) plus other policies regarding crime that are dictated either by your location or the nature of your business.

EMPOWERMENT STRATEGY #146: Make sure your employment application has specific questions regarding criminal convictions as well as background information required for the specific jobs you will be filling.

EMPOWERMENT STRATEGY #147: Carefully screen new employees before hiring. It is your best defense against dishonest employees.

EMPOWERMENT STRATEGY #148: Check out such things as gaps in employment in the application process.

EMPOWERMENT STRATEGY #149: Make telephone calls to verify training, education or certifications, or previous employment. Always try to talk with direct supervisors if possible and always ask if they would rehire the person for the same job.

EMPOWERMENT STRATEGY #150: Verify home address and telephone numbers of your employees.

EMPOWERMENT STRATEGY #151: Consider paper and pencil honesty testing. Some methods have been developed recently that also determine tendency toward violence.

EMPOWERMENT STRATEGY #152: Provide your employees with a copy of company policies and procedures and keep a form signed by them indicating they have read and understand the policies (especially the policy on theft).

EMPOWERMENT STRATEGY #153: Apply the same standards you would use to hire an employee to select a custodial company or security company.

EMPOWERMENT STRATEGY #154: Managers should always set a good example for honesty with employees.

EMPOWERMENT STRATEGY #155: Managers should strictly adhere to company policies and insist that employees do the same.

EMPOWERMENT STRATEGY #156: Managers should be aware of problems that employees may have in their private lives such as marital problems or money problems; offer assistance within the company's medical, overtime, or leave policies.

EMPOWERMENT STRATEGY #157: Keep a running accounting of gross sales per shift per day.

EMPOWERMENT STRATEGY #158: Keep a record of cash register audits and investigate overages as well as shortages.

EMPOWERMENT STRATEGY #159: Keep an eye open for an employee that is obviously living beyond his or her income.

EMPOWERMENT STRATEGY #160: Train employees in till tapping, quick change artists, and shoplifting.

EMPOWERMENT STRATEGY #161: Use multi-copy numbered receipts and computerize the data so that if a receipt is missing, it is caught quickly.

EMPOWERMENT STRATEGY #162: Set up good receiving policies (especially if you have a loading dock).

EMPOWERMENT STRATEGY #163: Require two pieces of identification on checks.

EMPOWERMENT STRATEGY #164: Check cash register records to determine if you have people using receipts over again to cash refund the same item.

EMPOWERMENT STRATEGY #165: Have a stringent return policy—the best is to never give a cash refund. Refund by check or only allow exchanges for other merchandise. A good policy is NO RETURN without a receipt.

EMPOWERMENT STRATEGY #166: Consider mirrors: one-way glass from offices or closed circuit cameras to monitor problem areas.

EMPOWERMENT STRATEGY #167: Make sure the company has good opening and closing procedures to assure that a burglar would be caught at closing if they were hiding inside the building or that a burglary would be noticed as soon as the first person came to work.

EMPOWERMENT STRATEGY #168: If a burglary is discovered, protect the scene until the police arrive. This means keeping the people out of the area and not cleaning anything.

EMPOWERMENT STRATEGY #169: If there is an alarm system, be sure that everyone who must use it knows exactly how to use it.

EMPOWERMENT STRATEGY #170: Use a money chest (drop safe) to store any money on the premises.

EMPOWERMENT STRATEGY #171: Make sure there is a policy regarding who is responsible for locking up at night.

EMPOWERMENT STRATEGY #172: Specify a person to walk around the building on a regular basis (at least once per week, preferably after dark), to check for lights out or trees obscuring the light, pry marks on doors or windows, or signs of loitering in the parking lot or parking garages.

EMPOWERMENT STRATEGY #173: Never mark parking stalls with employee names or assign the same spot to one person if you can possibly avoid it.

EMPOWERMENT STRATEGY #174: Don't obstruct windows into the business (especially retail) so that people outside can't see the clerk and cash register area from outside.

EMPOWERMENT STRATEGY #175: Some businesses might need an alarm system with a duress code built in.

EMPOWERMENT STRATEGY #176: Robbery alarms should always be silent.

EMPOWERMENT STRATEGY #177: Institute good cash controls in your business.

EMPOWERMENT STRATEGY #178: Make sure that lighting is good inside and out of your business.

EMPOWERMENT STRATEGY #179: Consider uniforms or smocks that are readily identifiable for your employees where appropriate.

EMPOWERMENT STRATEGY #180: Train employees in prudent policies to follow before, during, and after a robbery or a robbery attempt.

EMPOWERMENT STRATEGY #181: Write down what should be done after a robbery and keep it on a laminated sheet near the cash register or in the office to be ready should a robbery occur.

EMPOWERMENT STRATEGY #182: Since observation and descriptive skills are important, role playing situations at various training events might be worthwhile.

EMPOWERMENT STRATEGY #183: Develop a strong policy on drugs (including alcohol use) in the workplace. This policy definitely needs to be reviewed by an attorney who specializes in labor law.

EMPOWERMENT STRATEGY #184: All levels of management need in-depth training in identifying the problem, whether it be an employee selling drugs in the facility or a person who is under the influence of alcoholic or other drugs during the course of the work day.

EMPOWERMENT STRATEGY #185: Use and abuse of alcohol or other drugs at company functions should be weighted against company policy and the message such use gives to employees, especially employees who may have a problem with substance abuse.

EMPOWERMENT STRATEGY #186: All on the job accidents should be evaluated in regards to possibility of drug or alcohol cause.

EMPOWERMENT STRATEGY #187: Company policies, procedures, hiring, evaluation, training and retention should all reflect the most up-to-date information regarding violence in the workplace, its causes, contributing factors and signs.

EMPOWERMENT STRATEGY #188: Special company policies need to address how the company can help protect an employee who is being stalked, the subject of kidnap/extortion (including, but not limited to corporate executives), or the victim of domestic violence.

EMPOWERMENT STRATEGY #189: Companies should have as part of any employee insurance plan counseling available for stress, family problems or anger management.

EMPOWERMENT STRATEGY #190: Company training should include such issues as ethnicity, religious freedom, and sexual harassment.

EMPOWERMENT STRATEGY #191: When downsizing, a prudent company will sponsor job training for employees to move into other jobs within the company or a program to help other employees find employment elsewhere.

EMPOWERMENT STRATEGY #192: The company should set up a crisis action team that would be designed to help cope with any workplace violence related problem.

OUTSMARTING CRIME AGAINST WOMEN

EMPOWERMENT STRATEGY #193: If you work in a large office building, find out which elevators shut down after a specified time and which elevators are still operable after normal business hours.

EMPOWERMENT STRATEGY #194: Check the identification of any stranger who asks for confidential information, or any delivery or repair person who wants to enter a restricted area or remove equipment.

EMPOWERMENT STRATEGY #195: Keep your purse or wallet locked in a drawer or cabinet at all times.

EMPOWERMENT STRATEGY #196: Post emergency numbers for security, police, and fire assistance near every phone.

EMPOWERMENT STRATEGY #197: If you notice any suspicious persons or vehicles, call security or the police.

EMPOWERMENT STRATEGY #198: Be alert when you go home. It is the hardest time to be alert because you're tired. Try to see if people are around.

EMPOWERMENT STRATEGY #199: Keep doors and windows locked at all times. On a warm weather day, don't leave a side door open.

EMPOWERMENT STRATEGY #200: Have keys ready when approaching your home.

EMPOWERMENT STRATEGY #201: If you arrive home to find that windows or doors have been tampered with, don't go inside but, instead, call the police from a neighbor's house.

EMPOWERMENT STRATEGY #202: If someone arrives unexpectedly at your house, find out who it is before opening the door. Install a peephole in the door.

EMPOWERMENT STRATEGY #203: Record only nonspecific messages on your answering machine and avoid messages like, "We'll be back at seven o'clock on Sunday."

EMPOWERMENT STRATEGY #204: Don't give personal information to unknown callers. If you receive an obscene or crank call, hang up immediately, saying nothing.

EMPOWERMENT STRATEGY #205: When walking, choose busy streets and avoid passing vacant lots, alleys, or deserted construction sites. At night, walk only in well-lighted areas and try to avoid walking or jogging alone.

EMPOWERMENT STRATEGY #206: Don't list your full name in the phone book. You should use a first initial only, your husband's name (especially if widowed), or not be listed at all. Such listings have the potential to invite prank calls.

EMPOWERMENT STRATEGY #207: Don't leave your purse in your shopping cart when you go to the grocery store.

EMPOWERMENT STRATEGY #208: If you go out dancing with friends, make sure at least one of you stays behind to watch the purses of the others.

EMPOWERMENT STRATEGY #209: While walking on the street, clutch your purse in hand, and do not rely on a shoulder strap for carrying purposes.

EMPOWERMENT STRATEGY #210: Avoid placing personal ads in the newspaper.

EMPOWERMENT STRATEGY #211: Consider carrying a fanny pack instead of a purse or some kind of bag that can wrap around your body.

EMPOWERMENT STRATEGY #212: If you carry a purse, consider carrying your wallet in an inside coat pocket.

EMPOWERMENT STRATEGY #213: If you get an obscene phone caller, consider getting a whistle and blowing the whistle into the phone as loud as you can.

EMPOWERMENT STRATEGY #214: If you get an obscene phone caller, another strategy is to click on the receiver and then say, "Operator this is the call I would like you to trace for me," and then hang up.

OUTSMARTING YOUTH VIOLENCE AND GANGS

EMPOWERMENT STRATEGY #215: Ensure that your child knows his/her full name, address, telephone number, and an emergency contact name and number. Teach your children how to use the telephone and dial 9-1-1, or 0.

EMPOWERMENT STRATEGY #216: Thoroughly check the background of baby-sitters and day care center personnel.

EMPOWERMENT STRATEGY #217: Set up procedures with your child's school or day care center as to whom the child will be released to other than yourself, and what notification procedure they are to follow if the child does not show up on time.

EMPOWERMENT STRATEGY #218: Practice with your child the route he or she should take to walk to school or to friends' homes.

EMPOWERMENT STRATEGY #219: Show your child safe places he can go in case of an emergency, like a neighbor's house.

EMPOWERMENT STRATEGY #220: Avoid putting your child's name on clothing, books, hats, bikes, or toys. Children may respond to a stranger who calls them by name.

EMPOWERMENT STRATEGY #221: Define what a stranger is. Let your children know that just because they see someone every day, for instance the mailman, paperboy, milkman, or neighbor, it does not mean that these people are not strangers. A stranger may be a man or a woman.

EMPOWERMENT STRATEGY #222: Teach your child that if she is approached by a stranger, not to talk to the person and to run away in the direction of people and light. If your child is grabbed by a stranger, teach her to scream, "Help," kick, and attempt to break loose.

EMPOWERMENT STRATEGY #223: Never leave a child alone; not at home, in a vehicle, at play, in the toy section of a store, or anywhere. Don't let your child go to a public restroom alone.

EMPOWERMENT STRATEGY #224: Instruct your child that if he or she is separated from you in a store, not to look for you but instead, go to the nearest check-out stand and ask the person at the register for help.

EMPOWERMENT STRATEGY #225: Teach your child that no one has a right to touch him or her on any part of the body and that your child should tell you if someone tries to do so.

EMPOWERMENT STRATEGY #226: If you and your spouse are not living together, make sure your child knows exactly what days he is supposed to be with each parent.

EMPOWERMENT STRATEGY #227: Evaluate for yourself how much gang activity is present at your child's school and then look for help from the school administration, gang intervention counselors, and the PTA for ways to help your child avoid joining.

EMPOWERMENT STRATEGY #228: Look into local youth programs available in your community.

EMPOWERMENT STRATEGY #229: Look for constructive activities to get your kids involved in, like summer employment and/or recreational activity camps.

EMPOWERMENT STRATEGY #230: Talk to your kids about guns and how to confront the presence of weapons in their school.

EMPOWERMENT STRATEGY #231: Consider developing a contract with your child that is jointly developed and signed by both parties regarding issues like drug and alcohol use, driving, and other safety issues.

EMPOWERMENT STRATEGY #232: It is important to teach your children from an early age on what "good touch" is and what "bad touch" is, which parts of their bodies are private, and which aren't.

EMPOWERMENT STRATEGY #233: An unattended child is a child at risk. Arrange with your child an alternative place to wait if you are delayed, especially in the darker winter evenings. Suggest a well-lit store or inside an arena or school.

EMPOWERMENT STRATEGY #234: Have children walk in pairs or groups.

EMPOWERMENT STRATEGY #235: Children should always travel the same way home.

EMPOWERMENT STRATEGY #236: Don't allow your young child to go to a public washroom unattended.

EMPOWERMENT STRATEGY #237: Check your baby-sitters' credentials thoroughly. In your absence, they are guardians of a priceless treasure.

EMPOWERMENT STRATEGY #238: Tell your child it is not rude to ignore an adult who is asking directions on the street. Another adult could be asked for more accurate information.

EMPOWERMENT STRATEGY #239: Tackle the subject of sexual abuse prevention with the same honest matter of fact manner you would attach to road safety.

EMPOWERMENT STRATEGY #240: Discuss with your child the difference between fact and fiction so that she may understand the nature of taking an oath. (This may be necessary for a court appearance.)

EMPOWERMENT STRATEGY #241: If you suspect that an abuse has taken place, encourage your child to talk about it.

EMPOWERMENT STRATEGY #242: When you are aware of an incident of sexual abuse, call the police or the child welfare authorities immediately. Ensure that a social worker, a police officer, and someone supportive to the child is present when evidence is given.

EMPOWERMENT STRATEGY #243: Make sure your child knows his or her own address.

EMPOWERMENT STRATEGY #244: Make sure your child knows where to go in an emergency.

EMPOWERMENT STRATEGY #245: Make sure your child knows never to get into a stranger's car.

EMPOWERMENT STRATEGY #246: Learn as much as you can about communicating with children and do it from early ages on.

EMPOWERMENT STRATEGY #247: Talk to adolescents about unusual drawings on notebooks, especially if you see similar drawings on walls in the neighborhood.

EMPOWERMENT STRATEGY #248: Look for changing styles of language in your child. If your child begins to drop specific letters from all words, it may be an indication that he or she is involved with gangs.

EMPOWERMENT STRATEGY #249: Learn all you can about gangs and indicators of gang membership. Many police agencies, teen centers, and schools offer classes for parents.

EMPOWERMENT STRATEGY #250: The most important way to deter your child from joining a gang is to listen to him and get him involved in positive activities like sports or outdoor activities like 4-H club, Outward Bound, or the Boy and Girl Scouts of America.

OUTSMARTING CRIME AGAINST OLDER ADULTS

EMPOWERMENT STRATEGY #251: Remember you cannot get something for nothing, no matter what anyone says.

EMPOWERMENT STRATEGY #252: If you think you know someone who is a potential victim of fraud, do something about it..

EMPOWERMENT STRATEGY #253: Take what you see on the news with a grain of salt.

EMPOWERMENT STRATEGY #254: Find out what the crime rate is in your community.

EMPOWERMENT STRATEGY #255: Remember that not only are older adults less victimized by crime, but burglars hate neighborhoods that have seniors.

EMPOWERMENT STRATEGY #256: Stay sociable as you age; maintain and increase your network of friends and acquaintances.

EMPOWERMENT STRATEGY #257: Keep in contact with old friends and neighbors if you move in with a relative or change to a new address.

EMPOWERMENT STRATEGY #258: Develop a "buddy" system with a friend outside the home. Plan for at least a weekly contact and share openly with this person.

EMPOWERMENT STRATEGY #259: Ask friends to visit you at home; even a brief visit can enhance your well-being.

EMPOWERMENT STRATEGY #260: Accept new opportunities for activities. They can bring new friends.

EMPOWERMENT STRATEGY #261: Participate in community activities as long as you are able.

EMPOWERMENT STRATEGY #262: Volunteer or become a member or officer of an organization.

EMPOWERMENT STRATEGY #263: Be sure that you have someone you are in regular contact with and share your concerns and fears with people and talk it out.

EMPOWERMENT STRATEGY #264: Make sure you lock your front door even when you are home, such as out in the back gardening or otherwise working in the yard.

EMPOWERMENT STRATEGY #265: When you go to your car in a parking lot, walk past it first to see if anything or anyone is lurking in or around the car.

Help your friends and colleagues
OUTSMART CRIME!

Dear Reader,

Since the release of *Outsmart Crime!* many business owners and leaders from other organizations have inquired about buying bulk supplies of the book to give to employees and/or clients to help reduce their chances of becoming victims of crime. Because of this huge demand, we have created a special 800 number specifically for such bulk order requests.

The cost of bulk orders varies depending on the amount purchased. Discounts range from a low of 46 percent to a high of 60 percent off the cover price. The minimum bulk order which qualifies for a discount is 30 copies.

Do your part to help yourself and others stop crime by ordering bulk supplies of *Outsmart Crime!* today.

OUTSMART CRIME!
Bulk Order Hotline:
(800) 932-4809

ABOUT THE AUTHORS

Doug Shadel has been in law enforcement since 1979, having spent ten years as an investigator for the Washington State Attorney General and four years as a special assistant to the Attorney General. He is currently the consumer affairs representative for the American Association of Retired Persons' Western region. Shadel has been an instructor for the National Crime Prevention Council, the International Society of Crime Prevention Practitioners, the Washington State Criminal Justice Training Commission, and the National Association of Attorneys General. Shadel is a former member of the board of directors of the Washington State Crime Prevention Association, and his crime prevention materials and programs have won six national awards. He is the co-author of the award-winning consumer guidebook *Schemes & Scams*, which chronicles consumer fraud in America.

Al Ward has been in law enforcement for over twenty-five years. He is a former crime prevention officer with the Bellevue Police Department, past president of the board of directors of the Washington State Crime Prevention Association, and past president of the International Society of Crime Prevention Practitioners. Additionally, Ward has been an instructor for the Washington State Criminal Justice Training Commission, the Federal Bureau of Investigation, the National Crime Prevention Council, and the National Crime Prevention Institute. In 1994, Ward won the prestigious Crime Prevention Practitioner of the Year Award given each year by the International Society of Crime Prevention Practitioners.